NELSON'S

Student

Bible

HANDBOOK

Gives you the who, what, when, where,
why and how for every book of the Bible!

Can be used with the NKJV, NCV, KJV, NIV, NRSV,
and other popular translations

THOMAS NELSON
Since 1798

NASHVILLE   DALLAS   MEXICO CITY   RIO DE JANEIRO   BEIJING

www.thomasnelson.com

Published in Nashville, Tennessee, by Thomas Nelson. Thomas Nelson is a trademark of Thomas Nelson, Inc.

Adapted from *The Layman's Overview of the Bible*, Copyright © 1987, Thomas Nelson, Inc. Compiled and Edited by George W. Knight and James R. Edwards.

Thomas Nelson, Inc. titles may also be purchased in bulk for ministry use by churches, parachurch ministries, and media ministries. For information, please call (800) 251-4000 ext. 2804 or email NelsonMinistryServices@thomasnelson.com.

All Scripture quotations, unless otherwise noted, are taken from the New King James Version (NKJV) Copyright © 1982 by Thomas Nelson, Inc. Used by permission. All rights reserved.

All photographs by Todd Bolen are Copyright © 2001, 2006 Todd Bolen. Used by contractual arrangement from www.bibleplaces.com.

Managing Editor, W. Mark Whitlock
Proofediting, Pam Darbonne
Book packaging, DesignPoint, Inc.
Interior Design, Rainbow Graphics

Library of Congress Cataloging-in-Publication Data available upon request.

Printed in the People's Republic of China

ISBN: 1418509116 (SS-1418509124)
      9781418509118
UPC 020049081648 (SS-020049081655)
EAN 9781418509118 (SS-9781418509125)

07 08 09 10 11 12 RRD 9 8 7 6 5 4 3 2 1

Contents

Thomas Nelson, Inc. appreciates the photography of Todd Bolen. Mr. Bolen is Associate Professor of Biblical Studies at the Israel Bible Extension (IBEX) of The Master's College. As part of his teaching in biblical history and archaeology, Mr. Bolen leads students on tours and archaeological excavations. In more than a decade of living in the Middle East, Mr. Bolen has developed a collection of more than 30,000 photographs of major sites, landscapes, and artifacts of the biblical world. Todd, his wife Kelli, and their four children live in the Judean Hills of Israel.

For more information about this collection of stunning photographs, please go to:

www.bibleplaces.com

Todd Bolen at Mount Gerizim and Mount Ebal.

Todd at work.

Introduction

THE THRILLING STORY OF THE BOOK OF BOOKS

The sacred book known as the Holy Bible is accepted by the church as uniquely inspired by God, and thus authoritative, providing guidelines for belief and behavior.

Major Divisions

The Bible contains two major divisions known as the Old Testament and the New Testament. The Old Testament tells of the preparation that was made for Christ's coming, His life and ministry, and the growth of the early church.

The English word *testament* normally refers to a person's will, the document which bequeaths property to those who will inherit it after the owner's death. But the meaning of testament from both the Hebrew and the Greek languages is "settlement," "treaty," or "covenant." Of these three English words, "covenant" best captures the meaning of the word *testament*. Thus, the two collections that make up the Bible can best be described as the books of the old covenant and the books of the new covenant.

The old covenant is the covenant settled at Mount Sinai in the days of Moses. By this covenant, the living and true God, who had delivered the Israelites from slavery in Egypt, promised to bless them as His special people. They were also to worship Him alone as their God and to accept His law as their rule for life (Ex. 19:3–6; 24:3–8).

The new covenant was announced by Jesus as He spoke to His disciples in the upper room in Jerusalem the night before His death. When He gave them a cup of wine to drink, Jesus declared that this symbolized "the new covenant in My blood" (Luke 22:20; 1 Cor. 11:25).

Between the times of Moses and Jesus, the prophet Jeremiah foresaw a day when God would make a new covenant with His people. Under this new covenant, God would inscribe His laws on the hearts of people rather than on tablets of stone (Jer. 31:31–34). In the New Testament, this new covenant of which Jeremiah spoke is identified with the covenant inaugurated by Jesus (Heb. 8:6–13).

While these two covenants, the old and the new, launched great spiritual movements, Christians believe these movements are actually two phases of one great act through which God has revealed His will to His people and called for their positive response. The second covenant is the fulfillment of what was promised in the first.

Authority of the Bible

The authority of the Bible is implied by its title, "the Word of God." It is the written record of the Word of God which came to prophets, apostles, and other spokesmen, and which "became flesh" in Jesus Christ. Christians believe Jesus Christ was the Word of God in a unique sense. Through Jesus, God communicated the perfect revelation of Himself to mankind. For Christians the authority of the Bible is related to the authority of Christ. The Old Testament was the Bible that Jesus used—the authority to which He made constant appeal and whose teachings He accepted and followed. When Jesus was arrested in the Garden of Gethsemane and led away to His execution, He submitted with the words, "The Scriptures must be fulfilled" (Mark 14:49). He saw His mission in the world as a fulfillment of the predictions of the Old Testament.

Revelation and Response

According to the Bible, God has made Himself known in a variety of ways. "The heavens declare the glory of God" (Ps. 19:1). "For since the creation of the world His invisible attributes are clearly seen, being understood by the things that are made, even His eternal power and Godhead" (Rom. 1:20). But while God is revealed in His creation and through the inner voice of man's conscience, the primary means by which He has made Himself known is through the Bible and through Jesus Christ, His Living Word.

God has revealed Himself through His mighty acts and in the words of His messengers, or spokesmen. Either of these ways is incomplete without the other. In the Old Testament record, none of the mighty acts of God is emphasized more than the Exodus—God's deliverance of the Israelites from Egyptian bondage. As He delivered His people, God repeatedly identified Himself as their redeemer God. "I am the Lord your God, who brought you out of the land of Egypt, out of the house of bondage. You shall have no other gods before Me" (Ex. 20:2–3).

In communicating with His people, God revealed both His identity and His purpose. His purpose was to make the Israelites a nation dedicated to His service alone. This message, conveyed to the Israelites through Moses, would have been ineffective if God had not delivered them personally. On the other hand, His deliverance would have been meaningless without the message. Together both constituted the Word of God to the Israelites—the saving message of the God who both speaks and acts.

In addition to God's revelation of Himself through the Bible, God's Word also records the response of those to whom the revelation was given. Too often the response was unbelief and disobedience. But at other times, people responded in faith and obedience. The Psalms, especially, proclaim the grateful response of men and women who experienced the grace and righteousness of God. These faithful people sometimes voiced their appreciation in words addressed directly to God. At other times they reported to others what God had come to mean to them.

In the New Testament writings, revelation and response came together in the person of Jesus Christ. On the one hand, Jesus was God's perfect revelation of Himself—He was the divine Word in human form. His works of mercy and power portrayed God in actions, especially His supreme act of sacrifice to bring about "the redemption that is in Christ Jesus" (Rom. 3:24). His teaching expressed the mind of God.

The words and acts of Jesus also proclaimed the meaning and purpose of His works. For example, His act of casting out demons "with the finger of God" (Luke 11:20) was a token that the kingdom of God had arrived. He also declared that His death, which He interpreted as the fulfillment of prophetic Scripture (Mark 14:49), was "a ransom for many" (Mark 10:45).

In His life and ministry, Jesus also illustrated the perfect human response of faith and obedience to God. Jesus was "the Apostle [God's Messenger to us] and High Priest [our Representative with God] of our confession" (Heb. 3:1). Thus, Jesus performed the mighty acts of God and He spoke authoritatively as God's Messenger and Prophet.

Preservation of the Bible

The Bible is a written, authoritative record by which any teaching or theory may be judged. But behind the writing lay periods of time when these messages were circulated in spoken form. The stories of the patriarchs (Abraham, Isaac, Jacob, and Jacob's twelve sons) were passed from generation to generation by word of mouth before they were written. The messages of the prophets were delivered orally before they were fixed in writing. Narratives of the life and ministry of Christ were repeated orally for three or more decades before they were given literary form. But the Bible owes its preservation to the fact that all these oral narratives were eventually reduced to writing. Just as God originally inspired the Bible, He has used this means to preserve His Word for future generations.

The first person in the Bible to write anything down was Moses. God instructed Moses to write as a permanent memorial the divine vow that the name of Amalek would be blotted out (Ex. 17:14). From that time until the end of the New Testament age, the writing of the many books and parts of the Bible continued.

None of the original biblical documents—referred to by scholars as the "original autographs"—has survived. No scrap of parchment or papyrus bearing the handwriting of any of the biblical authors has been discovered. But before the original documents disappeared, they were copied. These copies of the original writings are the texts on which current translations of the Bible are based.

The process of copying and recopying the Bible has continued to our time. Until the middle of the fifteenth century A.D., all the copying was done by hand. Then, with the invention of printing in Europe, copies could be made in greater quantities by using this new process. Each copy of the Bible had to be produced slowly by and with the old system, but now the printing press could produce thousands of copies in a short time. This made the Scriptures available to many people, rather than just the few who could afford handmade copies.

The older handwritten copies of Bible texts are called manuscripts. Early manuscripts for the books of the Bible were written on papyrus or skin. Papyrus was a type of ancient paper manufactured from a reed plant that grew in the Nile Valley of Egypt and similar environments. Papyrus was inexpensive but it was not very durable. It rotted quickly when exposed to moisture.

The ancient papyrus manuscripts which have been discovered were found in the dry sands off of Egypt and other arid places. Great quantities of inscribed papyri have been recovered from the Egyptian sands during the last hundred years dating from the period shortly before and after the beginning of the Christian era, about A.D. 30. A few scraps of papyri containing ancient texts of the Bible have been among the recovered manuscripts.

The skins of animals proved to be a much more durable writing material than papyrus. Many different writing materials were manufactured from such skins. Some were a coarse form of leather. Others were subjected to a special refining process, emerging as a writing material known as parchment. Vellum, another valued writing material, was made from calfskin. Some of the most important manuscripts of the Bible were written on vellum.

The Canon of the Bible. The word canon means a "rod"—specifically, a rod with graduated marks used for measuring length. Since the fourth century the word has come to be used for the collection of books officially recognized by the church as the Holy Bible. Every book in the canon was considered authoritative but not every authoritative book was in the canon. Christians recognized the entire Old Testament as their Bible from the earliest of times. Catholic Christianity sees the canon as an important source of authority along with the tradition of the church. Protestant and evangelical Christianity views the canon as the sole authority.

The exact process of canonization has faded through the ages. But it is known that the Pentateuch (first five books of the Old Testament) was considered authoritative from the earliest recorded time and that the other books were collected through the centuries as they were accepted as inspired writings. The Old Testament mentions several books which do not appear in our current Bibles (Num. 21:14; Josh. 10:13; 1 Kin. 11:41; 1 Chr. 29:29).

Differences still exist in the order and content of the Old Testament. Both Catholic and Protestant Bibles follow the order of the Vulgate, a Latin translation of the Bible produced about A.D. 400. However, the actual number of books in the Protestant Bible follows the Hebrew Bible, while the Catholic Bible follows the Vulgate's content by including the "extra books" known as the Apocrypha.

At least two letters from Paul that do not appear in Bibles today are mentioned in the New Testament. These are letters to the Corinthians (1 Cor. 5:9), and the Laodiceans (Col. 4:16). Only three of the twelve disciples of Jesus are recognized as authors in the New Testament. The belief that other disciples also wrote some material became the basis of third century apocryphal New Testament books. A list of accepted books from the third century has not been found, but several fourth century lists have been discovered. These lists point out the accepted, unaccepted, and doubtful books. During this time each locality had its own collection of books, but a number of them were held in common by all people. These eventually became the general canon although local canons continued to differ for centuries. The Holy Spirit's working has been manifested through the entire process of the canonization of God's Word.

The "Bible" which Jesus used was the Hebrew Old Testament. He left no instructions about forming a new collection of authoritative writings to stand beside the books which He and His disciples accepted as God's Word. The Old Testament was also the Bible of the early church, but it was the Old Testament as fulfilled by Jesus. Early Christians interpreted the Old Testament in the light of His person and work. This new perspective controlled the early church's interpretation to such a degree that, while Jews and Christians shared the same Bible, they understood it so differently that they might almost have been using two different Bibles.

The works and words of Jesus were first communicated in spoken form. The apostles and their associates proclaimed the gospel by word of mouth. Paul taught the believers orally in the churches which he founded when he was on the scene. But when he was absent, he communicated through his letters.

Quite early in its history, the church felt a need for a written account of the teachings of Jesus. His teachings did provide the basis for the new Christian way of life. But the church grew so large that many converts were unable to rely on the instructions of those who had heard and memorized the teachings of Jesus. From about A.D. 50 onward, probably more than one written collection of sayings of Jesus circulated in the churches. The earliest written gospel appears to have been the Gospel of Mark, written in the 60's.

An individual gospel, a letter from an apostle, or even several works circulating independently would not amount to a canon, or an authoritative list of books. A canon implies a collection of writings bearing a degree of authority for faith and life. There is evidence that two collections of Christian writings circulated among the churches at the beginning of the second century. One of these was the gospel collection—the four writings which are commonly called the four Gospels. The other collection was the Pauline collection, or the letters of the apostle Paul. The anonymous letter to the Hebrews was later added to this second collection.

Early Christians continued to accept the Old Testament as authoritative. But they could interpret the Old Testament in the light of Jesus' deeds and words only if they had a reliable record of them. So, alongside Moses and the prophets, they had these early writings about Jesus and letters from the apostles, who had known Jesus in the flesh.

When officials of the early church sought to make a list of books about Jesus and the early church which they considered authoritative, they kept the Old Testament, on the authority of Jesus and His apostles. Along with these books they recognized as authoritative the writings of the new age—four Gospels, or biographies, on the life and ministry of Jesus; the thirteen letters of Paul; and letters of other apostles and their companions. The gospel collection and the apostolic collection were joined together by the Book of Acts, which served as a sequel to the gospel story as well as a narrative background for the earlier epistles.

The primary standard applied to a book was that it must have been written either by an apostle or by someone close to the apostles. This guaranteed that their writing about Jesus and the early church would have the authenticity of an eyewitness account. As in the earlier phase of the church's existence, "the apostles' doctrine" (Acts 2:42) was the basis of its life and thought. The apostolic writings formed the charter, or foundation documents, of the church.

None of the books written after the death of the apostles was included in the New Testament, although early church officials recognized they did have some value as inspirational documents. The fact that they were written later ruled them out for consideration among the church's foundation documents. These other writings might be suitable for reading aloud in church because of their edifying character, but only the apostolic writings carried ultimate authority. They alone could be used as the basis of the church's belief and practice.

English Translations of the Bible

Shortly after James VI of Scotland ascended the throne of England as James I (1603), he convened a conference to settle matters under dispute in the Church of England. The only important result of this conference was an approval to begin work on the King James Version of the English Bible (KJV).

A group of forty-seven scholars, divided into six teams, was appointed to undertake the work of preparing the new version. Three teams worked on the Old Testament; two were responsible for the New Testament; and one worked on the Apocrypha. They used the 1602 edition of the Bishops' Bible as the basis of their revision, but they had access to many other versions and helps, as well as the texts in the original biblical languages. When the six groups had completed their task, the final draft was reviewed by a committee of twelve. The King James Version was published in 1611.

The new version won wide acceptance among the people of the English-speaking world. Nonsectarian in tone and approach, it did not favor one shade of theological or ecclesiastical opinion over another. The translators had an almost instinctive sense of good English style; the prose rhythm of the version gave it a secure place in the popular memory. Never before had an English version of the Bible been more admirably suited for reading aloud in public.

Although there was some resistance to the King James Version at first, it quickly made a place for itself. For more than three centuries, it has remained "The Bible" throughout the English-speaking world.

During the last fifty seventy years the Authorized, or King James, Version has been joined by a host of other English translations—all attempting to communicate God's Word clearly and concisely to a modern age. (Please see pages x and xi for a chart comparing these translations.)

Behind the Bible is a thrilling story of how God revealed Himself and His will to human spokesmen and then acted throughout history to preserve His Word and pass it along to future generations. The processes of canonization, preservation, and translation show that God is still involved in speaking His prophetic truth and calling His people to faith and obedience. In the words of the prophet Isaiah, "The grass withers, the flower fades, but the word of our God stands forever" (Is. 40:8).

Bible Translation Chart

Translation/ Paraphrase	Grade Level	Year of Release	Passage Comparison (John 15: 1–4)
Contemporary English Version (CEV)	5.6	1995	Jesus said to his disciples: I am the true vine, and my Father is the gardener. He cuts away every branch of mine that doesn't produce fruit. But he trims clean every branch that does produce fruit, so that it will produce even more fruit. You are already clean because of what I have said to you. Stay joined to me, and I will stay joined to you. Just as a branch cannot produce fruit unless it stays joined to the vine, you cannot produce fruit unless you stay joined to me.
English Standard Version	7.4	2001	I am the true vine, and my Father is the vinedresser. Every branch of mine that does not bear fruit he takes away, and every branch that does bear fruit he prunes, that it may bear more fruit. Already you are clean because of the word that I have spoken to you. Abide in me, and I in you. As the branch cannot bear fruit by itself, unless it abides in the vine, neither can you, unless you abide in me.
God's Word	4.5	1988	Then Jesus said, "I am the true vine, and my Father takes care of the vineyard. He removes every one of my branches that doesn't produce fruit. He also prunes every branch that does produce fruit to make it produce more fruit. You are already clean because of what I have told you. Live in me, and I will live in you. A branch cannot produce any fruit by itself. It has to stay attached to the vine. In the same way, you cannot produce fruit unless you live in me."
Good News Bible	7.3	1976	I am the real vine, and my Father is the gardener. He breaks off every branch in me that does not bear fruit, and he prunes every branch that does bear fruit, so that it will be clean and bear more fruit. You have been made clean already by the teaching I have given you. Remain united to me, and I will remain united to you. A branch cannot bear fruit by itself; it can do so only if it remains in the vine. In the same way you cannot bear fruit unless you remain in me.
Holman Christian Standard Version	7.5	2004	I am the true vine, and My Father is the vineyard keeper. Every branch in Me that does not produce fruit He removes, and He prunes every branch that produces fruit so that it will produce more fruit. You are already clean because of the word I have spoken to you. Remain in Me, and I in you. Just as a branch is unable to produce fruit by itself unless it remains on the vine, so neither can you unless you remain in Me.
International Children's Bible	3.9	1988	I am the true vine; my Father is the gardener. He cuts off every branch of mine that does not produce fruit. And he trims and cleans every branch that produces fruit so that it will produce even more fruit. You are already clean because of the words I have spoken to you. Remain in me, and I will remain in you. A branch cannot produce fruit alone but must remain in the vine. In the same way, you cannot produce fruit alone but must remain in me.
King James Version	12	1611	I am the true vine, and my Father is the husbandman. Every branch in me that beareth not fruit he taketh away: and every branch that beareth fruit, he purgeth it, that it may bring forth more fruit. Now ye are clean through the word which I have spoken unto you. Abide in me, and I in you. As the branch cannot bear fruit of itself, except it abide in the vine; no more can ye, except ye abide in me.
Living Bible	8.3	1971	I am the true Vine, and my Father is the Gardener. He lops off every branch that doesn't produce. And he prunes those branches that bear fruit for even larger crops. He has already tended you by pruning you back for greater strength and usefulness by means of the commands I gave you. Take care to live in me, and let me live in you. For a branch can't produce fruit when severed from the vine. Nor can you be fruitful apart from me.
New American Bible	6.6	1970	I am the true vine, and My Father is the vinedresser. Every branch in Me that does not bear fruit, He takes away; and every branch that bears fruit, He prunes it so that it may bear more fruit. You are already clean because of the word which I have spoken to you. Abide in Me, and I in you. As the branch cannot bear fruit of itself unless it abides in the vine, so neither can you unless you abide in Me.

New American Standard Version	11	1971	I am the true vine, and My Father is the vinedresser. Every branch in Me that does not bear fruit, He takes away; and every branch that bears fruit, He prunes it so that it may bear more fruit. You are already clean because of the word which I have spoken to you. Abide in Me, and I in you. As the branch cannot bear fruit of itself unless it abides in the vine, so neither can you unless you abide in Me.
New Century Version	5.6	1987	I am the true vine; my Father is the gardener. He cuts off every branch of mine that does not produce fruit. And he trims and cleans every branch that produces fruit so that it will produce even more fruit. You are already clean because of the words I have spoken to you. Remain in me, and I will remain in you. A branch cannot produce fruit alone but must remain in the vine. In the same way, you cannot produce fruit alone but must remain in me.
New International Reader's Version	3.5	1996	I am the true vine. My Father is the gardener. He cuts off every branch joined to me that does not bear fruit. He trims every branch that does bear fruit. Then it will bear even more fruit. You are already clean because of the word I have spoken to you. Remain joined to me, and I will remain joined to you. No branch can bear fruit by itself. It must remain joined to the vine. In the same way, you can't bear fruit unless you remain joined to me.
New International Version	7.8	1978	I am the true vine, and my Father is the gardener. He cuts off every branch in me that bears no fruit, while every branch that does bear fruit he prunes so that it will be even more fruitful. You are already clean because of the word I have spoken to you. Remain in me, and I will remain in you. No branch can bear fruit by itself; it must remain in the vine. Neither can you bear fruit unless you remain in me.
New King James Version	8.5	1982	I am the true vine, and My Father is the vinedresser. Every branch in Me that does not bear fruit He takes away; and every branch that bears fruit He prunes, that it may bear more fruit. You are already clean because of the word which I have spoken to you. Abide in Me, and I in you. As the branch cannot bear fruit of itself, unless it abides in the vine, neither can you, unless you abide in Me.
New Living Translation	6.3	1996	I am the true vine, and my Father is the gardener. He cuts off every branch of mine that doesn't produce fruit, and he prunes the branches that do bear fruit so they will produce even more. You have already been pruned and purified by the message I have given you. Remain in me, and I will remain in you. For a branch cannot produce fruit if it is severed from the vine, and you cannot be fruitful unless you remain in me.
New Revised Standard Version	8.1	1990	I am the true vine, and my Father is the vinegrower. He removes every branch in me that bears no fruit. Every branch that bears fruit he prunes to make it bear more fruit. You have already been cleansed by the word that I have spoken to you. Abide in me as I abide in you. Just as the branch cannot bear fruit by itself unless it abides in the vine, neither can you unless you abide in me.
Revised Standard Version	10	1952	I am the true vine, and my Father is the vinedresser. Every branch of mine that bears no fruit, he takes away, and every branch that does bear fruit he prunes, that it may bear more fruit. You are already made clean by the word which I have spoken to you. Abide in me, and I in you. As the branch cannot bear fruit by itself, unless it abides in the vine, neither can you, unless you abide in me.
The Message	8.5	1993	I am the Real Vine and my Father is the Farmer. He cuts off every branch of me that doesn't bear grapes. And every branch that is grape-bearing he prunes back so it will bear even more. You are already pruned back by the message I have spoken. Live in me. Make your home in me just as I do in you. In the same way that a branch can't bear grapes by itself but only by being joined to the vine, you can't bear fruit unless you are joined with me.
The Voice	In progress	In progress	I am the true vine, and My Father is the keeper of the vineyard. My Father examines every branch in Me and cuts away those who do not bear fruit. He leaves those bearing fruit and carefully prunes them so that they will bear more fruit; already, you are clean because you have heard My voice. Abide in Me, and I will abide in you. A branch cannot bear fruit if it is disconnected from the vine, and neither will you if you are not connected to Me.
Today's New International Version	8.3	2005	I am the true vine, and my Father is the gardener. He cuts off every branch in me that bears no fruit, while every branch that does bear fruit he prunes so that it will be even more fruitful. You are already clean because of the word I have spoken to you. Remain in me, as I also remain in you. No branch can bear fruit by itself; it must remain in the vine. Neither can you bear fruit unless you remain in me.

PART I

THE OLD TESTAMENT

The Sinai Desert near Hazeroth, showing some of the rocky outcroppings that almost seem to magnify its desolation. (Todd Bolen, bibleplaces.com)

CHAPTER 1

BOOKS OF THE LAW

The first five books of the Old Testament are called the Books of the Law or the Pentateuch, a Greek term meaning "five volumed." The Hebrew word for this collection is Torah, meaning "instruction, teaching, or doctrine."

This ancient division of the Law into five sections is supported by the Septaugint, a third-century B.C. translation of the Hebrew Old Testament into Greek. The five books together present a history of humanity from creation to the death of Moses, with particular attention to the development of the Hebrew people. The activity of God receives special emphasis throughout, and the Books of the Law reveal a great deal about God's nature and His purposes for mankind.

From the time it was written, the Pentateuch was consistently accepted as the work of Moses. His specific writing or compiling activity is mentioned in Exodus 17:14; 24:4; 34:27, while in the postexilic writings the Law, or Torah, was often attributed directly to Moses (Neh. 8:1; 2 Chr. 25:4; 35:12). This tradition was supported by Christ in New Testament times (Mark 12:26; John 7:23).

The chart below gives an overview of the Pentateuch by showing the individual books that make up this section of the Old Testament. These books are then discussed in detail in their appropriate order to give you a better understanding of this important major division of God's Word.

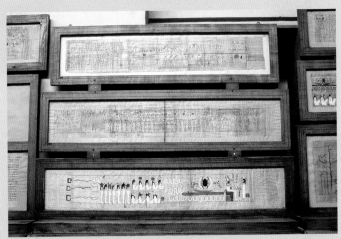

These strips of papyrus—made from a reed that grows along the Nile River in Egypt—were written during the same era as the books of Moses. (Daniel Gebhardt, bibleplaces.com)

Books of the Law

Book	Summary
Genesis	Creation and the establishment of the covenant relationship
Exodus	Deliverance of the people of Israel from slavery in Egypt
Leviticus	The ceremonial law
Numbers	Wandering of God's people in the wilderness
Deuteronomy	The second giving of the law by Moses before the people occupy the Promised Land

Touching the Torah scroll is a time-honored Jewish tradition—a visible sign of honor and respect. (Todd Bolen, bibleplaces.com)

The Book of Genesis

Genesis is the book of beginnings. The word *Genesis* means "the origin, source, creation, or coming into being of something." The Hebrew name for the book is *bereshith*, the first word in the Hebrew text, which is translated as "in the beginning" (Gen. 1:1). Genesis describes such important beginnings as the Creation, the fall of man, and the early years of the nation of Israel.

The beginning of salvation history—the story of God and man, sin and grace, wrath and mercy, covenant and redemption—also begins in the book of Genesis. These themes are repeated often throughout the rest of the Bible. As the Book of Revelation is the climax and conclusion of the Bible, so the Book of Genesis is the beginning and essential seed-plot of the Bible. Thus, Genesis is an important book for understanding the meaning of the entire Bible.

As the sun rises over the Negev Highlands the countours of the landscape stand out in stark relief, dominated by flat plateaus. (Todd Bolen, bibleplaces.com)

STRUCTURE OF THE BOOK

The Book of Genesis may conveniently be divided into four major parts:

- the Creation and the early days of mankind (Gen. 1:1—11:26);
- the story of Abraham and Isaac (Gen. 12:1—25:18);
- the story of Jacob and Esau (Gen. 25:19—36:43); and
- the story of Joseph and his brothers (Gen. 37:1—50:26).

The first major part of the Book of Genesis (chaps. 1—11) contains five great events:

- the history of creation and a description of life in the Garden of Eden before the Fall (Gen. 1:1—2:25);
- the story of Adam and Eve in the Garden of Eden: the temptation and fall of man (Gen. 3:1–24);
- the story of Cain and Abel (Gen. 4:1–16);
- the story of Noah and the Flood: the wickedness and judgment of man (Gen. 6:5—9:29); and
- the story of the Tower of Babel: the proud presumption of man, the confusion of tongues, and the scattering of mankind upon the earth (Gen. 11:1–9). Each of these great events relates to the whole of humanity, and each is filled with significance that continues throughout Scripture.

The rest of the Book of Genesis (chaps. 12—50) relates the narrative of the four great patriarchs of Israel: Abraham, Isaac, Jacob, and Joseph. The theme of these chapters is God's sovereignty in calling out a Chosen People who would serve and worship Him.

AUTHORSHIP AND DATE

The Book of Genesis gives no notice about its author. The early church, however, held to the conviction that Moses wrote the book, as did the Jerusalem Talmud and the first-century Jewish historian Josephus. In spite of the number of modern scholars who reject the Mosaic authorship of Genesis, the traditional view has much to commend it. Both the Old Testament and the New Testament contain frequent testimony to the Mosaic authorship of the entire Pentateuch (Lev. 1:1–2; Neh. 13:1; Matt. 8:4; Acts 26:22).

It would be difficult to find a person in Israel's life who was better prepared or qualified than Moses to write the history recorded in the Book of Genesis. A man who "was learned in all the wisdom of the Egyptians" (Acts 7:22), Moses was providentially prepared to understand and integrate, under the inspiration of God, all the available records, manuscripts, and oral narratives. Moses may have written the book during the years of the wilderness wandering to prepare the new generation to enter the land of Canaan.

As a prophet who enjoyed the unusual privilege of unhurried hours of communion with God on Mount Sinai, Moses was well equipped to record for all generations this magnificent account of God's dealings with the human race and the nation of Israel.

HISTORICAL SETTING

Moses may have finished writing the Book of Genesis not long before his death on Mount Nebo (Deut. 34). During this time the children of Israel, now led by Joshua, were camped east of the Jordan River, poised for the invasion of Canaan. In such a crucial historical context, the message of the Book of Genesis would have been of tremendous spiritual help to its first hearers. The creation of the world, the beginning of sin and disobedience, the principle of judgment and deliverance, the scattering of the na-

A Concise Outline of
Genesis

The Jordan River, mirroring some of the lush growth along its banks. The Jordan is home to 35 species of fish, 16 of which are found nowhere else. (Todd Bolen, bibleplaces.com)

tions, the call and covenant God made with Abraham, the checkered careers of the first descendants of Abraham—all of these accounts would bear directly on the attitudes and faith of the new community.

The first readers, or hearers, of the Book of Genesis were the covenant community, the Chosen People of God. Like Abraham, they were on a journey—a great venture of faith into the unknown (Gen. 12:1–9). Like Abraham, they needed to respond to God in wholehearted faith and in the fear of the Lord (Gen. 22:1–19). They needed to hear such words as were spoken to Isaac: "I am the God of your father Abraham; do not fear, for I am with you. I will bless you and multiply your descendants for My servant Abraham's sake" (Gen. 26:24).

THEOLOGICAL CONTRIBUTION

The Book of Genesis is a primary source for several basic doctrines of the Bible. The book focuses on God primarily in two areas: He is the Creator of the universe, and He is the one who initiates covenant with His people. Genesis ties creation and covenant together in a stunning manner: the God who initiates covenant is the same God who has created the entire universe. The eternal God and almighty Creator enters into covenant with His people (Gen. 1:1; John 1:1).

God's covenant with Abraham is the basic plot of the Scripture. God's work from that day forward was to accomplish His plan for the nations of the world through His people Israel, the descendants of Abraham. God's covenant with Abraham (Gen. 12:1–3; 15:1–21) contains a number of personal blessings on the father of the faith. But the climax of the text is in the words of worldwide import: "And in you all the families of the earth shall be blessed" (Gen. 12:3).

This promise is realized in the person of the Lord Jesus Christ, the Seed of Abraham (Gal. 3:16, 19), through whom peoples of all nations and families may enter into the joy of knowing the God of Abraham. God's promise is realized also in the church, in those who believe in Christ, which the apostle Paul calls "the Israel of God" (Gal. 6:16). The true "seed," or descendants, of Abraham, Paul argued, are not Abraham's physical descendants but those who have the same faith as Abraham (Rom. 9:7–8; Gal. 3:29).

Genesis presents the creation of man as male and female in the image of God (Gen. 1:26–27; 5:3; 9:6), man's fall and ruin, his judgment, and his possible triumph in God's grace. In the context of man's judgment came the first whisper of the gospel message of the final triumph of Christ over Satan: "And I will put enmity between you [the serpent] and the woman, and between your seed and her seed; He shall bruise your head, and you shall bruise His heel" (Gen. 3:15). This prophecy was fulfilled by the death of Jesus on the cross, a sacrifice that destroyed the works of the devil (1 John 3:8).

The apostle Paul referred to the story of Adam's fall (Gen. 3) by comparing Adam to Christ (Rom. 5:12, 18). Christ is portrayed as a "second Adam" who, by His atonement, reverses the effects on the Fall. Some scholars see another type, or foreshadowing truth, of Calvary in the fact that God, in order to cover the nakedness of Adam and Eve (symbolic of sin, guilt, and shame), killed an animal (thereby shedding blood) and made tunics of skin with which to clothe them (Gen. 3:21). For, as the writer of the Book of Hebrews says, "Without shedding of blood there is no remission [of sin]" (Heb. 9:22).

SPECIAL CONSIDERATIONS

Some scholars organize the literary structure of the Book of Genesis around the Hebrew word *toledoth* (literally, genealogy), which Moses seems to use ten times in Genesis to indicate major blocks of material. The NKJV translates *toledoth* as "this is the history of" (Gen. 2:4) and "this is the genealogy of" (Gen. 5:1; 6:9; 10:1; 11:10; 11:27; 25:12; 25:19; 36:1; 37:2).

The Book of Genesis takes the reader to the moment when the Creator spoke into being the sun, moon, stars, planets, galaxies, plants, moving creatures, and mankind. Those who seek to discredit the

Book of Genesis by pointing to alleged discrepancies between religion and science are blind to the exalted spiritual content of this work. If a student expects to find in Genesis a scientific account of how the world came into existence, with all questions concerning primitive life answered in technical language, he will be disappointed. Genesis is not an attempt to answer such technical questions.

Genesis is marked by exquisite prose, such as chapter 22 (the account of the binding of Isaac) and chapter 37—50 (the Joseph narrative). Literacy critics often point to Genesis 24, the story of a bride for Isaac, as a classic example of great narrative style. Genesis also has poetic sections such as the solemn curses by God (Gen. 3:14–19) and the prophetic blessing of Jacob (Gen. 49:3–27). Genesis 1, the history of creation, is written in a highly elevated prose with a poetic tone.

At times attention is focused on the men in the Book of Genesis. But women of major significance also appear in the book: Eve is the mother of all living (Gen. 3:20); Sarah had a faith that was complementary to Abraham's (Gen. 21:1–7); and Leah, Rachel, Bilhah, and Zilpah are the mothers of the 12 patriarchs of Israel (Gen. 29:31—30:24; 35:23–26).

Genesis is also a book of firsts. Genesis records the first birth (Gen. 4:1), the first death (Gen. 4:8), the first musical instruments (Gen. 4:21), and the first rainbow (Gen. 9:12–17). Genesis is indeed the book of beginnings. As the children of Israel read this book in the wilderness, or after they crossed the Jordan River; they knew that their experiences with God were just beginning.

This marble relief from the 6th century A.D., now in the Ephesus Museum, shows Abraham about to sacrifice Isaac just before the Lord provided a substitute. (Todd Bolen, bibleplaces.com)

The Book of Exodus

This book outlines Israel's beginning and early years as a nation. It takes its name from the event known as the Exodus, the dramatic deliverance of the Hebrew people from enslavement in Egypt under the leadership of Moses. Throughout Exodus we meet a God who is the Lord of history and the Redeemer of His people. These themes, repeated throughout the rest of the Bible, make Exodus one of the foundational books of the Scriptures.

Jebel Musa is the traditional site of Mount Sinai, on which Moses received the 10 commandments from God. It's hard to imagine a more forbidding landscape. (Todd Bolen, bibleplaces.com)

STRUCTURE OF THE BOOK

Exodus begins where the Book of Genesis leaves off—with the descendants of Joseph who moved to Egypt to escape famine and hardship in their own land. For many years the Hebrew people grew and prospered with the blessings of the Egyptian ruler. But then with one transitional verse, Exodus explains the changing political climate that brought an end to their favored position: "Now there arose a new king over Egypt, who did not know Joseph" (1:8). The Hebrews were reduced to the status of slaves and put to work on the Pharaoh's building projects.

The Book of Exodus falls naturally into three major divisions:

- Israel in Egypt (1:1—12:36);
- Israel in the wilderness (12:37—18:37); and
- Israel at Mount Sinai (19:1—40:38).

Some of the major events covered by this rapidly moving book include God's call to Moses through the burning bush to lead His people out of bondage (3:1—4:17); the series of plagues sent upon the Egyptians because of Pharaoh's stubbornness (7:1—12:30); the release of the captives and their miraculous crossing of the Red Sea, followed by the destruction of Pharaoh's army (15:1–31); God's provision for the people in the wilderness through bread, quail, and water (16:1—17:7); the giving of the Ten Commandments and other parts of the Law to Moses at Mount Sinai (20:1—23:33); and the renewal of the covenant between God and His people (24:1–8).

The book ends as Moses and the workmen under his supervision build a tabernacle in the wilderness around Mount Sinai at God's command. A cloud, symbolizing God's presence, rests on the tabernacle; and the entire building is filled with His glory (36:1—40:38).

AUTHORSHIP AND DATE

Exodus is one of the first five books of the Old Testament—books that have traditionally been assigned to Moses as author. But some scholars insist that Exodus was compiled by an unknown writer or editor who drew from several different historical documents. There are two sound reasons why Moses can be accepted without question as the divinely inspired author of this book.

First, Exodus itself speaks of the writing activity of Moses. In Exodus 34:27 God commands to "write these words." Another passage tells us that "Moses wrote all the words of the Lord" in obedience to God's command (24:4). It is reasonable to assume that these verses refer to Moses's writing of material that appears in the Book of Exodus. Second, Moses either observed or participated in the events described in Exodus. He was well qualified to write about these experiences, since he had been educated in the household of the Pharaoh during his early life.

Since Moses wrote Exodus, it must be dated some time before his death about 1400 B.C. Israel spent the 40 years preceding this date wandering in the wilderness because of their unfaithfulness. This is the most likely time for the writing of the book.

HISTORICAL SETTING

Exodus covers a crucial period in Israel's early history as a nation. Most conservative scholars believe the Hebrews left Egypt about 1440 B.C. Some believe it took place much later, around 1280 B.C. About two-thirds of the book describes Israel's experiences during the two years after this date. This was the period when Israel traveled through the wilderness toward Mount Sinai and received instructions from God through Moses as he met with God on the mountain.

A Concise Outline of **Exodus**	**I. Redemption from Egypt**	
	1. The Need for Redemption from Egypt	1:1–22
	2. The Preparation of the Leaders of the Redemption	2:1—4:31
	3. The Redemption of Israel from Egypt by God	5:1—15:21
	4. The Preservation of Israel in the Wilderness	15:22—18:27
	II. Revelation from God	
	1. The Revelation of the Old Testament	19:1—31:18
	2. The Response of Israel to the Covenant	32:1—40:38

The mudbricks of Moses's day looked a lot like these, still made from one of the most available materials in Egypt. (Daniel Gebhardt, bibleplaces.com)

THEOLOGICAL CONTRIBUTION

The Book of Exodus has exercised much influence over the faith of Israel, as well as Christian theology. The Bible's entire message of redemption grows out of the covenant relationship between God and His people first described in this book. In addition, several themes in the book can be clearly traced in the life and ministry of Jesus. Moses received the Law on Mount Sinai; Jesus delivered the Sermon on the Mount. Moses lifted up the serpent in the wilderness to give life to the people; Jesus was lifted up on the cross to bring eternal life to all who trust in Him.

The Passover (see Ex. 12), first instituted by God for the deliverance of the Hebrews from slavery, became one of the focal points of Israel's faith. It also served as the base on which Jesus developed the Last Supper as a lasting memorial for His followers. With clear insight into Exodus, the message of the Bible and the meaning of the life of Jesus dawns with greater understanding for Christian believers.

SPECIAL CONSIDERATIONS

The Book of Exodus is a dramatic testimony to the power of God. The signs and plagues sent by God to break Pharaoh's stubbornness are clear demonstrations of His power. In addition to setting the Israelites free, they also dramatize the weakness of Egypt's false gods. The puny idols of Egypt are powerless before the mighty God of Israel.

The crossing of the Red Sea is one of the most dramatic events in all of the Bible; the biblical writers repeatedly refer to it as the most significant sign of God's love for Israel. A helpless slave people had been delivered from their enemies by their powerful Redeemer God. They celebrated their victory with a song of praise that emphasizes the theme of the Book of Exodus.

> I will sing to the Lord,
> For He has triumphed gloriously!
> The horse and its rider
> He has thrown into the sea!
> The Lord is my strength and song,
> And He has become my salvation.

This ancient frieze shows Ramses II in a heroic position, ready for action with a fully drawn bow. (Daniel Gebhardt, bibleplaces.com)

The Book of Leviticus

This book is filled with worship instructions for God's Chosen People, the Hebrew nation. The Levites, members of the tribe of Levi, were the priestly family of the nation; the title of the book seems to indicate these instructions were given specifically for them. But Leviticus was actually a manual of worship for all the people. Because of its emphasis on holiness, sacrifice, and atonement, the book has an important message for modern believers.

Flames such as these would consume even the largest burnt offering. (© 2007 JupiterImages Corporation)

STRUCTURE OF THE BOOK

Leviticus is difficult reading for most Bible students. It contains page after page of detailed instructions about strange worship rituals that seem to have no clear organizing principle. But with careful analysis, the book breaks down into six divisions.

The first several chapters of the book contain instructions about the ritual of sacrifice, including animal sacrifice, or the burnt offering—a key ingredient of Old Testament worship. Other segments of the book deal with the consecration of the priesthood, personal purification and dietary laws, laws of atonement, holiness of the people, and the redemption of tithes and vows.

AUTHORSHIP AND DATE

Most conservative Bible students acknowledge Moses as the author of the Book of Leviticus. But some scholars insist the book was pulled together from many different sources by an unknown editor several centuries after Moses's death. This theory overlooks the dozens of instances in Leviticus where God spoke directly to Moses and Moses wrote down His instructions to be passed along to the people (4:1; 6:1, 8:1, 11:1).

In addition, nothing was more important to the nation of Israel in its earliest years than the development of its system of worship. Thus, worship rules would have been established at a very early stage in Israel's history. This argues convincingly for the early writing of these rules at the hand of Moses, probably about 1445 B.C.

HISTORY SETTING

The Book of Leviticus belongs to the period in Israel's history when the people were encamped at Mount Sinai following their miraculous deliverance from slavery in Egypt. At Sinai Moses received the Ten Commandments and other parts of the Law directly from God. He also built and furnished the tabernacle as a place where the people could worship God (Ex. 40). Just after the tabernacle was filled with God's glory, Moses received instructions for the people regarding worship of God in this holy place. It is these instructions which we find in the Book of Leviticus.

THEOLOGICAL CONTRIBUTION

The Book of Leviticus is important because of its clear teachings on three vital spiritual truths: Atonement, Sacrifice, and Holiness. Without the background of these concepts in Leviticus, we could not understand their later fulfillment in the life and ministry of Jesus.

Atonement—Chapter 16 of Leviticus contains God's instructions for observing the Day of Atonement. On that day the high priest of Israel entered the most sacred place in the tabernacle and offered an animal sacrifice to atone for his own sins. Then he killed another animal and sprinkled its blood on the altar to atone for the sins of the people. New Testament writers later compared this familiar picture to the sacrifice of Jesus on our behalf. But unlike a human priest, Jesus did not have to offer sacrifices, "first for His own sins and then for the people's, for this He did once for all when He offered up Himself" (Heb. 7:27).

Sacrifice—The Book of Leviticus instructs the Covenant People to bring many types of sacrifices or offerings to God: burnt offerings, grain offerings, peace offerings, sin offerings, and guilt or trespass offerings. These were considered gifts by which a worshiper expressed his loyalty and devotion to God. But a blood offering—presenting the blood of a sacrificed animal to God—went beyond the idea of a gift. It symbolized that the worshiper was offering his own life to God, since the Hebrews believed that

A Concise Outline of
Leviticus

This reproduction shows the tabernacle as seen from the outer court. The altar usually appears bigger than most people expect; the bronze laver typically appears smaller. (Todd Bolen, bibleplaces.com)

"the life of the flesh is in the blood" (Lev. 17:11). Again, this familiar teaching assumed deeper meaning in the New Testament when applied to Jesus. He gave His life on our behalf when He shed His blood to take away our sins.

Holiness—The basic meaning of holiness as presented in the Book of Leviticus is that God demands absolute obedience of His people. The root meaning of the word is "separation." God's people were to be separate from, and different than, the surrounding pagan peoples. This is actually the reason for God's instruction that His people were not to eat certain unclean foods. Only a clean, undefiled people could be used by Him to bring about His purpose of world redemption. Leviticus also makes it clear that the holiness demanded by God extended to the daily behavior of His people. They were expected to practice kindness, honesty, and justice and to show compassion toward the poor (Lev. 19:9–18).

SPECIAL CONSIDERATIONS

The blood of bulls and goats so prominent in Leviticus had no power to take away sin. But each of these rituals was "a shadow of the good things to come" (Heb. 10:1). They pointed forward to God's ultimate sacrifice, given freely on our behalf: "So Christ was offered once to bear the sins of many" (Heb. 9:28).

Known as the "choice fruit" of Leviticus 23:40, the citron is better known in modern days in its preserved form, as a main ingredient in less-expensive fruitcakes. (Kim Guess, bibleplaces.com)

The Book of Numbers

This book traces the Israelites through their long period of wandering in the wilderness as they prepared to enter the Promised Land. Numbers takes its name from the two censuses or "numberings" of the people recorded in the book (chaps. 1 and 26). But Numbers contains a great deal more than a listing of names and figures.

The Isrealites had to pass through the valley called the Wadi Punon to reach the King's Highway on the plateau, at which point they were denied access by the Moabites. (Todd Bolen, bibleplaces.com)

STRUCTURE OF THE BOOK

Numbers is actually a sequel to the Book of Exodus. Exodus follows the Hebrew people as they escape from slavery in Egypt and cross the wilderness, arriving finally at Mount Sinai, where they receive the Ten Commandments and other parts of God's Law. The Book of Numbers picks up this story with the people still encamped at Sinai. It follows their wanderings through the Wilderness of Sinai for the next 40 years until they finally arrive at Moab on the eastern side of the Jordan River, ready to occupy the land of Canaan. Thus, the books of Exodus and Numbers together show how an enslaved people were prepared to take possession of the land that God himself had promised many centuries earlier to Abraham and his descendants.

Just as Moses is the central figure in Exodus, he also is the dominant personality in Numbers. His leadership ability is pushed to the limit in Numbers as the people grumble about everything from their food to the water supply. Time after time God supplied their needs by sending manna, quail, and water; but still they cried out in a stubborn spirit. Finally, in exasperation, Moses struck a rock with his rod to produce drinking water. This was a clear violation of God's command, since He had instructed Moses to *speak* to the rock. Because of his disobedience, Moses was not allowed to enter the Promised Land. He died shortly after viewing the land at a distance from atop Mount Nebo in Moab (Deut. 34).

HISTORICAL SETTING

The events in the Book of Numbers cover a span of about 39 or 40 years in Israel's history—from 1445 B.C., when they left their encampment at Mount Sinai, to 1405 B.C., when they entered the land of Canaan by crossing the Jordan River near Jericho. These were years of preparation as well as punishment. Their harsh life in the desert wilderness prepared them for the task of pushing out the Canaanites.

The Book of Numbers clearly shows why the Israelites did not proceed immediately to take the land after leaving Mount Sinai. Moses chose 12 spies or scouts and sent them into Canaan along its southern border to explore the land and check its defenses. Ten of them returned with a pessimistic report about the warlike Canaanites who held the land. But two of the spies, Joshua and Caleb, encouraged the people to take the land; for God had promised to prepare the way. When the Israelites refused, God sentenced them to two generations of aimless wandering in the wilderness before they could enter the Promised Land (Num. 14:1–38).

AUTHORSHIP AND DATE

Numbers is one of the first five books of the Old Testament—books that have traditionally been assigned to Moses as author. He is the central personality of the book, and it is reasonable to assume that he wrote about these events in which he played such a prominent role. One passage in Numbers states, "Now Moses wrote down the starting points of their journeys at the command of the Lord" (33:2). Other similar references to Moses's writings are found throughout Numbers, giving strong support to the conviction that he wrote the book.

Moses must have written Numbers some time just before his death as the Hebrew people prepared to enter the land. This would place the time of writing at about 1404 B.C.

THEOLOGICAL CONTRIBUTION

The Book of Numbers presents the concept of God's correcting wrath upon His own disobedient people. Through their rebellion, the Hebrews had broken the covenant. Even Moses was not exempt from God's wrath when he disobeyed God.

A Concise Outline of
Numbers

The King's Highway, showing a fallen-down milestone. The ancient Moabites forbade the Israelites to cross modern-day Transjordan on this highway, on their way to the Promised Land. (Todd Bolen, bibleplaces.com)

But even in His wrath, God did not give up on His people. While He might punish them in the present, He was still determined to bless them and bring them ultimately into a land of their own. Even the false prophet Balaam recognized this truth about God's sovereign purpose. Balaam declares: "God is not a man, that He should lie, nor a son of man, that He should repent. Has He said, and will He not do it? Or has He spoken, and will He not make it good?" (23:19).

SPECIAL CONSIDERATIONS

The Israelite warriors counted in the two censuses in the Book of Numbers have been a puzzle to Bible scholars (see chaps. 1 and 26). In each case, they add up to an army of more than 600,000. If this is correct, then the total Israelite population must have been more than 2,000,000 people. Such a figure seems out of line for this period of ancient history when most nations were small.

One possible explanation is that the word translated *thousands* in English could have meant something like units, tents, or clans in the Hebrew language. If so, a much smaller number was in mind. But other scholars believe there is no reason to question the numbers, since the Israelites did increase dramatically during their years of enslavement in Egypt (Ex. 1:7–12).

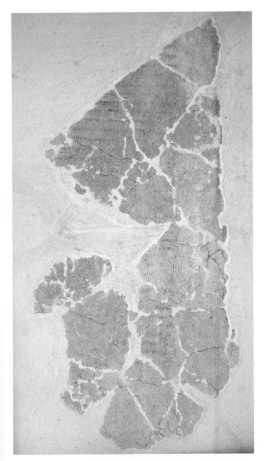

This ancient inscription mentions Balaam four separate times—the same Balaam we encounter in the book of Numbers. It is the first specific mention of an Old Testament prophet from an archeological source. (Todd Bolen, bibleplaces.com)

The Book of Deuteronomy

This book is commonly identified as the farewell speech of Moses to the people of Israel just before his death. The title of the book comes from the Greek word *Deuteronomion*, which means "second law." In his address, Moses underscored and repeated many of the laws of God that the people received at Mount Sinai about 40 years earlier. He also challenged the people to remain faithful to their God and His commands as they prepared to enter the Promised Land.

A beautiful wheat field, ready for harvest. Note the irregular shape of the field in the background, conforming to the contours of the land. (Todd Bolen, bibleplaces.com)

STRUCTURE OF THE BOOK

Because it is written in the format of a series of warmhearted speeches, Deuteronomy is unique among the books of the Bible. Following a brief introduction of Moses as the speaker, the book begins with a series of speeches and addresses from Moses to the people. These speeches continue through chapter 33, with only brief narrative interruptions of his spoken words. The final chapter departs from the speech format to report on Moses's death and the selection of Joshua as his successor.

In his addresses, Moses reminded the people of their days of slavery in Egypt and how God had delivered them safely through the wilderness to the borders of the Promised Land. He also restated the Ten Commandments and indicated that these great moral principles should direct their lives. As God's special people, they were to be holy and righteous as an example for surrounding pagan nations. Moses also warned Israel of the perils of idolatry and called the people to worship the one true God, who demanded their total commitment: "Hear, O Israel: The Lord our God, the Lord is one! You shall love the Lord your God with all your heart, with all your soul, and with all your might" (6:4–5).

As he spoke to the people, Moses also repeated many of the laws and regulations that dealt with observance of the Sabbath, proper forms of worship, treatment of the poor, religious feasts and festivals, inheritance rights, sexual morality, property rights, treatment of servants, and the administration of justice. Finally Moses ended his words of caution and counsel with a beautiful song of praise to God. Then he pronounced an individual blessing on each of the tribes of the nation that would go into Canaan with Joshua to possess the land.

AUTHORSHIP AND DATE

Conservative Bible students are united in their conviction that Moses wrote this book. But many liberal scholars theorize that Deuteronomy was written several centuries after Moses's time by an unknown author who wanted to bring about the religious reforms of the nation of Judah under King Josiah (2 Kings 22—23). These sweeping reforms began when a copy of the Book of Deuteronomy was discovered as workmen repaired the Temple in Jerusalem. According to this theory, Deuteronomy was placed in the Temple to call the Jewish people back to observance of the laws which God had revealed to Moses and the people of Israel many centuries earlier.

This theory unfortunately overlooks the statement of the book itself that Moses wrote Deuteronomy and directed that it be read regularly by the people (31:9–13).

The first-person pronoun *I* appears throughout the book as Moses refers to himself and his experiences. The logical conclusion is that Moses wrote the first 33 chapters of the book. Chapter 34, about his death, probably was added by his successor Joshua as a tribute to Moses. The date of the writing must have been some time around 1400 B.C.

HISTORICAL SETTING

The Book of Deuteronomy marks a turning point in the history of God's Chosen People. For the previous 40 years, they had been through many unforgettable experiences under the leadership of Moses. He had led them out of enslavement in Egypt and through the wilderness to receive God's laws at Mount Sinai. Then, because of their rebellion and unfaithfulness, they had wandered aimlessly in the desert for two generations. Now they were camped on the eastern border of Canaan, the land which God had promised as their homeland.

Moses sensed that the people would face many new temptations as they settled in the land and established permanent dwellings among the pagan Canaanites. He also realized that his days as their

A Concise Outline of
Deuteronomy

A modern Passover seder plate with its six traditional items, including a roasted egg, an unbroken shankbone of a lamb, and bitter herbs. (Todd Bolen, bibleplaces.com)

leader were drawing to a close. He used this occasion to remind the people of their heritage as God's special people and to challenge them to remain faithful to God and His laws. Thus, the Book of Deuteronomy becomes a stirring conclusion to the life of this statesman and prophet. One of the final verses of the book pays this fitting tribute to Moses's visionary leadership: "Since then there has not arisen in Israel a prophet like Moses, whom the Lord knew face to face" (34:10).

THEOLOGICAL CONTRIBUTION

The New Testament contains more than 80 quotations from Deuteronomy, so it must be rated as one of the foundational books of the Bible. Jesus Himself often quoted from Deuteronomy. During His temptation, He answered Satan with four quotations from Scripture. Three of these came from this key Old Testament book (Matt. 4:4, Luke 4:4—Deut. 8:3; Matt. 4:7, Luke 4:12—Deut. 6:16; Matt. 4:10, Luke 4:8—Deut. 6:13).

When Jesus was asked to name the most important commandment in the law, He responded with the familiar call from Deuteronomy: "You shall love the Lord your God with all your heart, with all your soul, and with all your mind" (Matt. 22:37; Deut. 6:5; Mark 12:30; Luke 10:27). He then added some other important words from Leviticus to show that He was carrying the law one step further: "The second [commandment] is like it: 'You shall love your neighbor as yourself'" (Matt. 22:39; Lev. 19:18; Mark 12:31; Luke 10:27).

Another great truth underscored by the Book of Deuteronomy is that God is faithful to His Covenant People, those whom He has called to carry out His purpose of redemption in the world. The Hebrews were chosen as God's instruments not because they were a worthy, powerful people, but because He loved them and desired to bless the rest of the world through their influence (7:6, 11). This is still God's purpose as He continues to call people to follow Him and commit themselves to His purpose in their lives.

SPECIAL CONSIDERATIONS

Some people look upon the laws of God in the Old Testament as burdensome and restrictive. The Book of Deuteronomy, however, teaches that God's laws are given for our own good to help us stay close to Him in our attitudes and behavior. Thus, Moses called on the people to keep God's statutes, "which I command you today for your good" (10:13). The intention of God's law is positive; passages in the New Testament that seem to condemn the law must be interpreted in this light. It is the misuse of the law— trusting it rather than God's mercy as the basis of our salvation—that we should avoid. God's law is actually fulfilled in the person of our Lord and Savior Jesus Christ (Matt. 5:17, 20).

A modern scribe, copying Torah by hand in the traditional way. Note the position of his hand—Hebrew is written from right to left. (Kim Guess, bibleplaces.com)

CHAPTER 2

BOOKS OF HISTORY

The story of the nation of Israel continues in the twelve historical books—the second major division of the Old Testament. These books contain descriptions of the settlement of God's Covenant People in the Promised Land after their escape from Egypt and the years of wandering in the wilderness; the transition from rule by judges to rule by kings; the division of the nation into northern and southern factions; the destruction of the Northern Kingdom; and the captivity and return of the Southern Kingdom. The time period represented by these books covers about 700 years.

The chart on page 26 gives an overview of this historical material by showing the individual books that make up this section of the Old Testament. These books are then discussed in detail in their appropriate order to give you a better understanding of this important major division of God's Word.

This is the 1750-foot-long tunnel, dug by King Hezekiah to bring water into the City of David from the Gihon Spring to the Pool of Siloam. (Todd Bolen, bibleplaces.com)

Books of History

Book	Summary
Joshua	The capture and settlement of the Promised Land
Judges	The nation of Israel is rescued by a series of judges, or military leaders
Ruth	A beautiful story of God's love and care
1 and 2 Samuel	The early history of Israel, including the reigns of Saul and David
1 and 2 Kings	A political history of Israel, focusing on the reigns of selected kings from the time of Solomon to the captivity of the Jewish people by Babylon
1 and 2 Chronicles	A religious history of Israel, covering the same period of time as 2 Samuel and 1 and 2 Kings
Ezra	The return of the Jewish people from captivity in Babylon
Nehemiah	The rebuilding of the walls of Jerusalem after the exiles returned from Babylon
Esther	God's care for His people under Gentile rule

The modern city of Gibeon, shown from the south. Gibeon was once part of the tribe of Benjamin, but was designated a levitical city in Joshua 21:17. (Todd Bolen, bibleplaces.com)

The Book of Joshua

This Old Testament book describes the conquest and division of the land of Canaan by the Hebrew people. The book is named for its central figure, Joshua, who succeeded Moses as leader in this vigorous campaign.

Portions of a Jericho mudbrick wall, collapsed in front of a revetment (barricade) wall dating from the time of Joshua. (Todd Bolen, bibleplaces.com)

STRUCTURE OF THE BOOK

The Book of Joshua has a natural, flowing structure that makes it a joy to read and study. In a brief pro-logue, the warrior Joshua is introduced as the capable leader selected by God to lead the people. Then the book launches immediately into narratives about the military victories of the Hebrews as they drove the Canaanites out of the land. Joshua's strategy was to divide and conquer. He struck first in cen-tral Canaan by taking the city of Jericho and surrounding territory. Then he launched rapid attacks to the south and north. This strategy quickly gave the Covenant People a foothold in the land. After weak-ening the enemy's position with this strategy, Joshua led numerous minor attacks against them during the next several years.

These accounts of Joshua's military campaigns are followed by a long description of the division of the land among the 12 tribes of Israel. Finally, the book ends with the death of Joshua after he leads the people to renew the covenant and charges them to remain faithful to God.

AUTHORSHIP AND DATE

Early Jewish tradition credited Joshua with writing this book. But this is disputed by many modern scholars. One of the strongest objections to his authorship is the final section of the book, which de-scribes Joshua's death and burial (24:29–33). Obviously, Joshua could not have written this material.

But other sections of the book strongly suggest that they were written by Joshua. One passage de-clares that after giving his farewell address, "Joshua wrote these words in the Book of the Law of God" (24:26). Some of the battle narratives are also written with vivid description and minute detail, sug-gesting that they may have been composed by the commander on the scene, Joshua himself (see espe-cially chaps. 6—8).

The most logical and believable theory about authorship is that Joshua wrote a major part of the book. But it probably did not reach its finished form until several years after his death. An editor must have added some additional narratives, such as the one about Joshua's death and burial, to complete this important book about Joshua and his contribution. A commonly accepted date for the death of Joshua is about 1375 B.C., so the book must have been completely shortly after this date.

HISTORICAL SETTING

The Book of Joshua covers about 25 years in one of the most important periods of Israel's history—their conquest and final settlement of the land which God had promised to Abraham and his descen-dants many centuries earlier. The specific years for this occupation must have been from about 1400 to 1375 B.C.

THEOLOGICAL CONTRIBUTION

One important message of the Book of Joshua is that true and false religions do not mix. Joshua's or-ders were to destroy the Canaanites because of their pagan and immoral worship practices. But these people never were totally subdued or destroyed. Traces of their false religion remained to tempt the Is-raelites. Again and again throughout their history, the Hebrew people departed from worship of the one true God. This tendency toward false worship was the main reason for Joshua's moving farewell speech. He warned the people against worshiping these false gods and challenged them to remain faithful to their great deliverer Jehovah. The point of Joshua's message was, you cannot worship these false gods and remain faithful to the Lord: "But as for me and my house, we will serve the Lord" (24:15).

A Concise Outline of
Joshua

SPECIAL CONSIDERATIONS

Some people have difficulty with God commanding Joshua to destroy the Canaanites. But behind this command lay God's concern for His Covenant People. He wanted to remove the Canaanites' idolatrous worship practices so they would not be a temptation to the Israelites. This command to Joshua also represented God's judgment against sin and immorality. God used Israel as an instrument of His judgment against a pagan nation.

The "tell" portion of this modern photo refers to the mound near the middle, containing mudbricks and other artifacts from the original walls of Jericho. (Todd Bolen, bibleplaces.com)

The Book of Judges

This historical book covers the chaotic time between Joshua's death and the beginning of a centralized government under King Saul—a period of about 300 years. The "judges" for whom the book is named were actually military leaders whom God raised up to deliver His people from their enemies. Twelve of these heroic deliverers are mentioned in the book.

Both Abraham and Jacob undoubtedly crossed over the Jabbok River, shown just beyond the strip of grass in the foreground, on their way to Shechem. (Todd Bolen, bibleplaces.com)

STRUCTURE OF THE BOOK

The introduction to Judges (1:1—3:6) describes the period after Joshua's death as a time of instability and moral depravity. Without a strong religious leader like Joshua to give them clear direction, the people of Israel fell into the worship of false gods. To punish the people, God delivered them into the hands of enemy nations. In their distress the people repented and cried out to God for help, and God answered their pleas by sending a "judge" or deliverer. In each instance after a period of faithfulness and security, the people once again forgot God, renewing the cycle of unfaithfulness all over again. This theme of sin-punishment-repentance-deliverance runs seven times throughout the book; it is introduced by the refrain, "The children of Israel again did evil in the sight of the Lord" (4:1).

The three best-known judges or deliverers described in the book are Deborah (4:1—5:31), Gideon (6:1—9:57), and Samson (13:1—16:31). The other nine heroic figures from this period in Israel's history are Othniel, Ehud, Shamgar, Tola, Jair, Jephthah, Ibzan, Elon, and Abdon.

The Book of Judges contains some of the best-known stories in the Bible. One judge, Gideon, routed a Midianite army of several thousand with a group of 300 warriors. Under the cover of darkness, Gideon and his men hid lighted torches inside empty pitchers, then broke the pitchers and blew trumpets to catch the army by surprise. The mighty Midianites fled in panic (7:15–25).

An interesting part of the Gideon story is the way in which this judge of Israel tested what he perceived to be God's call. First, Gideon spread a piece of wool on the ground and asked God to saturate it with dew but leave the ground under it dry if he wanted Gideon to deliver Israel. This happened exactly that way. Still not satisfied, Gideon asked God to reverse this procedure the second night—to leave the wool dry with wet ground all around it. After this happened, Gideon agreed to lead his band of warriors against the Midianites (6:36–40).

Another famous story in the Book of Judges is about Samson and Delilah. A judge of superhuman strength, Samson defeated superior forces of the Philistine tribe several times by himself. They finally captured him after Delilah betrayed him by cutting his long hair, which was the secret of his strength. In captivity, Samson took thousands of his enemies to their death by pulling down the pillars of the temple where the Philistines were worshiping their pagan god Dagon (16:1–31).

AUTHORSHIP AND DATE

Like the authors of several other historical books of the Old Testament, the author of Judges is unknown. But internal evidence gives us a clue about the probable date when it was written. The writer reminds us, "In those days there was no king in Israel; everyone did what was right in his own eyes" (17:6; 21:25). This statement tells us the book was written after the events described in Judges, probably during the days of King Saul or King David, about 1050 to 1000 B.C. Early Jewish scholars believed the book was written by Samuel, Israel's first prophet, who anointed Saul as the nation's first king. But this is impossible to determine from evidence presented by the book itself. At least we know that the unknown writer was a contemporary of Samuel.

HISTORICAL SETTING

Israel's entry into the Promised Land under Joshua was not so much a total conquest as an occupation. Even after the land was divided among Israel's twelve tribes, the Israelites continued to face the possibility of domination by the warlike Canaanites who were never driven entirely out of the land. These were the enemies who threatened Israel repeatedly during the 300-year period of the judges, from 1380 to 1050 B.C.

A Concise Outline of

Judges

Samson is one of the best-known characters of the Old Testament, a flawed yet beloved hero. His tomb at Zorah lies quite close to his birthplace. (Todd Bolen, bibleplaces.com)

The Canaanite problem was intensified by Israel's loose form of tribal organization. The Israelites were easy targets for a well-organized enemy like the Canaanites. The first big task of the judges whom God raised up as deliverers was to rally the separate tribes behind them to rout the common enemy.

THEOLOGICAL CONTRIBUTION

The Book of Judges points out the problems of the nation of Israel when the people had a succession of "judges" or military leaders to deliver them from their enemies. This is a subtle way of emphasizing the nation's need for a king or a strong, centralized form of government. But even the establishment of the kingship failed to lead to a state of perfection. Only after the right king, David, was placed on the throne did the nation break free of its tragic cycle of despair and decline. David, of course, as God's chosen servant, points to the great King to come, the Lord Jesus.

Judges also speaks of man's need for an eternal deliverer or a savior. The deliverance of the human judges was always temporary, partial, and imperfect. Some of the judges themselves were flawed and misdirected. The book points forward to Jesus Christ, the great Judge (Ps. 110:6), who is King and Savior of His people.

SPECIAL CONSIDERATIONS

Many readers are troubled by the rash vow of the judge Jephthah in the Book of Judges. He promised God that if he were victorious in battle, he would offer as a sacrifice the first thing to come out of his house to greet him on his return. The Lord did give Jephthah victory. On his return, his daughter came out of the house to greet him, and he was forced to carry out his terrible vow (11:29–40). This text is so troubling to some people that they seek to weaken it by claiming that Jephthah did not actually kill his daughter but only made her remain a virgin. This claim is based on the words, "she knew no man" (11:39). But the text indicates clearly that Jephthah did what he had vowed.

Human sacrifice was never sanctioned by the nation of Israel. Indeed, God condemned it as an evil of the surrounding nations. The point the author of Judges made in recording this deed is the same he had in mind as he recorded the sins and excesses of Samson. The period of the judges was a time of such religious and political chaos that even the best of God's servants were seriously flawed.

Deborah's song of victory (chap. 5) demonstrates a high degree of literary skill at this early period in Israel's history. It also shows that women have made great contributions to God's work across the centuries. Another insight is that God deserves the praise when His people are victorious in battle.

The Book of Ruth

A very devoted Gentile woman, Ruth of Moab, became an ancestor of King David of Israel (4:18–22). The story is one of friendship and faithfulness, of God's grace to one outside of Israel, of romantic love and of covenant continuity. The book is a sparkling jewel in the setting of the chaos of the period of the judges. The woman Ruth is a counterpart of Abraham, a woman of noble faith—a fitting ancestress of the Savior Jesus (Matt. 1:5).

These are the fields of Moab, surely quite similar to those that Ruth left behind to travel to Israel with Naomi, her beloved mother-in-law. (Todd Bolen, bibleplaces.com)

STRUCTURE OF THE BOOK

The Book of Ruth tells the story of a Moabite woman who married into a family of Israelites. Her father-in-law, Elimelech, had moved his wife and two sons from Bethlehem in Judah to the country of Moab. After the death of Elimelech the two sons married Moabite women, Ruth and Orpah. They continued to dwell in Moab another ten years until the deaths of the two brothers. With all of the men in the family gone, this left Ruth, Orpah, and their mother-in-law, Naomi, in a desperate situation. Ruth accompanied Naomi back to Judah when Naomi learned that the famine in the land had passed. They began to scratch out an existence by gathering leftover grain in the fields. This led to Ruth's encounter with Boaz, a wealthy Israelite and distant kinsman of Naomi who eventually married the Moabite woman. Their son became the father of David's father, making Ruth and Boaz the great-grandparents of Judah's most famous king.

AUTHORSHIP AND DATE

The author of Ruth is unknown, although some scholars credit it to the prophet Samuel. The book was not written too late in Israel's history. Some of the verbal forms are archaic; it is not likely that a later writer of integrity would consciously use forms that would make the book appear to be older than it really was. The book had to be written some time after the birth of David because he is the last entry in the genealogy. Because Samuel anointed David as the future king and knew his upcoming position in Israel, he would be the obvious person to recognize the importance of placing David in this historical perspective.

HISTORICAL SETTING

The events in the book occurred at a dark time in Israel's history—"in the days when the judges ruled" (1:1), according to the historical introduction. This was a period of unrelieved chaos, a time when "everyone did what was right in his own eyes" (Judg. 21:25), when the nation lapsed again and again into worship of false gods. What a contrast this is to Ruth, who remained faithful to God, although she was a Moabite by birth—one considered an alien by God's Chosen People. She exemplified many of the ideals that God desired in His own people.

THEOLOGICAL CONTRIBUTION

The book is a treatise on the right use of the law of God. By leaving his people, Elimelech was denying the rule of God indicated by his name "My God is King." He averted his part in the process of response to judgment. Perhaps he was motivated by a concern for the welfare of his family. The names of his sons indicate the stress of the time of famine; Mahlon and Chilion mean "sickly" and "failing"—names likely occasioned by the effects of the famine on the health of their mother while they were in her womb. Nonetheless, Elimelech was judged by God and died in Moab (1:3). The law is not something to trifle with.

In the case of Ruth, she is marked out as an exception to the ban on full participation by people from Moab because of her loyal love (2:22; 3:10) and her profound faith in God (2:12). Ruth's life gives us a beautiful example of the providence of God. He brought Ruth to precisely the right field where she could meet Boaz. God is also portrayed in the book as the model of loyal and abiding love (2:20).

SPECIAL CONSIDERATIONS

The name *Ruth* means "friendship," and this book contains one of the most touching examples of friendship in the Bible. Ruth's mother-in-law changes her name to Mara, meaning "bitterness," in verse

A Concise Outline of
Ruth

I. Ruth's Love Demonstrated

1. Ruth's Decision to Remain with Naomi   1:1–18
2. Ruth's Devotion to Care for Naomi   1:19—2:23

II. Ruth's Love Rewarded

1. Ruth's Request for Redemption by Boaz   3:1–18
2. Ruth's Reward of Redemption by Boaz   4:1–22

1:20, but she becomes Naomi again, meaning "pleasantness" at the end of the story when her new grandson is nursing at her breast (4:16). A new fullness has come to the family of Elimelech in the form of the daughter-in-law, Ruth, whom the village women judged to be of more value to Naomi than seven sons (4:15).

Ruth's words to her mother-in-law are quoted often as a pledge of love and devotion. "Entreat me not to leave you, or to turn back from following after you, for wherever you go, I will go; and wherever you lodge, I will lodge; your people shall be my people, and your God, my God" (1:16).

Stone benches flanking the gate of Beersheba. This is where the local elders would have gathered to handle the business of the city. (Todd Bolen, bibleplaces.com)

The Books of First and Second Samuel

These two historical books cover the nation of Israel's transition from a loose tribal form of government to a united kingship under Saul and David. The books are named for the prophet Samuel, who anointed these two leaders.

This is a portion of Michelangelo's 17-foot marble Statue of David, now more than 500 years old and probably the most recognized sculpture in the world. David is at his moment of decision to meet Goliath. (© 2007 JupiterImages Corporation)

STRUCTURE OF THE BOOKS

In the Bible used by the Hebrew people during Old Testament days, the books of Samuel consisted of one continuous narrative. This long book was divided into 1 and 2 Samuel when the Hebrew Bible was translated into the Greek language in the second century B.C. All Bibles since that time have followed the two-book pattern.

First Samuel covers the lives of the prophet Samuel and King Saul, introducing David as a warrior and a possible successor to the throne. Second Samuel picks up the story at David's anointing and focuses on his career as Israel's greatest king.

Some of the most dramatic stories in the Bible are found in these two Old Testament books. First Samuel reports Samuel's own experience as a boy when he heard God's call to a prophetic ministry (chap. 2). It also reveals that David was a shepherd boy destined for greatness when he defeated the Philistine giant Goliath with nothing but a slingshot and a stone (1 Sam. 17:19–51).

Contrast this triumphant moment, however, with David's great sin, when he committed adultery with Bathsheba, then arranged for the killing of her husband, Uriah. David repented of his sin and claimed God's forgiveness, but from that day on his fortunes were clouded and his family was troubled.

AUTHORSHIP AND DATE

Since the name of the great prophet Samuel is associated with these books, it is logical to assume that he wrote 1 and 2 Samuel. But the problem with this theory is that all of 2 Samuel and a major portion of 1 Samuel deal with events that happened after Samuel's death. However, there is strong support for Samuel's authorship of some of the material, since the Book of 1 Chronicles refers to "the book of Samuel the seer" (1 Chr. 29:29).

Before Samuel's death about 1000 B.C., he must have written accounts of the kingship of Saul and the early life of David that appear as part of 1 Samuel. Many scholars believe that Abiathar the priest wrote those parts of these two books that deal with the court life of David. He served as a priest during David's administration; so he may have had access to the royal records that provided the historical facts for these accounts.

HISTORICAL SETTING

The Books of 1 and 2 Samuel describe a turning point in Israel's history. This was a time when the people became dissatisfied with their loose tribal form of organization and insisted on a united kingdom under the ruling authority of a king. For hundreds of years they had existed as a tribal society, with each tribe living on its own portion of the land and minding its own affairs. If a superior enemy threatened the entire nation, they depended on deliverance at the hands of judges, those military leaders described in the Book of Judges, who would raise a volunteer army to make their borders secure.

This system of defense, however, proved woefully inadequate when the Philistines began to flex their muscles against the nation with renewed intensity about 1100 B.C. These warlike people boasted of iron chariots, a well-organized army, and other superior weapons which they used with military precision against the poorly organized Israelites. The threat of this superior force led the nation to clamor for a king—a ruler who could unite all the tribes against a common enemy.

Saul was anointed by Samuel about 1050 B.C. to serve as first king of the nation. A gifted young man of great promise, he ruled for 40 years (Acts 13:21) before taking his life by falling on his own sword when the Philistines prevailed against him in a decisive battle (1 Sam. 31:1–7). David, his successor, also ruled 40 years (2 Sam. 5:4; 1 Chr. 29: 27), from 1010 to 971 B.C. Building on Saul's beginning, David

A Concise Outline of **First Samuel**	**I. Samuel, the Last Judge**	
	1. The First Phase of National Leadership: Eli-Samuel	1:1—3:21
	2. The Judgeship of Samuel	4:1—7:17
	II. Saul, the First King	
	1. The Second Phase of National Leadership: Samuel-Saul	8:1—12:25
	2. The Reign of King Saul	13:1—15:9
	3. The Third Phase of National Leadership: Saul-David	15:10—31:13

A Concise Outline of **Second Samuel**	**I. The Triumphs of David**	
	1. The Political Triumphs of David	1:1—5:25
	2. The Spiritual Triumphs of David	6:1—7:29
	3. The Military Triumphs of David	8:1—10:19
	II. The Transgressions of David	
	1. The Sin of Adultery	11:1–5
	2. The Sin of Murder	11:6–27
	III. The Troubles of David	
	1. The Troubles in David's House	12:1—13:36
	2. The Troubles in David's Kingdom	13:37—24:25

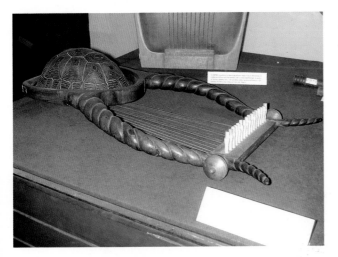

A Roman lyre. David's own instrument was probably simpler, made entirely of wood and carved in a circular pattern with cow-gut strings stretched across an open center. (Todd Bolen, bibleplaces.com)

succeeded in driving out the Philistines, unifying the people, and conquering or establishing peaceful relationships with surrounding nations.

THEOLOGICAL CONTRIBUTION

The major theological contribution of 1 and 2 Samuel is the negative and positive views of the kingship which they present. On the negative side, the books make it clear that in calling for a king the people were rejecting God's rule. Because Israel was unable to live under God's rule through the judges, God gave in to their demands and granted them a king. But He also warned them about the dangers of the kingship (1 Sam. 8:9–21).

On the positive side, 1 and 2 Samuel portray the kingship as established through David as a clear picture of God's purpose for His people. The covenant that God established with David demonstrated God's purpose through David's family line; David's ancestors would be adopted as the sons of God in a special sense (2 Sam. 7). David's line would continue through the centuries, and his throne would be established forever (2 Sam. 7:13). In the person of Jesus Christ the Messiah, this great covenant came to its fulfillment.

SPECIAL CONSIDERATIONS

The story of David and Goliath (1 Sam. 17) presents more than a dramatic encounter between two warriors. It also points up the contrast between David and Saul. Since he was tall himself, Saul should have been the one to face the giant (1 Sam. 9:2). By his failure to meet Goliath, Saul demonstrated both his folly and his inability to rule. By rising to the challenge, David demonstrated his wisdom and faith, proving that he was God's man for the throne of Israel.

In addition to its stories, the books of 1 and 2 Samuel contain several poems, or psalms of praise to God. One such poem is the lovely Psalm of Hannah (1 Sam. 2), in which Hannah rejoices in God's goodness in allowing her to conceive. The dramatic Psalm of the Bow (2 Sam. 1), in which David laments the death of Saul and Jonathan, is another of these poems.

The brook of Elah runs dry in the summer months. Even so it is probably the brook from which the young David chose the stone that killed Goliath. (Todd Bolen, bibleplaces.com)

The Books of First and Second Kings

The history of God's Chosen People during four turbulent centuries, from 970 to 587 B.C., is recounted in these books. The narratives in these books of history are organized around the various kings who reigned during these centuries, thus explaining the titles by which the books are known.

This small, flat plain—on the side of Mount Carmel—is called Muhraqa and is generally considered the site of the prophet Elijah's battle with the prophets of Baal. (Todd Bolen, bibleplaces.com)

STRUCTURE OF THE BOOKS

As originally written in the Hebrew language, 1 and 2 Kings consisted of one unbroken book. It formed a natural sequel to the books of 1 and 2 Samuel, which also appeared originally in the Hebrew Bible as a single book. The writer of Samuel traced the history of the Hebrew people up to the final days of David's reign. This is where the Book of 1 Kings begins—with the death of David and the succession of his son, Solomon, to the throne.

The first half of the Book of 1 Kings describes Solomon's reign. Included are accounts about his vast wealth, his great wisdom, his marriages to foreign wives, and his completion of the Temple of Jerusalem. But 1 Kings also reveals that all was not well in Solomon's empire. Many of the people grew restless and rebellious because of the king's excesses and the high taxes required to support his ambitious projects. At his death the people in the northern part of the empire rebelled and formed their own nation, known as the Northern Kingdom of Israel. Those who remained loyal to the house of David and Solomon continued as the Southern Kingdom, or the nation of Judah.

From this point on in the Books of 1 and 2 Kings, the narrative grows complex and difficult to follow. The historical writer traces the history of a king of Israel, then switches over to touch on the high points in the administration of the parallel king of Judah. This can be very confusing to the Bible reader unless this parallel structure is known.

But we do these books a great injustice if we assume they are filled with nothing but dry historical statistics and minute details. First and Second Kings contains some of the most interesting stories in the Bible. Here we come face to face with the fiery prophet Elijah, who challenged the false god Baal and hundreds of his prophets in a dramatic showdown on Mount Carmel. The prophet's faith was verified as God proved himself superior to Baal by answering Elijah's fervent prayer.

In these books we also meet a proud Syrian commander, Naaman the leper, who almost passed up his opportunity to be healed because of his reluctance to dip himself in the waters of the Jordan River. Fortunately, his servants convinced him to drop his pride, and he emerged from the river with his skin restored "like the flesh of a little child" (2 Kin. 5:14).

During the four centuries covered by these books, a total of 19 different kings ruled the nation of Israel, while 22 different kings (if David and Solomon are included) occupied Judah's throne. The writer covers some of these kings with a few sentences, while he devotes several pages to others. Apparently, this author selected certain kings for major attention because they illustrated the conditions that led to the eventual collapse of the nations of Judah and Israel.

Some of these kings were honest, ethical, and morally pure. But the good kings always were the exception. The majority of the rulers led the people astray, some even openly encouraging them to worship false gods. Thus, the most familiar refrain in 1 and 2 Kings is the phrase, "He did evil in the sight of the Lord" (2 Kin. 8:18).

Israel was the first nation to collapse under the weight of its disobedience and depravity. This kingdom ended in 722 B.C. with the fall of its capital city, Samaria, to the Assyrians. The citizens of the Southern Kingdom of Judah struggled on for another 136 years under a succession of kings before their nation was overrun by the Babylonians in 587 B.C. The Book of 2 Kings comes to a close with the leading citizens of Judah being held captive in Babylon.

AUTHORSHIP AND DATE

These books cover, in chronological fashion, about 400 years of Judah's and Israel's history. The last event mentioned in this chronology is the captivity of Judah's citizens by the Babylonians. This means

A Concise Outline of
First Kings

I. The United Kingdom

1. The Establishment of Solomon as King   1:1—2:46
2. The Rise of Solomon as King   3:1—8:66
3. The Decline of Solomon as King   9:1—11:43

II. The Divided Kingdom

1. The Division of the Kingdom   12:1—14:31
2. The Reigns of Two Kings in Judah   15:1–24
3. The Reigns of Five Kings in Israel   15:25—16:28
4. The Reign of Ahab in Israel   16:29—22:40
5. The Reign of Jehoshaphat in Judah   22:41–50
6. The Reign of Ahaziah in Israel   22:51–53

A Concise Outline of
Second Kings

I. The Divided Kingdom

1. The Reign of Ahaziah in Israel   1:1–18
2. The Reign of Jehoram in Israel   2:1—8:15
3. The Reign of Jehoram in Judah   8:16–24
4. The Reign of Ahaziah in Judah   8:25—9:29
5. The Reign of Jehu in Israel   9:30—10:36
6. The Reign of Queen Athaliah in Judah   11:1–16
7. The Reign of Joash in Judah   11:17—12:21
8. The Reign of Jehoahaz in Israel   13:1–9
9. The Reign of Jehoash in Israel   13:10–25
10. The Reign of Amaziah in Judah   14:1–22
11. The Reign of Jeroboam II in Israel   14:23–29
12. The Reign of Azariah in Judah   15:1–7
13. The Reign of Zechariah in Israel   15:8–12
14. The Reign of Shallum in Israel   15:13–15
15. The Reign of Menahem in Israel   15:16–22
16. The Reign of Pekahiah in Israel   15:23–26
17. The Reign of Pekah in Israel   15:27–31
18. The Reign of Jotham in Judah   15:32–38
19. The Reign of Ahaz in Judah   16:1–20
20. The Reign of Hoshea in Israel   17:1–41

II. The Surviving Kingdom of Judah

1. The Reign of Hezekiah in Judah   18:1—20:21
2. The Reign of Manasseh in Judah   21:1–18
3. The Reign of Amon in Judah   21:19–26
4. The Reign of Josiah in Judah   22:1—23:30
5. The Reign of Jehoahaz in Judah   23:31–34
6. The Reign of Jehoiakim in Judah   23:35—24:7
7. The Reign of Jehoiachin in Judah   24:8–16
8. The Reign of Zedekiah in Judah   24:17—25:21
9. The Governorship of Gedaliah   25:22–26
10. The Release of Jehoiachin in Babylon   25:27–30

the book had to be compiled in its final form some time after the Babylonians overran Jerusalem in 587 B.C.

Early tradition credited the prophet Jeremiah with the writing of these two books. Whether this is correct is uncertain. We do know that this famous prophet preached in Jerusalem before and after the fall of the city. Two chapters from 2 Kings also appear in the Book of Jeremiah (compare 2 Kin. 24—25 and Jer. 39—42; 52). This led many scholars to the natural assumption that Jeremiah wrote the book.

Most scholars today no longer hold to the Jeremiah theory. The evidence points to an unknown prophet who worked at the same time as Jeremiah to compile this long history of his nation's religious and political life. His purpose was to show that the two kingdoms fell because of their unfaithfulness and to call the people back to renewal of the covenant.

While this prophet-writer is not named in the Books of 1 and 2 Kings, he does reveal the sources which he used. He speaks of "the chronicles of the kings of Israel" (1 Kin. 14:19) and "the chronicles of the kings of Judah" (1 Kin. 14:29). These were probably the official court documents and historical archives of the two nations. He must have drawn from them freely as he wrote.

HISTORICAL SETTING

The four centuries covered by 1 and 2 Kings were times of change and political upheaval in the ancient world as the balance of power shifted from one nation to another. Surrounding nations that posed a threat to Israel and Judah at various times during this period included Syria, Assyria, and Babylon.

The Assyrian threat was particularly strong during the last 50 years of the Northern Kingdom. Under Tiglath-Pileser III, this conquering nation launched three devastating campaigns against Israel in 734, 733, and 732 B.C. It was a blow from which Israel never recovered, and the nation fell to Assyrian forces just 10 years later in 722 B.C.

While Syria and Assyria were threats to Judah at various times, their worst enemy turned out to be the nation of Babylon. The Babylonians took captives and goods from Jerusalem in three campaigns— in 605 and 597 B.C. and in a two-year siege beginning in 588 B.C. in which Jerusalem finally fell in 587 B.C. The Temple was destroyed, and thousands of Judah's leading citizens were carried into captivity in Babylon.

THEOLOGICAL CONTRIBUTION

The Books of 1 and 2 Kings present an interesting contrast between King David of Judah and King Jeroboam I, the first king of the Northern Kingdom of Israel.

Jeroboam established a legacy of idol worship in this new nation by setting up golden calves at Bethel and Dan (1 Kin. 12:25–33). These were symbols of the fertility religion of Baal. His strategy was to mix this false religion with worship of the one true God in an attempt to win the loyalty and good will of the people and bind them together as a distinctive nation. This act of idolatry was condemned by the writer of 1 and 2 Kings. Each succeeding king of Israel was measured against the standard of Jeroboam's idolatry. Of each king who led the people astray, it was written, "He did not depart from the sins of Jeroboam the son of Nebat, who had made Israel sin" (2 Kin. 15:9).

Just as Jeroboam was used as a bad example by the writer of 1 and 2 Kings, King David was used as a standard of righteousness and justice. In spite of David's moral lapses, he became the measure of righteousness for all kings who followed him. The Northern Kingdom was marked by rebellion and strife as opposing factions struggled for the right to reign, but the house of David continued in the Kingdom of Judah without interruption for nearly four centuries. The writer explained that the evils of kings such as Abijam (or Abijah) did not cancel out the love and mercy that God had promised to the house of David: "Nevertheless for David's sake the Lord his God gave him a lamp in Jerusalem, by setting up his son after him and by establishing Jerusalem; because David did what was right in the eyes of the Lord" (1 Kin. 15:4–5).

SPECIAL CONSIDERATIONS

The writer of 1 Kings reported that Solomon had "seven hundred wives, princesses, and three hundred concubines" (1 Kin. 11:3). In the ancient world, the number of wives held by a ruler symbolized his might and power. Rulers also took on wives to seal political alliances and trade agreements. But Solomon cannot be totally excused for his excesses because of these cultural factors. According to the writer of 1 Kings, he let his foreign wives turn away his heart from worshiping the one true God (1 Kin. 11:1–3). This was a fatal flaw in his character that eventually led to rebellion and the separation of Solomon's empire into two opposing nations (1 Kin. 11:11–13).

The Books of 1 and 2 Kings describe several miracles wrought by God through the prophets Elijah and Elisha. In addition to proving God's power, these miracles are also direct attacks on the pagan worship practices of the followers of Baal. Elijah's encounter with the prophets of Baal on Mount Carmel, for example, was a test of the power of Baal—whether he could send fire from heaven (lightning bolts) to ignite the sacrifice and bring the rains that were needed to end the drought. Baal was silent, but God thundered—and the rains came, as Elijah had predicted (1 Kin. 18:20–46).

This is the traditional location of Elijah's spring, where the prophet was given food and water in the wilderness after fleeing from the wicked Jezebel. (Daniel Gebhardt, bibleplaces.com)

The Books of First and Second Chronicles

O ften these books are characterized as "books of hope." In broad, selective strokes, they trace the history of the nation of Israel from Adam to the Captivity and Restoration. Much of this material is a repetition of that found in the Books of 1 and 2 Samuel and 1 and 2 Kings. But the writer of Chronicles apparently wrote his history to encourage the exiles who had returned to Jerusalem after more than 50 years of captivity in Babylon. This selective history reminded them of Israel's glorious days from the past and gave them hope for the future as they pondered God's promises to His Covenant People.

This is the city of Jerusalem, shown at dawn just as the sky begins to lighten in the east. (Daniel Frese, bibleplaces.com)

STRUCTURE OF THE BOOKS

The Books of 1 and 2 Chronicles were written originally as one unbroken book. In later translations of the Bible, however, this long narrative was divided into two shorter books. Each of these books falls naturally into two major divisions.

The first nine chapters of 1 Chronicles contain long genealogies, or family histories, that are composed of information from the earliest historical books of the Bible. These genealogies take the reader from the descendants of Adam up through the ancestors of King David. Special attention is given to the families of priests and Levites (6:1–81; 9:1–34), Saul's family, and particularly to the family of David (chaps. 2—3). The second major section of the book (chaps. 10—29) focuses on the reign of King David. This long account begins with the death of Saul (chap. 10) omitting the historical facts that preceded this event. Saul's death is reported to establish the fact that he was unqualified for office and that David was God's choice for this responsibility (10:14).

The account of David's reign is presented in a positive light, with all the details about David's great sin omitted. First Chronicles also lists the names of all those associated with him as mighty men (chaps. 11—12) and records his great victories (chaps. 14, 18—20). This section of the book also lists the names of the Levites, priests, and musicians in David's administration (chaps. 23—26), as well as other state officials (chaps. 27). Also included is David's work in establishing Jerusalem as his capital city (11:4–9) and as the center of worship (chaps. 13, 15—16, 22, 28—29).

The Book of 2 Chronicles also contains two major sections. Chapters 1—9 focus on the rule of King Solomon, whose greatest accomplishment was the building of the Temple in Jerusalem. Included is correspondence between Solomon and Hiram, king of Tyre, about building materials (chap. 2), as well as a full account of the dedication service when the Temple was completed (chaps. 10—36) is a highly selective account of the kings of Judah—from Rehoboam (chaps. 10—12) until the time of the Captivity (chaps. 14—16), Jehoshaphat (chaps. 17—20), Joash (chaps. 23—24), Amaziah (chap. 25), Uzziah or Azariah (chap. 26), Hezekiah (chaps. 29—32), and Josiah (chaps. 34—35). The book ends with the proclamation of King Cyrus of Persia allowing the return of the Jews to rebuild their Temple in Jerusalem (36:22—23).

One particularly interesting fact about the Book of 2 Chronicles is that it includes little information about the kings of the Northern Kingdom, Israel. And the facts which it gives about the kings of Judah are mostly positive. This indicates the author was interested in tracing the line of David and showing that Judah was the nation which remained faithful to the covenant between God and His people. This fact would have been encouraging to the exiles who returned to Jerusalem to rebuild the Temple. They felt they were continuing the forms and traditions which set them apart as the true worshipers of God and gave them a sense of identity as God's Covenant People.

AUTHORSHIP AND DATE

The author of the Books of 1 and 2 Chronicles is unknown, although Ezra the priest and scribe seems the most likely possibility. As in 1 and 2 Chronicles, the books of Ezra and Nehemiah were written originally as one unbroken book in the Hebrew language. And the last two verses of 2 Chronicles are repeated in the first three verses of the Book of Ezra, probably indicating they went together in the original version. Most scholars agree that these four books were written and compiled by the same person, but not all accept the theory of Ezra's authorship.

Ezra, however, remains the best candidate for this honor because of his important role among the community of exiles in Jerusalem. After leading a group to return to their homeland, he worked with

A Concise Outline of
First Chronicles

I. The Royal Line of David

1. The Family of Adam   1:1–27
2. The Family of Israel   1:28–54
3. The Family of Israel   2:1–55
4. The Family of David   3:1–24
5. The Descendants of the Twelve Tribes   4:1—8:40
6. The Descendants of the Remnant   9:1–34
7. The Family of Saul   9:35–44

II. The Reign of David

1. David Becomes King   10:1—12:40
2. The Removal of the Ark of the Covenant   13:1—17:27
3. The Military Victories of King David   18:1—20:8
4. The Preparation and Organization
   of Israel for the Temple   21:1—27:34
5. The Last Days of David   28:1—29:30

A Concise Outline of
Second Chronicles

I. The Reign of Solomon

1. The Succession of Solomon as King   1:1–17
2. The Completion of the Temple   2:1—7:22
3. The Glory of the Reign of Solomon   8:1—9:28
4. The Death of Solomon   9:29–31

II. The Reigns of Selected Kings of Judah

1. The Reign of Rehoboam   10:1—12:16
2. The Reign of Abijah   13:1–22
3. The Reign of Asa   14:1—16:14
4. The Reign of Jehoshaphat   17:1—20:37
5. The Reign of Jehoram   21:1–20
6. The Reign of Ahaziah   22:1–9
7. The Reign of Athaliah   22:10—23:15
8. The Reign of Joash   23:16—24:27
9. The Reign of Amaziah   25:1–28
10. The Reign of Uzziah   26:1–23
11. The Reign of Jotham   27:1–9
12. The Reign of Ahaz   28:1–27
13. The Reign of Hezekiah   29:1—32:33
14. The Reign of Manasseh   33:1–20
15. The Reign of Amon   33:21–25
16. The Reign of Josiah   34:1—35:27
17. The Reign of Jehoahaz   36:1–3
18. The Reign of Jehoiakim   36:4–8
19. The Reign of Jehoiachin   36:9–10
20. The Reign of Zedekiah   36:11–21
21. The Proclamation by Cyrus to Return
    to Jerusalem   36:22–23

another Jewish leader, Nehemiah, to strengthen the people's commitment to God's law (Ezra 10:17–19; Neh. 8:1–8; 9:1–3). He must have written all four of these books—1 and 2 Chronicles, Ezra and Nehemiah—after he arrived in Jerusalem about 457 B.C. and led the reforms among the people.

The Chronicler used many sources in writing his book, including the Books of Samuel and Kings. He also used court histories, as did earlier writers, and prophetic narratives. One illustration of this procedure can be observed in 2 Chronicles 9:29, at the end of the story of Solomon.

HISTORICAL SETTING

The Books of 1 and 2 Chronicles cover several centuries of the history of God's Covenant People—from the founders of the nation until the end of their captivity in Babylon and Persia about 538 B.C. But the books were written with a specific purpose in mind—to give comfort and hope to those who returned to Jerusalem.

The stage was set for the return of the Jewish people to Jerusalem after the Persians defeated Babylon and became the dominant power of the ancient world. The Babylonians had held the Jewish people captive for more than 50 years, but the Persians had a different foreign policy. They believed in letting their subject nations live in their own native regions under the authority of a ruling governor. They allowed the Jewish people to return to Jerusalem in several different stages, beginning with the first wave under Zerubbabel about 530 B.C. (2 Chr. 36:22–23).

After they returned to Jerusalem and rebuilt the Temple, the remnant of God's Covenant People needed constant encouragement. Keeping their faith and traditions alive required continual struggle. The situation called for determination and a strong sense of hope—hope that the promises of God to David would not be forgotten, and that a king from this royal line would rule again one day among God's people. This was the unique situation to which the Books of 1 and 2 Chronicles were addressed.

THEOLOGICAL CONTRIBUTION

The Books of 1 and 2 Chronicles tie the entire sweep of the Old Testament together into one great affirmation of hope. These books should not only be read as histories, but for their insights into how God has kept faith with His Covenant People across the centuries. By selecting events that show how God has kept His promises, the author presents a beautiful doctrine of hope that begins with Adam (1 Chr. 1:1) and stretches to the end of the captivity of God's people thousands of years later (2 Chr. 36:22–23). The clear implication for Christians today is that He is still a God of hope whose ultimate purpose will prevail in the world and in the lives of His people.

The Book of Ezra

This book describes the resettlement of the Hebrew people in their homeland after their long exile in Babylon. The book is named for its author and central figure, Ezra the priest, who led the exiles in a new commitment to God's Law after their return.

The remains of the Ammon acropolis, once a strong fortification at the highest point in the city of Ammon. (Todd Bolen, bibleplaces.com)

STRUCTURE OF THE BOOK

The ten chapters of this book fall naturally into two main divisions, chapters 1—6, which report the return of the first wave of exiles to Jerusalem under the leadership of Zerubbabel, about 530 B.C., and chapters 7—10, which describe the return of a second group under Ezra's leadership, about 458 B.C. One of the most unusual facts about the Book of Ezra is that its two major sections are separated by a time gap of about 80 years.

The book opens with a brief introduction that explains how the first return from exile happened. Cyrus, the king of Persia, issued a proclamation allowing the Jewish people to return to Jerusalem to rebuild their Temple and resettle their native land. About 50,000 of the people returned under the leadership of Zerubbabel, a Jewish citizen appointed by Cyrus as governor of Jerusalem (2:64–65). Arriving about 530 B.C., they set to work immediately on the rebuilding project. In spite of some shrewd political maneuvering by their enemies, the work moved forward until the Temple was completed in 515 B.C. (6:14–15).

The second major section of the book (chaps. 7—10) reports on the arrival of Ezra in Jerusalem with another group of exiles about 60 years after the Temple had been completed. Just as Zerubbabel had led the people to rebuild God's house, Ezra's mission was to lead his countrymen to rebuild the Law of God in their hearts. Ezra worked with another Jewish leader, Nehemiah, to bring about several reforms among the Jewish people in Jerusalem during this period. From the Book of Nehemiah (Neh. 8:1–8), we learn that Ezra read the books of the Law (Genesis, Exodus, Leviticus, Numbers, and Deuteronomy) aloud to the people. This led to a great religious revival throughout Jerusalem as the people committed themselves again to God's law, confessed their sins (Neh. 9:1–3), and renewed the covenant with their redeemer God (Neh. 10).

We also learn from the final chapter of his book that Ezra was distressed at the Jewish men who had married non-Jewish women. He led these men to repent of their sin and divorce their pagan wives (10:17–44).

AUTHORSHIP AND DATE

Ezra has traditionally been accepted as the author of this book that bears his name, as well as the companion book of Nehemiah. In the Hebrew Old Testament, Ezra and Nehemiah appeared as one unbroken book, closely connected in theme and style to the books of 1 and 2 Chronicles. The last two verses of 2 Chronicles are repeated in the first three verses of the Book of Ezra, probably indicating that they belonged together in the original version. For this reason, many scholars believe Ezra served as writer and editor-compiler of all four of these books: 1 and 2 Chronicles, Ezra, and Nehemiah. He probably drew from official court documents to compile 1 and 2 Chronicles.

This compilation theory also helps explain the strange 80-year gap between the two major sections of Ezra's book. He probably wrote about Zerubbabel's return many years after it happened, drawing from official court records or some other account of the event. To this he added his own personal memoirs, now contained in chapters 7—10 of the Book of Ezra as well as chapters 8—10 of the Book of Nehemiah. The rest of the material in the Book of Nehemiah may have come from Nehemiah's memoirs, which Ezra incorporated into the book of Ezra-Nehemiah. The time for the final writing and compilation of all this material must have been some time late in the fifth century B.C.

HISTORICAL SETTING

The Book of Ezra belongs to the post-exilic period. These were the years just after a remnant of the nation returned to Jerusalem following their exile of about 50 years in Babylon. The return came about

A Concise Outline of **Ezra**	**I. The Restoration of the Temple of God**	
	1. The First Return to Jerusalem Under Zerubbabel	1:1—2:70
	2. The Construction of the Temple	3:1—6:22
	II. The Reformation of the People of God	
	1. The Second Return to Jerusalem Under Ezra	7:1—8:36
	2. The Restoration of the People	9:1—10:44

This picture shows a sycamore, which is actually a fig tree—although its fruit is generally not as desirable as that of the common fig tree. (Kim Guess, bibleplaces.com)

after the defeat of Babylon by the Persian Empire. Unlike the Babylonians, the Persians allowed their subject nations to live in their own native regions under the authority of a ruling governor. The Persians also practiced religious tolerance, allowing each nation to worship its own god. This explains the proclamation of Cyrus of Persia, which allowed the Jewish people to return to Jerusalem and rebuild their Temple. Cyrus even returned the Temple treasures that the Babylonians took when they destroyed Jerusalem about 50 years earlier (1:7–11).

THEOLOGICAL CONTRIBUTION

The theme of the Book of Ezra is the restoration of the remnant of God's Covenant People in Jerusalem in obedience to His Law. The book shows clearly that God had acted to preserve His people, even when they were being held captive in a pagan land. But in their absence, the people had not been able to carry on the true form of Temple worship. Only in their Temple in Jerusalem, they believed, could authentic worship and sacrifice to their redeemer God be offered. This is why the rebuilding of the Temple was so important. Here they could restore their worship of God and find their true identity as God's people of destiny in the world.

The Book of Ezra also teaches a valuable lesson about the providence of God. Several different Persian kings are mentioned in this book. Each king played a significant role in returning God's Covenant People to their homeland and helping them restore the Temple as the center of their religious life. This shows that God can use the unrighteous as well as the righteous to work His ultimate will in the lives of His people.

SPECIAL CONSIDERATIONS

Many scholars believe the Jewish people in Babylon and Persia must have numbered at least two million. Yet only about 50,000 chose to return to Jerusalem with the first group under Zerubbabel (2:64–65). This indicates that most of them probably had become comfortable with their lives in these foreign lands. Or perhaps the certainties of their present existence were more appealing than the uncertainties of life in Jerusalem—a city which most of them had never seen.

Some Bible readers are bothered by Ezra's treatment of the pagan women whom the Jewish men had married (10:10–19). How could he be so cruel as to insist that these wives be "put away" (divorced) with no means of support? His actions must be understood in light of the drastic situation that faced the Jewish community in Jerusalem following the Exile. Only a small remnant of the Covenant People had returned, and it was important for them to keep themselves from pagan idolatry and foreign cultural influence at all costs. Ezra must have realized too, that this was one of the problems which had led to their downfall and captivity as a people in the first place. Yet even the horrors of defeat and exile by the Babylonians had failed to teach the people a lesson. He was determined to stamp out the problem this time before it became a widespread practice among God's Covenant People.

The Book of Nehemiah

The theme of this book is the rebuilding of the city walls around Jerusalem. The book is named for its major personality, a Jewish servant of a Persian king and effective leader, who organized and guided the building project.

A closeup of the ancient city walls of Jerusalem. These were worked on by Nehemiah when he directed the rebuilding of the city's walls. (Todd Bolen, bibleplaces.com)

STRUCTURE OF THE BOOK

Nehemiah was serving as cupbearer to the Persian king Artaxerxes (1:11—2:1) in 444 B.C., when he received distressing news about his native land. Jerusalem's wall was still in ruins, although the project to rebuild the city and its beautiful Temple had been under way for many years. So Nehemiah went to Jerusalem himself on special assignment from the king to oversee the building project. In spite of harassment by their enemies, Nehemiah rallied the people to the challenge and completed the wall in less than two months.

Nehemiah remained as Persian governor of Jerusalem for the next 12 years, leading the people in several important religious reforms. The priest Ezra assisted Nehemiah in interpreting God's Law for His people. He had accompanied a group of captives back to Jerusalem about 13 years before Nehemiah arrived on the scene.

AUTHORSHIP AND DATE

As written originally in the Hebrew language, Nehemiah was connected to the books of 1 and 2 Chronicles and Ezra. The material in these books formed one unbroken book, written probably by the priest, Ezra. The purposes of this work was to show how God's blessings sustained His Covenant People after they returned to their native land following the years of captivity in Babylon and Persia. Most conservative scholars, however, believe Nehemiah contributed some of the material that appears in the book which bears his name. This is the only logical explanation for chapters 1—7 and 11—13, which are written by Nehemiah as a first-person report. Ezra could have picked up these passages from Nehemiah's personal diary.

HISTORICAL SETTING

The Book of Nehemiah is set in that crucial time in Jewish history known as the post-exilic period. These were the years after the return of the Covenant People to their homeland about 530 B.C. following 70 years of captivity in Babylon and Persia. At first the exiles were excited about rebuilding their lives and restoring their city; but the work was slow and tiring, and the living conditions were primitive. Their enemies often exploited them in their plight. These were the desperate circumstances that motivated Nehemiah to return to Jerusalem to encourage his countrymen.

THEOLOGICAL CONTRIBUTION

Nehemiah is an excellent case study in courageous, resourceful leadership. Against overwhelming odds, he encouraged the people to "rise up and build" (2:18). Their rapid completion of the wall has been an inspiration to countless Christians across the centuries who have faced the challenge of completing some major task to the glory of God.

Nehemiah also teaches that prayer is an important part of the faith of every follower of God. At several crucial points in his book, he prayed for God's direction (1:5–11; 2:1–20; 4:1–14; 6:9–14). If this courageous leader needed to claim God's strength and guidance through prayer, how much more fervently should we pray for God's will to be done through us as we face the important decisions of life? Nehemiah is an excellent object lesson on the power of prayer for all believers.

SPECIAL CONSIDERATIONS

Scholars have debated who returned to Jerusalem first, Ezra or Nehemiah. But the Bible makes it plain that Ezra arrived about 13 years before Nehemiah. Ezra went back to Jerusalem in the seventh year of

A Concise Outline of
Nehemiah

This picture shows a "seam" on the southeastern portion of the Temple Mount, where a later addition to the original wall leans up against the northern portion. (Todd Bolen, bibleplaces.com)

King Artaxerxes' reign (Ezra 7:8), while Nehemiah returned during this Persian king's 20th year (Neh. 2:1). The debate arises because of the account of the religious revival under Ezra, which is inserted as chapters 8—10 of Nehemiah.

Perhaps there is a simple reason why this "Ezra story" was included in the Book of Nehemiah. It was used to emphasize the truth that rebuilding the Law of God in the hearts of the people was just as important as rebuilding a wall of stone around the nation's capital city. This was a spiritual, life-sustaining wall that no enemy could batter down.

Observant Jews live in sukkot ("booths") on the Feast of Tabernacles, as it is known in English. Palm branches typically form a temporary roof. (Todd Bolen, bibleplaces.com)

The Book of Esther

This book shows how God preserved His Chosen People. The book is named for its main personality, Queen Esther of Persia, whose courage and quick thinking saved the Jewish people from disaster.

This is the base for a pillar in a Persian palace near the town of Lachish. Undoubtedly the palace of Xerxes (also called Ahasuerus), the king who honored Esther's request to spare her people, featured similar pillars. (Todd Bolen, bibleplaces.com)

STRUCTURE OF THE BOOK

The Book of Esther reports on actual events, but it is written like a short story. The main characters in this powerful drama are King Xerxes of Persia; his wife Queen Esther, a Jewish woman; his second in command, Haman, recently promoted by the king; and Mordecai, a leader among the Jewish people who are scattered throughout the Persian Empire. In an attempt to stamp out the Jews, Haman manipulates the king into issuing an order calling for their execution. But Esther uses her royal favor to intervene and expose Haman's plot. Ironically, in a dramatic twist of plot, Haman is hanged on the gallows he built for Mordecai's execution, and Mordecai is promoted to prime minister. The Jewish people are granted revenge against their enemies. They also celebrate by instituting the Feast of Purim to mark their miraculous deliverance.

AUTHORSHIP AND DATE

For centuries scholars have debated the question of who wrote the Book of Esther. The Jewish historian Josephus claimed it was written by Mordecai. But many modern scholars dispute this because Mordecai is mentioned in the past tense in the final chapter of the book. Until new evidence emerges, the author must remain unknown.

The question of date can be answered with greater certainty. The reign of the Persian king Xerxes (Esth. 1:1, NIV) lasted for about 20 years, beginning about 485 B.C. So Esther must have been written some time shortly after 465 B.C.

HISTORICAL SETTING

The Book of Esther is valuable historically because it gives us a view of the Jewish people who were scattered throughout the ancient world about 475 B.C. The events in the book occurred about 100 years after the leading citizens of the Jewish nation were carried into exile by Babylon in 587 B.C. Shortly after the Persians overthrew the Babylonians, they allowed the Jewish exiles to return to their native land. Many did return to Jerusalem, but thousands of Jewish citizens chose to remain in Persia, probably because this had become home to them during their long separation from their native land. Thus, this book shows clearly that God protects His Chosen People, even when they are scattered among the nations of the world.

THEOLOGICAL CONTRIBUTION

The Book of Esther is a major chapter in the struggle of the people of God to survive in the midst of a hostile world. Beginning with the Book of Genesis, God had made it clear that He would bless His Covenant People and bring a curse upon those who tried to do them harm (Gen. 12:1, 3). The Book of Esther shows how God has kept this promise at every stage of history. Just as Haman met his death on the gallows, we can trust God to protect us from the enemy, Satan, and to work out His ultimate purpose of redemption in our lives.

SPECIAL CONSIDERATIONS

One unusual fact about this book is that it never mentions the name of God. For this reason some people believe Esther has no place in the Bible. They see it as nothing but a fiercely patriotic Jewish book that celebrates the victory of the Jews over their enemies.

This harsh criticism is unfair to Esther. A careful reading will reveal that the book does have a spiritual base. Queen Esther calls the people to prayer and fasting (4:16), and God's protection of His people speaks of His providence. The book also teaches a valuable lesson about the sovereignty of God: although the enemies of the Covenant People may triumph for a season, He holds the key to ultimate victory.

A Concise Outline of
Esther

A modern gallows, perhaps somewhat similar to the one on which the evil Haman met his end. (© 2007 JupiterImages Corporation)

CHAPTER 3

BOOKS OF POETRY AND WISDOM

Beautiful poetry occurs in both the Old and New Testaments. Approximately one-third of the Old Testament is written in poetry. This includes entire books (except for short prose sections), such as Job, Psalms, Proverbs, the Song of Solomon, and Lamentations. Many scholars consider the Book of Job to be not only the greatest poem in the Old Testament but also one of the greatest poems in all literature.

The five poetical books illustrate three kinds of poetry:

- lyric poetry—originally accompanied by music on the lyre, this poetry often has strong emotional elements (most of Psalms);
- didactic poetry—teaches principles about life by means of wise sayings (Proverbs, Ecclesiastes); and
- dramatic poetry—dialogue in poetic form (Job, the Song of Solomon).

Poetic elements such as assonance, alliteration, and rhyme occur rarely in Hebrew poetry. The essential formal characteristic of Hebrew poetry is parallelism. This is a construction in which the content of one line is repeated, contrasted, or advanced by the content of the next (see the article on the book of Psalms below for an explanation of parallelism).

The wisdom literature of the Old Testament consists of the Books of Job, Proverbs, and Ecclesiastes, and certain of the Psalms (Pss. 1; 19; 27; 49; 104; 107; 112; 119; 127; 128; 133; 147; 148).

In general, two principal types of wisdom are found in these books—practical and speculative. Practical wisdom consists mainly of wise sayings that offer guidelines for a successful and happy life. These are maxims of common sense, insight, and observation about how an intelligent person should conduct himself. The Book of Proverbs is a good example of practical wisdom.

Speculative wisdom goes beyond practical maxims about daily conduct. It reflects upon the deeper issues of the meaning of life, the worth and value of life, and the existence of evil in the world. The Book of Job and the Book of Ecclesiastes are classified among the works of speculative wisdom.

The chart on page 64 gives an overview of the books of poetry and wisdom by showing the individual books that make up this section of the Old Testament. These books are then discussed in detail in their appropriate order to give you a better understanding of this important major division of God's Word.

Books of Poetry and Wisdom

Book	Summary
Job	An examination of the problems of evil and human suffering
Psalms	The song book or hymnal of ancient Israel
Proverbs	Wise sayings and observations designed to develop proper attitudes and behavior
Ecclesiastes	A philosophical description of the emptiness of life without God
Song of Solomon	A love song portraying the beauty of a human love relationship as a symbol of divine love

All the biblical books of poetry and wisdom were written on scrolls from which fragments such as this one, found with the Dead Sea Scrolls, still survive. (Todd Bolen, bibleplaces.com)

The Book of Job

Written in the form of a dramatic poem, this book deals with the age-old question of why the righteous suffer. The book takes its name from the main character in the poem, the patriarch Job. Because Job deals with one of man's universal questions, it is classified as one of the Wisdom Books of the Old Testament.

The ancient Canaanite city of Dor, now an archeological mound in the background of this photo, shown from the south across an ocean lagoon. (Daniel Frese, bibleplaces.com)

STRUCTURE OF THE BOOK

Job begins with two introductory chapters, in the form of a narrative or prologue, that set the stage for the rest of the book. Chapters 3 through 37 form the main body of the book. These chapters are poems in the form of dramatic dialogues between Job and his friends. Four additional chapters containing God's response to their arguments are also written in poetic form. The book ends with a final narrative or epilogue (42:7–17) that tells what happened to Job after these discussions had ended.

This prologue-poetry-epilogue format was used often in writings of this type in the ancient world. The author of Job was a literary craftsman who knew how to bring words together in dramatic fashion to drive home his message about the eternal purpose of life.

The story of Job opens with a brief description of the man, his possessions, and his family. "Blameless and upright" (1:1), he owned thousands of sheep, camels, oxen, and donkeys. He also had seven sons and three daughters. In simple terms, Job was considered a wealthy man in the tribal culture of the ancient world. But Satan insists that the integrity of this upright man has never been tested. He accuses Job of serving God only because God has protected him and made him wealthy. God grants permission for the testing to begin.

In rapid fashion, Job's sons and daughters are killed and all his flocks are driven away by his enemies. Finally, Job himself is stricken with a terrible skin disease. In his sorrow he sits mourning on an ash heap, scraping his sores with a piece of pottery while he laments his misfortune. This is when Job's three friends—Eliphaz, Bildad, and Zophar—arrive to mourn with him and to offer their comfort.

But instead of comforting Job, these friends launch into long lectures and philosophical debates to show Job the reason for his suffering. Their line of reasoning follows the generally accepted view of their time—that misfortune is always sent by God as punishment for sin. Job argues just as strongly that he is an upright man who has done nothing to deserve such treatment at the hand of God.

Finally, after Job and his friends have debated this question at length and have failed to arrive at a satisfactory solution, God himself speaks from a whirlwind. He does not enter their discussion about why the righteous suffer; He reveals Himself as the powerful, all-knowing God. God's message to Job is that He does not have to explain or justify His actions. He is the sovereign, all-powerful God who always does what is right, although His ways may be beyond man's understanding.

Job is humbled by this outpouring of God's power, and he learns to trust where he cannot understand. This leads to his great affirmation of faith, "I have heard of You by the hearing of the ear, but now my eye sees You" (42:5). Then the book closes with the birth of more sons and daughters and Job's rise to a position of even greater wealth and prominence. Job lived out his additional years as a happy, contended man: "So Job died, old and full of days" (42:17).

AUTHORSHIP AND DATE

No one knows who wrote the Book of Job. A few scholars have taken the position that it may have been written by Moses. Others have suggested that the patriarch Job himself may have written this account of his experiences. But these theories have no solid evidence to support them. The only thing we can say for certain is that the book was written by an unknown author.

The exact date of the book's writing is still something of a mystery. Some believe its unknown author put it in writing as late as the second century B.C. Others insist it must have been written about the time the people of Israel returned from the captivity in Babylon about 450 B.C. But many conservative scholars assign the writing of the book to the time of King Solomon, about 950 B.C. Historical evidence favors this date, since this was the golden age of biblical Wisdom literature.

A Concise Outline of

Job

The oryx, a desert antelope. From the side an oryx can appear to have only one horn and can sometimes be mistaken for a unicorn. (Matt Floreen, bibleplaces.com)

HISTORICAL SETTING

The events described in the Book of Job must have occurred many centuries before they were finally written. Job probably lived during the time of the patriarch Abraham, about 2000 to 1800 B.C. Like Abraham, Job's wealth was measured in flocks and herds. In patriarchal fashion, Job's married children were a part of his household, living in separate tents but subject to his rule as leader of the family clan.

This story of Job and his misfortunes was probably passed down by word of mouth from generation to generation for several hundred years. Finally, it was put in writing by an unknown writer during Solomon's time, thus assuring its preservation for all future generations.

THEOLOGICAL CONTRIBUTION

The Book of Job teaches us to trust God in all circumstances. When we suffer, it usually is a fruitless effort to try to understand the reasons for the difficulty. Sometimes the righteous must suffer without knowing the reason why; that is why it is important to learn to trust God in everything.

This masterful book also shows very clearly that God is not captive to His world, His people, or our views of His nature. God is free; He is subject to no will but His own. He is not bound by our understanding or by our lack of it. Job also discovered that God is a God of great power and majesty. When we see how great He is, we realize just how little we are. Like Job, we want to bow down in humble submission.

The Book of Job also teaches us that God is good, just, and fair in His dealings. He restored Job's fortunes and gave him more than He had ever enjoyed. God always replaces the darkness of our existence with the light of His presence when we remain faithful to Him.

SPECIAL CONSIDERATIONS

The dialogue sections of the Book of Job are written in poetry. Great truths are often expressed in such poetic language. These great truths are worth the slow, reflective reading it sometimes takes to grasp their meaning. Great art like that in this book often challenges our understanding. That is why we need to come back to it again and again.

The Book of Psalms

This inspiring book is a collection of prayers, poems, and hymns that focus the worshiper's thoughts on God in praise and adoration. Parts of this book were used as a hymnal in the worship services of ancient Israel. The musical heritage of the psalms is demonstrated by its title. It comes from a Greek word which means "a song sung to the accompaniment of a musical instrument."

Looking out over the sea, at sunset, from Acco, a northwestern city in Israel on the eastern coast of the Mediterranean. (Todd Bolen, bibleplaces.com)

STRUCTURE OF THE BOOK

With 150 individual psalms, this book is clearly the longest in the Bible. It is also one of the most diverse, since the psalms deal with such subjects as God and His creation, war, worship, wisdom, sin and evil, judgment, justice, and the coming of the Messiah. In the original Hebrew manuscripts, this long collection of 150 psalms was divided into five sections:

- Book 1 (1—41);
- Book 2 (42—72);
- Book 3 (73—89);
- Book 4 (90—106); and
- Book 5 (107—150).

Each of these major sections close with a brief prayer of praise. Many modern translations of the Bible, including the NKJV, retain this fivefold division.

Scholars are not sure exactly why the Book of Psalms was organized in this manner. One theory is that it was divided into five sections as a sort of parallel to the Pentateuch—the first five books of the Old Testament (Genesis, Exodus, Leviticus, Numbers, and Deuteronomy). But other scholars believe the five sections were different collections of psalms that circulated at different times in Israel's history. These five small collections were finally placed together, they believe, to form the large compilation which we know today as the Book of Psalms.

The second theory does seem to make sense when we examine the content of the psalms themselves. Individual psalms attributed to David appear in all five of these sections of the Book. Within these five sections, different types of psalms also appear. These include songs of thanksgiving, hymns of praise, psalms of repentance and confession, psalms which invoke evil upon one's enemies, messianic psalms, and songs sung by pilgrims as they traveled to Jerusalem to observe one of the great festivals of their faith. Such variety among the psalms within these five sections may indicate they were complete collections within themselves before they were placed with other groups of psalms to form this larger body of material.

But no matter how the present arrangement of the book came about, these individual psalms were clearly inspired by God's Spirit. Through these hymns of praise, we come face to face with our Maker and Redeemer. In the glory of His presence, we are compelled to exclaim along with the psalmist, "O Lord, our Lord, how excellent is Your name in all the earth!" (8:9).

AUTHORSHIP AND DATE

Most people automatically think of David when they consider the question of who wrote the Book of Psalms. A shepherd boy who rose to become the most famous king of Judah, he was also known as "the sweet psalmist of Israel" (2 Sam. 23:1). He lived during the most creative age of Hebrew song and poetry. As king, he organized the services of worship in the tabernacle, appointing priests and Levites for the specific purpose of providing songs and music. So it is not surprising that his name should be clearly associated with this beautiful book of praise.

The brief descriptions that introduce the psalms have David listed as author in 73 instances. But some scholars believe the phrase "A psalm of David" should not be interpreted as a certain indication that David actually wrote all these psalms. They point out the Hebrew word translated as *of* can also be translated *to* or *for*. Thus, these psalms could have been written by anonymous authors and dedicated to David or even written on his behalf (for David) and added to a special collection of his material already being used in the sanctuary.

While this is an interesting theory, there is no strong reason to question the traditional view that David actually wrote all the psalms that are attributed to him. David's personality and identity are clearly stamped on many of these psalms. For example, Psalm 18 is a psalm of David which sings praises to God as the sovereign Savior. The title indicates it was written after David was delivered "from the hand of all his enemies and from the hand of Saul." The same psalm in almost identical wording appears in 2 Samuel 22. This passage indicates that David sang this song after the death of Saul and upon his succession to the throne as the new king of Judah.

While it is clear that David wrote many of the individual psalms, he is definitely not the author of the entire collection. Two of the psalms (72 and 127) are attributed to Solomon, David's son and successor. Psalm 90 is a prayer assigned to Moses. Another group of 12 psalms (50 and 73—83) is ascribed to the family of Asaph. The sons of Korah wrote 11 psalms (42, 44—49, 84—85, 87—88). Psalm 88 is attributed to Heman, while Psalm 89 is assigned to Ethan the Ezrahite. With the exception of Solomon and Moses, all these additional authors were priests or Levites who were responsible for providing music for sanctuary worship during David's reign. Fifty of the psalms designate no specific person as author. They were probably written by many different people.

A careful examination of the authorship question, as well as the subject matter covered by the psalms themselves, reveals they span a period of many centuries. The oldest psalm in the collection is probably the prayer of Moses (90), a reflection of the frailty of man as compared to the eternity of God. The latest psalm is probably 137, a song of lament clearly written during the days when the Hebrew were being held captive by the Babylonians, from about 586 to 538 B.C.

It is clear that the 150 individual psalms were written by many different people across a period of a thousand years in Israel's history. They must have been compiled and put together in their present form by some unknown editor shortly after the Captivity ended about 537 B.C.

HISTORICAL SETTING

Some of the psalms written by David grew out of specific experiences in his life. For example, Psalm 3 is described as "a Psalm of David when he fled from Absalom his son" (see also 51, 52, 54, 56, 57, 59). But others seem to be general psalms that arose from no specific life situation (53, 55, 58). Knowing the particular historical background of a psalm can help the student interpret it correctly and apply its message to life today.

THEOLOGICAL CONTRIBUTION

We may think of the psalms as a description of our human response to God. At times God is presented in all His majesty and glory. Our response is wonder, awe, and fear: "Sing to God, you kingdoms of the earth" (68:32). But other psalms portray God as a loving Lord who is involved in our lives. Our response in these cases is to draw close to His comfort and security: "I will fear no evil; for You are with me" (23:4).

God is the same Lord in both these psalms. But we respond to Him in different ways, according to the specific needs of our lives. What a marvelous God we worship, the psalmist declares—One who is high and lifted up beyond our human experiences but also one who is close enough to touch and who walks beside us along life's way.

Other psalms might be described as outcries against God and the circumstances of life rather than responses to God because of His glory and His presence in our lives. The psalmist admits he sometimes feels abandoned by God as well as his human friends (88). He agonizes over the lies directed against him by his false accusers (109). He calls upon God to deliver him from his enemies and to wipe them out with His wrath (59). Whatever else we may say about the psalms, we must admit they are realistic about human feelings and the way we sometimes respond to the problems and inequities of life.

But even in these strong psalms of lament, the psalmist is never totally engulfed by a feeling of despair. The fact that he uttered his protest to the Lord is a sign of hope in God and His sense of justice. This has a significant message for all believers. We can bring all our feelings to God, no matter how negative or complaining they may be. And we can rest assured that he will hear and understand. The psalmist teaches us that the most profound prayer of all is a cry for help as we find ourselves overwhelmed by the problems of life.

The psalms also have a great deal to say about the person and work of Christ. Psalm 22 contains a remarkable prophecy of the crucifixion of the Savior. Jesus quoted from this psalm as He was dying on the cross (Ps. 22:1; Matt. 27:46; Mark 15:34). Other statements about the Messiah from the psalms that were fulfilled in the life of Jesus include these predictions: He would be a priest like Melchizedek (Ps. 110:4; Heb. 5:6); He would pray for His enemies (Ps. 109:4; Luke 23:34); and His throne would be established forever (Ps. 45:6; Heb 1:8).

SPECIAL CONSIDERATIONS

The Book of Psalms is the best example in the Bible of the nature of Hebrew poetry. The principle upon which this poetry is based is not rhythm or rhyme but parallelism. In parallelism, one phrase is followed by another that says essentially the same thing but in a more creative, expressive way. Here is a good example of this poetic technique:

The Lord of hosts is with us;
The God of Jacob is our refuge (46:11).

This example is known as synonymous parallelism because the second phrase expresses the same thought as the first. But sometimes the succeeding line introduces a thought that is directly opposite to the first idea. This is known as antithetic parallelism. Here is a familiar couplet that demonstrates this form:

For the Lord knows the way of the righteous,
But the way of the ungodly shall perish (1:6).

A third kind of parallelism in Hebrew poetry may be called progressive, or climbing—in which part of the first line is repeated in the second, but also something more is added. For example:

The floods have lifted up, O Lord,
The floods have lifted up their voice (93:3).

Another literary device which the Hebrew writers used to give their psalms a peculiar style and rhythm was the alphabetical acrostic. The best example of this technique is Psalm 119—the longest in the collection—which contains 22 different sections of eight verses each. Each major section is headed by a different letter of the Hebrew alphabet. In the original language, each verse in these major divisions of the psalm begins with the Hebrew letter which appears as the heading for that section. Many modern translations of the Bible include these Hebrew letters as a part of the structure required a high degree of literary skill.

The peculiar poetic structure of the 150 psalms makes them ideal for believers who like to create their own devotional exercises. You can easily combine the lines from many different psalms into a fresh, authentic expression of praise to God. Here is an example of such a combined psalm:

Oh, give thanks to the Lord, for He is good!
For His mercy endures forever (136:1).
He has not dealt with us according to our sins,
Nor punished us according to our iniquities (103:10).
For You, O God, have heard my vows;
You have given me the heritage of those who fear Your name (61:5).
Your testimonies are very sure;
Holiness adorns Your house, O Lord, forever (93:5).
So teach us to number our days,
That we may gain a heart of wisdom (90:12).
The fear of the Lord is the beginning of wisdom;
A good understanding have all those who do His commandments (111:10).
Oh, give thanks to the God of heaven!
For His mercy endures forever (136:26).

The cave to which David escaped from Saul, after leaving Gath. Some scholars believe he wrote Psalm 57 while holed-up here. (Todd Bolen, bibleplaces.com)

The Book of Proverbs

This "wisdom book" of the Old Testament contains instructions on many on the practical matters of daily life. The proverb was a familiar literary form in all ancient cultures; it was a very suitable device for collecting and summarizing the wisdom of the centuries. But the Book of Proverbs has one important difference: It points the believer to God with instructions on how to live a holy, upright life.

A rock badger, or hyrax (also called a coney) on a rocky outcropping overlooking the Dead Sea. (Todd Bolen, bibleplaces.com)

STRUCTURE OF THE BOOK

The Book of Proverbs has the longest title (in essence covering the first six verses of chapter 1) of any Old Testament book. The author introduces himself as a teacher, one of the Wise Men of Israel, who has written this book as a manual of instruction on the ways of wisdom. His declaration, "The fear of the Lord is the beginning of knowledge" (1:7), summarizes the theme of Proverbs, a point which he emphasizes again and again throughout the book.

In its 31 chapters, Proverbs discusses many practical matters to help the believer live in harmony with God as well as his fellow man. Subjects covered in this wise and realistic gook include how to choose the right kind of friends, the perils of adultery, the value of hard work, dealing justly with others in business, the dangers of strong drink, treating the poor with compassion, the values of strong family ties, the folly of pride and anger, and the characteristics of genuine friendship.

Scholars agree that Proverbs is a compilation of material from several different sources. This gives the book a unique internal structure. But the book itself tells us which parts were written by one author and which came from another's hand.

AUTHORSHIP AND DATE

The name of Solomon as author is associated with the Book of Proverbs from the very beginning. Verse 1 of chapter 1 states: "The proverbs of Solomon the son of David." We also know that Solomon was noted throughout the ancient world for his superior wisdom (1 Kin. 4:29–34). Additional evidence of his authorship is found within the book itself, where Solomon is identified as author of the section from 10:1 to 22:16 as well as writer of chapters 25—29.

But what about those portions of Proverbs that clearly are attributed to other writers, such as "the wise" (22:17), Agur (30:1), and King Lemuel (31:1)? Although Solomon wrote a major portion of Proverbs, he did not write the entire book. Many scholars believe he wrote the basic core of Proverbs but added some writings from other sources, giving proper credit to their writers.

Another interesting fact about this book and its writing is that the second collection of proverbs attributed to Solomon (chaps. 25—29) were not added to the book until more than 200 years after his death. The heading over this material reads: "These also are proverbs of Solomon which the men of Hezekiah king of Judah copied" (25:1). Perhaps these writings of Solomon were not discovered and inserted in to the book until Hezekiah's time.

Because of the strong evidence that the Book of Proverbs is, indeed, a compilation; some scholars dismiss the idea that Solomon wrote any of the material. But evidence for this authorship of some sections is too strong to be dismissed that lightly. In its original version the book must have been written and compiled by Solomon some time during his reign from 970 B.C. to 931 B.C. then, about 720 B.C. the material now contained in chapters 25—29 was added to the book.

HISTORICAL SETTING

The Book of Proverbs is the classical example of the type of writing in the Old Testament known as Wisdom Literature. Other books so categorized are Job, Ecclesiastes, and the Song of Solomon. These books are called wisdom writings because they were written by a distinctive group of people in Israel's history who grappled with some of the eternal questions of life. This type of writing flourished especially during Solomon's time, and he was known as the wisest of the wise throughout the ancient world. "Thus Solomon's wisdom excelled the wisdom of all the men of the East and all the wisdom of Egypt. For he was wiser than all men ... and his fame was in all the surrounding nations" (1 Kin. 4:30–31).

A Concise Outline of **Proverbs**		
	1. The Purpose of Proverbs	1:1–7
	2. Proverbs to the Youth	1:8—9:18
	3. Proverbs of Solomon	10:1—24:34
	4. Proverbs of Solomon Copied by Hezekiah's Men	25:1—29:27
	5. The Words of Agur	30:1–33
	6. The Words of King Lemuel	31:1–31

This stone inscription once contained the Book of Proverbs. Written in Sumerian cuneiform, it comes from the city of Nippur, in Sumeria. (Todd Bolen, bibleplaces.com)

THEOLOGICAL CONTRIBUTION

Israel's distinctive contribution to the thinking of the wise men of all nations and times is that true wisdom is centered in respect and reverence for God. This is the great underlying theme of the Book of Proverbs.

SPECIAL CONSIDERATIONS

In reading the Book of Proverbs, we need to make sure we do not turn these wise sayings into literal promises. Proverbs are statements of the ways things generally turn out in God's world. For example, it is generally true that those who keep God's commandments will enjoy "length of days and long life" (3:2). But this should not be interpreted as an ironclad guarantee. It is important to keep God's laws, no matter how long or short our earthly life may be.

The Book of Ecclesiastes

This wisdom book wrestles with the question of the meaning of life. It takes its name from the Greek word *ekklesiastes*, meaning "convener of an assembly." The book is often referred to by its Hebrew name, *qoheleth*, which means "preacher" or "speaker."

Dried mud along the spice route that went through Israel, from Arabia and Persia (modern Iran) to China. (Todd Bolen, bibleplaces.com)

STRUCTURE OF THE BOOK

The second verse of Ecclesiastes, "Vanity of vanities, all is vanity" (1:2), eloquently summarizes the underlying theme of the book—that all human achievements are empty and disappointing when pursued as ends in themselves. Many passages in Ecclesiastes appear to be as pessimistic and depressing as this statement because they point out the folly of pursuing selfish goals. One after the other, the author shows how wisdom, pleasure, hard work, popularity, wealth, and fame fail to bring lasting satisfaction. But the book ends on a triumphant note as the reader is asked to consider life's highest good: "Fear God and keep His commandments, for this is the whole duty of man" (12:13).

AUTHORSHIP AND DATE

King Solomon of Israel, a ruler noted for his great wisdom and vast riches, has traditionally been accepted as the author of Ecclesiastes. Evidence for this is strong, since Solomon fits the author's description of himself given in the book: "I, the Preacher, was king over Israel in Jerusalem. And I set my heart to seek and to search out by wisdom concerning all that is done under heaven" (1:12–13).

But some scholars claim that Solomon could not have written the book because it uses certain words and phrases that belong to a much later time in Israel's history. These objections by themselves are not strong enough to undermine Solomon's authorship. The book was probably written some time during his long reign of 40 years, from 970 to 931 B.C.

HISTORICAL SETTING

King Solomon amassed great riches during his long reign. He also developed a great reputation as a man of wisdom. He must have written Ecclesiastes as he looked back over his life accomplishments.

THEOLOGICAL CONTRIBUTION

The Book of Ecclesiastes has a powerful message for our selfish, materialistic age. It teaches that great accomplishments and earthly possessions alone do not bring lasting happiness. True satisfaction comes from serving God and following His will for our lives.

But another important truth from Ecclesiastes, which we often overlook, is that life is to be enjoyed. The preacher of this book repeats this truth several times so it does not escape our attention: "There is nothing better for them than to rejoice, and to do good in their lives, and also that every man should eat and drink and enjoy the good of all his labor—it is the gift of God" (3:12–13). God wants us to enjoy life's simple pleasures.

SPECIAL CONSIDERATIONS

One of the most moving passages in the Bible is the poem from Ecclesiastes on the proper time for all events: "A time to be born, and a time to die" (3:2). This text, if taken seriously, can restore balance to our living. Another powerful passage is the figurative description of the aging process (12:1–7). The preacher realizes that old age with its afflictions looms ahead for every person. So he counsels his audience, "Remember now your Creator in the days of your youth, before the difficult days come" (12:1).

A Concise Outline of
Ecclesiastes

I. "All Is Vanity"

1. Introduction of Vanity   1:1–3
2. Illustrations of Vanity   1:4–11

II. Proof That "All Is Vanity"

1. Proof of "All Is Vanity" from Experience   1:12—2:26
2. Proof of "All Is Vanity" from Observation   3:1—6:12

III. Counsel for Living with Vanity

1. Coping in a Wicked World   7:1—9:18
2. Counsel for the Uncertainties of Life   10:1—12:8
3. Conclusion: Fear God and Keep His Commandments   12:9–14

Almond trees in Jerusalem, blossoming in the snow. (Todd Bolen, bibleplaces.com)

The Song of Solomon

This book is written in the form of a lyrical love song. Some interpreters believe this song speaks symbolically of the love of God for the nation of Israel. But others insist it should be interpreted literally—as a healthy expression of romantic love between a man and a woman. No matter how the book is interpreted, it is certainly one of the most unusual in the Bible. Its subtitle, "the song of songs" (1:1), implies it was the loveliest and best-known of all the songs of Solomon.

Goats on a hillside in Gilead. Note the long hair and several different colors. (Todd Bolen, bibleplaces.com)

STRUCTURE OF THE BOOK

The Song of Solomon is a brief book of only eight chapters. But in spite of its brevity, it has a complicated structure that sometimes confuses the reader. Several different characters or personalities have speaking parts within this long lyrical poem. In some translations of the Bible, these speakers change abruptly with no identification to help the reader follow the narrative. But the NKJV clears up this confusion by publishing identification lines within the text. This helps the reader gain a clearer understanding of this beautiful song.

The three main parties with speaking parts of this long poem are:

• the groom, King Solomon;
• the bride, a woman referred to as "the Shulamite" (6:13); and
• the "daughters of Jerusalem" (2:7).

These women of Jerusalem may have been royal servants who served as attendants to Solomon's Shulamite bride. In this love song, they serve as a chorus to echo the sentiments of the Shulamite, emphasizing her love and affection for Solomon.

In addition to these main personalities, the brothers of the Shulamite bride are also mentioned in the poem (8:8–9). These may have been her step-brothers. The poem indicates she worked under their command as "the keeper of the vineyards" (1:6).

This beautiful love song falls naturally into two major sections of about equal length—the beginning of love (chaps. 1—4) and the broadening of love (chaps. 5—8).

In the first section, the Shulamite tells about Solomon's visit to her home in the country in the springtime (2:8–17). She also recalls the many happy experiences of their courtship when she visited Solomon in his palace in Jerusalem (2:4–7). She thinks about the painful separations from his love during this time (3:1–5), as well as the joyous wedding procession to Jerusalem to become the king's bride (3:6–11). Solomon also praises his bride-to-be in a beautiful poem on the magic and wonder of love (chap. 4).

In the second section of the book, the love of the Shulamite and Solomon for each other continues to deepen after their marriage. She has a troubled dream when he seems distant and unconcerned (5:2–8), praises her beauty (6:4—7:9). Longing to visit her country home (7:10—8:4), she finally makes the trip with Solomon; and their love grows even stronger (8:5–7). The song closes with an assurance of each to the other that they will always remain close in their love.

AUTHORSHIP AND DATE

Traditionally, authorship of the Song of Solomon has been assigned to Solomon, since the book itself makes this claim (1:1). But some scholars reject this theory. They insist it was a later collection of songs attributed to Solomon because of his reputation as a writer of psalms and proverbs (1 Kin. 4:32). A careful analysis of the internal evidence, however, gives strong support to the view that Solomon wrote the book.

Solomon is mentioned by name several times in the song (1:1, 5; 3:7, 9, 11; 8:11–12), and he is specifically identified as the groom. The book also gives evidence of wealth, luxury, and exotic imported goods (3:6–11)—a characteristic of his administration. The groom of the song also assures the Shulamite bride that she is "the only one" (6:9) among his "sixty queens and eighty concubines" (6:8)—probably a reference by Solomon to his royal harem. At the height of his power and influence, Solomon was known to have 700 wives and 300 concubines (1 Kin. 11:3).

This strong internal evidence clearly supports the traditional view that Solomon himself wrote this song that bears his name. It must have been written early in his reign, probably about 965 B.C.

This leopard is in a nature preserve in Israel. Zoologists estimate that a small number of leopards still live in the wilds, mostly on Mount Carmel. (Todd Bolen, bibleplaces.com)

HISTORICAL SETTING

With his large harem, how could King Solomon write such a beautiful love song to one specific wife? Perhaps his union with the Shulamite woman was the only authentic marriage relationship with Solomon ever knew. Most of his marriages were political arrangements with other nations. In contrast, the Shulamite woman was not a cultured princess but a lowly vineyard keeper whose skin had been darkened by her long exposure to the sun (1:6). Yet, she was the bride to whom Solomon declared, "How much better than wine is your love, and the scent of your perfumes than all spices!" (4:10).

This has a real message about the nature of true love. Authentic love is much more than a surface relationship; it extends to the very core of one's being. Love like this cannot be bought and sold like some commodity on the open market. Solomon had many wives, but the Shulamite may have been the only one with whom he enjoyed a warm, enriching relationship.

THEOLOGICAL CONTRIBUTION

The great message of the Song of Solomon is the beauty of love between a man and a woman as experienced in the relationship of marriage. In its frank but beautiful language, the song praises the mutual love which husband and wife feel toward each other in this highest of all human relationships.

The sexual and physical side of marriage is a natural and proper part of God's plan, reflecting His purpose and desire for the human race. This is the same truth so evident at the beginning of time in the Creation itself. God created man and woman and brought them together to serve as companions and to share their lives with one another: "Therefore a man shall leave his father and mother and be joined to his wife, and they shall become one flesh" (Gen. 2:24). Like the Book of Genesis, the Song of Solomon says a bold **yes** to the beauty and sanctity of married love.

But this book also points beyond human love to the great Author of love. Authentic love is possible in the world because God brought love into being and planted that emotion in the hearts of His people. Even husbands and wives should remember that the love which they share for one another is not a product of their human goodness or kindness. We are able to love because the love of God is working in our lives: "In this is love, not that we loved God, but that He loves us and sent His Son to be the propitiation for our sins. Beloved, if God so loved us, we also ought to love one another" (1 John 4:10–11).

SPECIAL CONSIDERATIONS

The symbols and images that the groom uses to describe the beauty of his Shulamite bride may seem strange to modern readers. He portrays her hair as "a flock of goats, going down from Mount Gilead" (4:1). Her neck, he says, is like "the tower of David, built for an armory, on which hang a thousand bucklers" (4:4). Such compliments today would certainly not be flattering to most women!

In his use of these symbols, the groom is reflecting the cultural patterns of the ancient world. To those who lived in Solomon's time, the rippling effect of a flock of goats moving down a hillside was, indeed, a thing of beauty. And a stately tower atop a city was reflected an aura of stability and nobility. The Shulamite woman would have been very pleased at such creative compliments from her poetic groom.

Scholars are not certain of the exact meaning of the phrase, "the Shulamite" (6:13), which has come to be used as title for the bride in this song. No city or region known as Shulam has been identified in Palestine or any of the surrounding territories. Because the poem makes several references to Lebanon (3:9; 4:8, 11, 15; 5:15; 7:4), some scholars believe she came from this mountainous territory along the Mediterranean coast in northwestern Palestine.

CHAPTER 4

BOOKS OF THE MAJOR PROPHETS

The last 17 books of the Old Testament are books of prophecy. As a unit, these books make up about one-fourth of the total Bible. These books of the prophets were written across a period of about 450 years—from the ninth to the fifth centuries B.C.

The prophets of Old Testament times who wrote these books were known by many titles, including seers, watchmen, men of God, messengers, and servants of the Lord. The title *prophet* is used more than 300 times in the Old Testament. It refers to one who has been called or appointed to proclaim the message of God. The English word *prophet* is derived from two Greek words that literally mean "speak for." This emphasizes the role of these people as divinely chosen spokesmen who received and related God's messages, whether in oral, visual, or written form. God communicated to them through a variety of means including dreams, visions, angels, nature, miracles, and an audible voice.

Although the prophets had a ministry of foretelling future events, their primary role was that of forthtelling. This demanded spiritual insight as well as foresight, because they proclaimed the consequences of specific attitudes and practices of their day. They dipped into the past for lessons and exhortations concerning the present. They spoke of the need of people to turn back to God to avoid future judgment.

The terms *major prophets* and *minor prophets* may suggest that some of these spokesmen for God are more important than others, but this is clearly not the case. As the Bible was compiled across the centuries, the longest prophetic books—Isaiah, Jeremiah, Lamentations, Ezekiel, and Daniel—were placed at the beginning of the prophetic section, while the shorter prophetic books were placed after these. That is why they are referred to as the "major prophets" and the "minor prophets."

The chart on page 86 gives an overview of the first group of prophetic books by showing the individual books that make up this section of the Old Testament. These books are then discussed in detail in their appropriate order to give you a better understanding of this important major division of God's Word.

Books of the Major Prophets

Book	Summary
Isaiah	The outstanding prophet of condemnation and Messianic consolation
Jeremiah	A message of judgment against Judah's moral and spiritual decay
Lamentations	Jeremiah's five poems of lament over fallen Jerusalem
Ezekiel	A prophecy of judgment during the Babylonian Captivity
Daniel	A book of prophecy about the end time

The church of St. Paul Outside the Wall, built over the traditional site of Paul's grave and refurbished several times down through the centuries. (Todd Bolen, bibleplaces.com)

The Book of Isaiah

This book is noted for its description of the coming Messiah as God's Suffering Servant. Because of its lofty portrayal of God and His purpose of salvation, the book is sometimes called "the fifth gospel," implying it is similar in theme to the gospels of the New Testament. The book is named for its author, the great prophet Isaiah, whose name means "God is salvation."

A solidly built mini-fortress, ideal for observing the surrounding lands. (Todd Bolen, bibleplaces.com)

STRUCTURE OF THE BOOK

With its 66 chapters, Isaiah is the longest prophetic book of the Old Testament. Most scholars agree that the book falls naturally into two major sections, chapters 1—39 and chapters 40—66. One good way to remember the grand design of the book is to think of the sections as a parallel to the two main parts of the Bible. The first section of Isaiah contains the same number of chapters as the numbers of books in the Old Testament (39). The second part of the book parallels the New Testament in the same way— 27 chapters for the 27 books of this section of the Bible.

The general theme of the first part of Isaiah's book is God's approaching judgment on the nation of Judah. In some of the most striking passages in all the Bible, the prophet announces that God will punish His people because of their sin, rebellion, and worship of false gods. But this message of stern judgment is also mixed with beautiful poems of comfort and promise. Although judgment is surely coming, better days for God's Covenant People lie just ahead. This section of Isaiah's book refers several times to the coming Messiah. His name will be called Immanuel (7:14). As a ruler on the throne of David, He will establish an everlasting kingdom (9:7).

Other significant events and prophecies covered in the first section of Isaiah's book include his call as a prophet (chap. 6), God's judgment against the nations surrounding Judah (chaps. 13—23), and a warning to Judah not to seek help through vain alliances with Egypt (chaps. 30—31).

During Isaiah's time, Judah's safety was threatened by the advancing Assyrian Empire. When the king of Judah sought to protect the nation's interests by forming an alliance with Egypt to turn back the Assyrians, Isaiah advised the nation to look to their God for deliverance—not to a pagan nation led by an earthly ruler. He also prophesied that the Assyrian army would be turned back by God before it succeeded in overthrowing the nation of Judah (30:27–33).

The second major section of Isaiah's book (chaps. 40—66) is filled with prophecies of comfort for the nation of Judah. Just as Isaiah warned of God's approaching judgment in the first part of his book, the 27 concluding chapters were written to comfort God's people in the midst of their suffering after His judgment had fallen. The theme of this entire section may be illustrated with Isaiah's famous hymn of comfort that God directed the prophet to address to the people: "Comfort, yes, comfort My people!" says your God. "Speak comfort to Jerusalem, and cry out to her, that her warfare is ended, that her iniquity is pardoned; for she has received from the Lord's hand double for all her sins" (40:1–2).

Isaiah's message in this part of his book is that after their period of judgment has passed, God's Covenant People will be restored to their place of responsibility in God's plan for the salvation of the world. The great suffering through which they were passing was their period of captivity as exiles of the pagan nation a of Babylon. This theme of suffering on the part of God's people is demonstrated dramatically by Isaiah's famous description of the Suffering Servant. The nation of Israel was God's suffering servant who would serve as God's instrument of blessing for the rest of the world after their release from captivity and restoration as His Chosen People (42:1–9).

But Isaiah's prophecy also points beyond the immediate future to the coming of Jesus Christ as the Messiah several centuries later. The heart of this stunning prophecy occurs in chapter 53, as Isaiah develops the description of God's Servant to its highest point. The Servant's suffering and death and the redemptive nature of His mission are clearly foretold. Although mankind deserved God's judgment because "we have turned, every one, to his own way" (53:6), God sent His Servant to take away our sins. According to Isaiah, it is through His suffering that we are made right with God, since "the Lord has laid on Him the iniquity of us all" (53:6).

Isaiah closes his book with a beautiful description of the glorious age to come (chaps. 60—66). In

A Concise Outline of
Isaiah

A very simple potter's wheel, kept spinning by the hands of the potter's assistant. (Todd Bolen, bibleplaces.com)

that day the city of Zion, or Jerusalem, will be restored. God's people will gather there to worship Him in all His majesty and glory. Peace and justice will reign, and God will make all things new.

AUTHORSHIP AND DATE

The question of who wrote the Book of Isaiah is a matter of much disagreement and debate among Bible scholars. In one camp are those who insist the entire book was written by the famous prophet Isaiah who ministered in the southern kingdom of Judah for 40 years, from about 740 to 700 B.C. But other scholars are just as insistent that the entire book was not written by this prophet. They agree that chapters 1—39 of the book belong to Isaiah, but they refer to chapters 40—66 as "Second Isaiah," insisting it was written by an unknown author long after the ministry of this famous prophet of Judah.

Those who assign chapters 40—66 to a "Second Isaiah" point out that the two major sections of the book seem to be set in different times. Chapters 1—39 clearly belong to the eighth century B.C., a turbulent period in the history of Judah. But Isaiah 40—66, according to these scholars, seems to be addressed to the citizens of Judah who were being held as captives in Babylon about 550 B.C. This was two centuries after Isaiah lived. In addition, these scholars point to the differences in tone, language, and style between these two major sections as proof that the book was written by two different authors.

But the traditional view cannot be dismissed so easily. Conservative scholars point out that the two sections of the book do have many similarities, although they are dramatically different in tone and theme. Many phrases and ideas that are peculiar to Isaiah appear in both sections of the book. A good example of this is Isaiah's unique reference to God as "the Holy One of Israel" (1:4; 17:7; 37:23; 45:11; 55:5; 60:14). The appearance of these words and phrases can be used to argue just as convincingly that the book was written by a single author.

Conservative scholars also are not convinced that the two major section of the book were addressed to different audiences living in different times. In the second section of his book, they believe Isaiah looked into the future and predicted the years of Captivity and the return of the Covenant People to their homeland after the Captivity ended. If the prophet could predict the coming of the Messiah over 700 years before that happened, he could certainly foresee this major event in the future of the nation of Judah.

After all the evidence is analyzed, there is no convincing reason to question the traditional view that the entire book was written by the prophet whose name it bears. The most likely time for its writing was about 700 B.C. or shortly thereafter.

Isaiah gives us few facts about himself, but we do know he was "the son of Amoz" (1:1). The quality of his writing indicates he was well educated and that he probably came from an upper-class family. Married, he had two children to whom he gave symbolic names to show that God was about to bring judgment against the nation of Judah. He was called to his prophetic ministry "in the year that King Uzziah [Azariah] died" (6:1)—about 740 B.C.—through a stirring vision of God as he worshiped in the Temple. He prophesied for about 40 years to the nation of Judah, calling the people and their rulers to place their trust in the Holy One of Israel.

HISTORICAL SETTING

Isaiah delivered his prophecies during a time of great moral and political upheaval. In the early part of his ministry, about 722 B.C., Judah's sister nation, the northern kingdom of Israel, fell to the invading Assyrians. For a while, it looked as if Judah advised the rulers of Isaiah not to enter alliances with foreign nations against the Assyrian threat. Instead, he called the people to put their trust in God, who alone could bring real salvation and offer lasting protection for the perilous times.

THEOLOGICAL CONTRIBUTION

The Book of Isaiah presents more insights into the nature of God than any other book of the Old Testament.

To Isaiah, God was first of all a holy God. His holiness was the first thing that impressed the prophet when he saw Him in all His glory in the Temple (6:1–8). But God's holiness also reminded Isaiah of his own sin and weakness. "Woe is me," he cried, "for I am a man of unclean lips, and I dwell in the midst of a people of unclean lips" (6:5). After this confession, Isaiah's lips were cleansed by a live coal from the altar, and he agreed to proclaim God's message of repentance and judgment to a wayward people.

Isaiah also tells us about a God who is interested in the salvation of His people. Even the prophet's name, "God is salvation, " emphasizes this truth. He uses the word *salvation* 28 times in his book, while all the other Old Testament prophets combined mentioned this word only 10 times. In Isaiah's thought, salvation is of God, not man. God is the sovereign ruler of history and the only one who has the power to save.

The Book of Isaiah also reveals that God's ultimate purpose of salvation will be realized through the coming Messiah, our Lord and Savior Jesus Christ. No other book of the Bible contains as many references to the coming Messiah as this magnificent book. Isaiah points us to a loving Savior who came to save His people from their sins. When Jesus began His public ministry in His hometown of Nazareth, He quoted from one of these beautiful messianic passages from Isaiah (61:1–2) to show that this prophecy was being fulfilled in His life and ministry. His purpose was "to set at liberty those who are oppressed, to preach the acceptable year of the Lord" (Luke 4:18–19).

SPECIAL CONSIDERATIONS

One unusual passage in the Book of Isaiah gives us a clue about how God views His work of judgment and salvation. The prophet describes God's judgment as "His unusual act" (28:21). If judgment is God's unusual act, does this not imply that salvation is the work more typical of Him as a loving God? It is an interesting question to think about as we express thanks to God for the marvelous insights of Isaiah and his important book.

The Book of Jeremiah

This major prophetic book was directed to the southern kingdom of Judah just before that nation fell to the Babylonians. The book is named for its author and central personality, the great prophet Jeremiah, who faithfully delivered God's message of judgment in spite of fierce opposition from his countrymen.

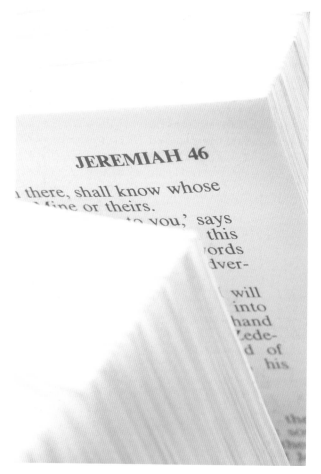

A page from a modern Bible, showing parts of the 46th chapter of the Book of Jeremiah. (© 2007 JupiterImages Corporation)

STRUCTURE OF THE BOOK

Jeremiah, consisting of 52 chapters, is one of the longest books in the Bible. It is also one of the hardest to follow and understand. Unlike most of the other prophetic books, which have a chronological arrangement, the material in Jeremiah seems to follow no logical pattern. Prophecies delivered in the final years of his ministry may appear at any point in the book, followed by messages that belong to other periods in his life. Mingled with his prophecies of God's approaching judgment are historical accounts of selected events in the life of Judah, personal experiences from Jeremiah's own life, and poetic laments about the fate of his country. It is important to be aware of this if one wants to understand the message of this great prophetic book.

Perhaps the best way to get a big picture of the Book of Jeremiah is to break it down by types of literature. Basically, the first half of the book (chaps. 1—25) consists of poetry, while the second half (chaps. 26—52) is in prose or narrative-style writing. The poetry section of the book contains Jeremiah's prophecies of God's approaching judgment against Judah because of its sin and idolatry. The prose section contains a few of his prophesies, but the main emphasis is on Jeremiah and his conflicts with the kings who ruled in Judah during his ministry. Also included near the end of his book is a report on the fall of Jerusalem and Judah's final days as a nation (chaps. 39—41; 52), along with a narrative about Jeremiah's flight into Egypt with other citizens of Judah following its fall (chaps. 42—44).

AUTHORSHIP AND DATE

Most conservative scholars agree that the author of the Book of Jeremiah was the famous prophet of that name who ministered in the southern kingdom of Judah during the final four decades of that nation's existence. But some scholars claim the book's disjointed arrangement proves it was compiled by an unknown author some time after Jeremiah's death. The book itself gives us a clue about how it may have taken its present form.

After prophesying against Judah for about 20 years, the prophet Jeremiah was commanded by God to put his messages in written form. He dictated these to his scribe or secretary, Baruch, who wrote them on a scroll (36:1–4). Because Jeremiah had been banned from entering the royal court, he sent Baruch to read the messages to king Jehoiakim. To show his contempt for Jeremiah and his message, the king cut the scroll apart and threw it in the fire (36:22–23). Jeremiah promptly dictated his book to Baruch again, adding "many similar words" (36:32) that had not been included in the first scroll.

This clear description of how a second version of Jeremiah came to be written shows the book was composed in several different stages during the prophet's ministry. The scribe Baruch was probably the one who added to the book at Jeremiah's command as it was shaped and refined over a period of several years. This is a possible explanation for the disjointed arrangement of the book. Baruch must have put the book in final form shortly after Jeremiah's death. This would place its final writing not long after 585 B.C.

We can learn a great deal about the prophet Jeremiah by reading his book. He was a sensitive poet who could weep over the sins of his nation: "Oh, that my head were waters, and my eyes a fountain of tears" (9:1). But he was also a courageous man of God who could endure persecution and affliction. He narrowly escaped death several times as he carried out God's command to preach His message of judgment to a wayward people. A patriot who passionately loved his nation, he drew the tough assignment of informing his countrymen that Judah was about to fall to a pagan power. Many of his fellow citizens branded him a traitor, but he never wavered from the prophetic ministry to which God had called him.

With the fall of Jerusalem in 587 B.C., most of the leading citizens of the nation were carried away

A Concise Outline of
Jeremiah

I. The Call of Jeremiah

1. Jeremiah's Call	1:1–10
2. Jeremiah's Signs	1:11–16
3. Jeremiah's Assurance	1:17–19

II. The Prophecies to Judah

1. The Condemnation of Judah	2:1—25:38
2. The Conflicts of Jeremiah	26:1—29:32
3. The Future Restoration of Jerusalem	30:1—33:26
4. The Present Fall of Jerusalem	34:1—45:5

III. The Prophecies to the Gentiles

1. Prophecies Against Egypt	46:1—28
2. Prophecies Against Philistia	47:1–7
3. Prophecies Against Moab	48:1–47
4. Prophecies Against Ammon	49:1–6
5. Prophecies Against Edom	49:7–22
6. Prophecies Against Damascus	49:23–27
7. Prophecies Against Kedar and Hazor	49:28–33
8. Prophecies Against Elam	49:34–39
9. Prophecies Against Babylon	50:1—51:64

IV. The Fall of Jerusalem

1. The Capture of Jerusalem	52:1–11
2. The Destruction of Jerusalem	52:12–23
3. The Exile to Babylon	52:24–30
4. The Release of Jehoiakim	52:31–34

as captives to Babylon. But Jeremiah was allowed to remain in Jerusalem with other citizens of Judah who were placed under the authority of a ruling governor appointed by Babylon. When the citizens of Jerusalem revolted against this official, Jeremiah and others were forced to seek safety in Egypt, where he continued his prophetic ministry (chaps. 43—44). This is the last we hear of this courageous prophet of the Lord.

HISTORICAL SETTING

The Book of Jeremiah belongs to a chaotic time in the history of God's Covenant People. Jeremiah's native land, the southern kingdom of Judah, was caught in a power squeeze between three great powers of the ancient world: Egypt, Assyria, and Babylon. As these empires struggled for dominance with one another, the noose grew tighter around Judah's neck.

To protect its borders, Judah entered into an alliance with Egypt against the Babylonians. But Jeremiah realized the alliance was too little too late. For years his beloved nation had risked disaster as it rejected worship of the one true God and turned to pagan gods instead. Immorality, injustice, graft, and corruption prevailed throughout the land. God revealed to the prophet that he intended to punish His Covenant People by sending the Babylonians to destroy Jerusalem and carry the people into captivity. Jeremiah preached this message of judgment faithfully for about 40 years.

At the beginning of his prophetic ministry, it appeared briefly that conditions might improve. King Josiah (ruled 641/40–609 B.C.) began reforms based on God's Law, but at his death the dark days of paganism returned. Josiah's successors continued their reckless pursuit of idolatry and foolish alliances with Egypt against the Babylonians. At the decisive battle of Carchemish in 605 B.C., the Egyptians were soundly defeated. About 18 years later the Babylonians completed their conquest of Judah by destroying the capital city of Jerusalem. Just as Jeremiah had predicted, the leading citizens of Judah were carried to Babylon, where they remained in captivity for half a century.

THEOLOGICAL CONTRIBUTION

Jeremiah's greatest theological contribution was his concept of the new covenant (31:31–34). A new covenant between God and His people was necessary because the old covenant had failed so miserably; the captivity of God's people by a foreign power was proof of that. Although the old covenant had been renewed again and again throughout Israel's history, the people still continued to break the promises they had made to God. What was needed was a new type of covenant between God and His people—a covenant of grace and forgiveness written in man's heart, rather than a covenant of law engraved in stone.

As Jeremiah reported God's plan for this new covenant, he anticipated the dawning of the era of grace in the person of Jesus Christ more than 500 years in the future: "No more shall every man teach his neighbor, and every man his brother, saying, 'Know the Lord,' for they all shall know Me, from the least of them to the greatest of them," says the Lord. "For I will forgive their iniquity, and their sin I will remember no more" (31:34).

SPECIAL CONSIDERATIONS

Jeremiah was a master at using figures of speech, metaphors, and symbolic behavior to drive home his messages. He carried a yoke around his neck to show the citizens of Judah they should submit to the inevitable rule of the pagan Babylonians (27:1–12). He watched a potter mar a piece of clay, then reshape it into a perfect vessel. He applied this lesson to the nation of Judah, which needed to submit to the divine will of the Master Potter while there was still time to repent and avoid God's judgment (18:1–11).

But perhaps his most unusual symbolic act was his purchase of a plot of land in his hometown, Anathoth, about three miles northeast of Jerusalem. Jeremiah knew this land would be practically worthless after the Babylonians overran Jerusalem, as he was predicting. But by buying the plot, he symbolized his hope for the future. Even in Judah's darkest hour, Jeremiah prophesied that a remnant would return from Babylon after their years in captivity to restore their way of life and to worship God again in the Temple (32:26–44). God directed Jeremiah to put the deed to the land in an earthen vessel so it would be preserved for the future: "For thus says the Lord of hosts, the God of Israel: 'Houses and fields and vineyards shall be possessed again in this land'" (32:15).

A modern potter plies an ancient trade at the HaAretz Museum in Tel Aviv. Note the foot pedal for spinning the wheel. (Kim Guess, bibleplaces.com)

The Book of Lamentations

Written in poetic form, Lamentations expresses deep grief over the destruction of the city of Jerusalem and the Temple. Its English title comes from a Greek verb meaning "to cry aloud," which accurately describes the contents of the book.

Looking down on a portion of ancient Jerusalem, at a moment when it looks as deserted as it must have been in verse 1 of Lamentations. (Todd Bolen, bibleplaces.com)

STRUCTURE OF THE BOOK

The book consists of poems, one for each chapter. The first, second, and fourth poems are written as acrostics, with each successive verse beginning with the next letter of the Hebrew alphabet. The third poem is also an acrostic, although in an expanded form giving three verses to each of the 22 letters of the Hebrew alphabet. The fifth poem departs from the acrostic pattern, but it contains 22 verses, the same number as poems one, two, and four.

It is clear that the writer of Lamentations went to much trouble to compose this book. He wove several literary devices together, under the inspiration of God's Spirit, to give these poems a somber tone. Nothing less could express his deep sorrow over the plight of Jerusalem at the hands of the invading Babylonians.

AUTHORSHIP AND DATE

Lamentations itself gives no clue concerning its author, but many conservative Bible scholars agree on the prophet Jeremiah as the most likely candidate. The book is realistic in its portrayal of conditions in Jerusalem just before its fall, suggesting the author was an eyewitness of these events. This supports Jeremiah's authorship, since he prophesied in Jerusalem during this period of his nation's history.

Some of the language in Lamentations and the Book of Jeremiah is also similar. For example, the phrase *daughter of* appears about 20 times in each book. In addition, Jeremiah was a very sensitive prophet who expressed his feelings about his nation's sins and approaching doom in rich symbols and metaphors. A deep outpouring of sorrow is characteristic of Lamentations as well as some sections of the Book of Jeremiah. All this evidence supports the traditional view that the prophet wrote the Book of Lamentations. The date of the writing was probably some time shortly after the fall of the city in 587 or 586 B.C.

HISTORICAL SETTING

The fall of Jerusalem to Babylonian forces under Nebuchadnezzar in 587/586 B.C. was one of Israel's most bitter experiences. Many of the nation's leading citizens were carried into captivity in Babylon. The people of Judah remained in that distant land for almost 50 years. Their idolatry and unfaithfulness had resulted in the loss of two of the focal points under their faith: Jerusalem and the Temple. Jeremiah must have expressed their collective shock and sorrow as he wrote his poetic book.

THEOLOGICAL CONTRIBUTION

Why was there such despondency over the destruction of a city? The reasons become clear when we sense the importance of Jerusalem in the purpose of God.

Jerusalem was more than the capital of the nation or the city of Israel's beloved King David. Jerusalem was the site of the Temple of God, the place where God's presence dwelt and where sacrifice could be made to Him. In later years Jerusalem became the focal point of God's final work of salvation in the person of Jesus Christ. The Book of Lamentations reminds us of the central role which this city has always played in God's work of redemption in the world.

SPECIAL CONSIDERATIONS

Lamentations has many strange expressions such as *daughter of Zion* (2:1), *daughter of Judah* (2:5), and *daughter of Jerusalem* (2:15). These do not refer to daughters of these cities but to the cities themselves as

A Concise Outline of
Lamentations

daughters of the Lord. In this context, these phrases refer to supreme grief. As such they remind us of the profound sorrow associated with God's judgment of His sinful people; yet, since they remain daughters, these cities speak of great hope during desperate times.

Ostriches in an Israeli nature preserve. Once indigenous to Israel, they no longer live there in the wild. (Todd Bolen, bibleplaces.com)

The Book of Ezekiel

The vivid, symbolic language of this book is similar to that in the Book of Revelation. The Book of Ezekiel is named for its author, the prophet Ezekiel, who received his prophetic messages from God in a series of visions. He addressed these prophesies to the Jewish exiles in Babylon.

Though it can't be seen clearly with the naked, untrained eye, there's copper in this Israeli mountainside, near Petra. (Todd Bolen, bibleplaces.com)

STRUCTURE OF THE BOOK

Although Ezekiel is a long book of 48 chapters, it has a logical, orderly structure that makes it easy to analyze and understand. After a brief introductory section about Ezekiel and the nature of his mission, the book falls naturally into three main divisions:

- judgment on the nation of Judah (chaps. 4—24);
- judgment on the surrounding nations (chaps. 25—32); and
- the future blessing of God's Covenant People (chaps. 33—48).

Ezekiel was a priest who lived among the other citizens of the nation of Judah as a captive of Babylon during the years of the Captivity. In the very first chapter of the book, he describes an amazing vision of God which came to him at the beginning of his ministry. He saw four living creatures, each with the face of a man, a lion, an ox, and an eagle. Clearly visible above these strange creatures was the likeness of a throne, symbolizing the might and power of God. The glory of the Lord was clearly visible to Ezekiel as He called the prophet to proclaim His message of judgment. This vision in the very first chapter sets the tone for the rest of Ezekiel. In other encounters with strange visions throughout the book, Ezekiel proclaims God's message for His Covenant People, as well as the Gentile nations surrounding the land of Israel.

In the first major section of the book (chaps. 4—24) Ezekiel describes God's judgment on the nation of Judah because of its rampant idolatry. Chapters 8—11 are especially interesting because their prophecies were delivered by Ezekiel in the city of Jerusalem after God transported him there during one of his visions (8:3). At the end of chapter 11, Ezekiel was taken back to Babylon, where he continued his messages (11:24–25).

The next major division of the book (chaps. 25—32) proclaims God's judgment against the Gentile nations surrounding the land of Israel. Included are judgments against Ammon, Moab, Edom, Philistia, Tyre and Sidon, and Egypt.

The final section of the book (chaps. 33—48) speaks of the future restoration of the people of Israel. It includes Ezekiel's famous vision of the valley of dry bones (chap. 37). At God's command, Ezekiel spoke to the bones and they arose. Then God declared to the bones, "I will put My spirit in you, and you shall live, and I will place you in your own land" (34:14). This was a clear promise from God that His Covenant People would be restored to their homeland after their period of exile in Babylon. This same theme is continued in chapters 40—48, which describe the restoration of the Temple in Jerusalem and renewal of sacrifices and authentic worship. These chapters are similar in tone and content to the closing chapters of the Book of Revelation. Ezekiel points forward to the glorious kingdom of Jesus the Messiah.

AUTHORSHIP AND DATE

The author of this book was clearly the prophet Ezekiel, a spokesman for the Lord who lived among the Jewish captives in Babylon. Some scholars have questioned Ezekiel's authorship, claiming instead that it was compiled by an unknown author from several different sources. But the book itself clearly states that Ezekiel delivered these prophecies. The prophet refers to himself with the personal pronoun "I" throughout the book. The uniformity of style and language in the book—including such phrases as "son of man" (2:1) and "as I live, says the Lord God" (5:11)—is also a convincing proof of authorship by a single person. There is no good reason to doubt the traditional theory that Ezekiel wrote the book.

A Concise Outline of
Ezekiel

The prophet identifies himself in the book as "Ezekiel the priest, the son of Buzi" (1:3). He also tells us he began his prophetic ministry "in the fifth year of King Jehoiakim's captivity" (1:2). This was the king of Judah who was taken captive by Babylon about 597 B.C. This would place the beginning of Ezekiel's prophecies at about 593 B.C. The last dates which he mentions in the book are the "twenty-seventh year" (29:17) and "the twenty-fifth year of our captivity" (40:1). So Ezekiel must have prophesied for at least 20 years among the captives, until 573 B.C. He probably wrote the Book of Ezekiel some time during the period or shortly thereafter.

HISTORICAL SETTING

The Book of Ezekiel belongs to the early years of the Babylonian captivity of God's Covenant People. The Babylonians took captives from Jerusalem in three stages. In an early campaign about 605 B.C., the prophet Daniel was among the Jews taken to Babylon. A second attack against the city occurred in 597 B.C., when many additional captives were taken. Ezekiel must have been among those carried away at this time. Then in the extensive campaign of 587–586 B.C., Nebuchadnezzar destroyed Jerusalem and took most of the remaining inhabitants into exile.

In the early prophecies of the Book of Ezekiel, the author wrote as a captive in Babylon who expected Jerusalem to be destroyed. Chapter 24 describes the beginning of the final siege of the city. This date was so important the Lord had the prophet write it down as a memorial of the dreaded event (24:2). This was followed by the symbol of the cooking pot with scum rising from the boiling meat, a clear judgment against Judah. Also on this day, the prophet's beloved wife died. Ezekiel was forbidden to mourn her death as a symbol of God's wrath upon the wayward nation (24:15–24).

Portions of the Book of Ezekiel were written during the long siege of Jerusalem. While Ezekiel and the other captives lived in Babylon, they must have heard of the suffering of their fellow citizens back home. At last they received word that the city had fallen, and Ezekiel translated this event into an unforgettable message for the people (33:21–29). Such were the perilous times in which Ezekiel prophesied.

THEOLOGICAL CONTRIBUTION

One of the greatest insights of the Book of Ezekiel is its teaching of individual responsibility. This prophet proclaimed the truth that every person is responsible for his own sin as he stands exposed before God. In Ezekiel's time the Jewish people had such a strong sense of group identity as God's Covenant People that they tended to gloss over their need as individuals to follow God and His will. Some even believed that future generations were held accountable for the sins of their ancestors. But Ezekiel declared: "The soul who sins shall die. The son shall not bear the guilt of the father, nor the father bear the guilt of the son. The righteousness of the righteous shall be upon himself, and the wickedness of the wicked shall be upon himself" (18:20).

This underscores the need for every person to make his own decision to follow the Lord. No person can depend on the faith of his ancestors to gain entrance into God's kingdom.

Ezekiel also paints a beautiful picture of the future age in which God will rule triumphantly among His people. Although God's people were suffering at the hands of a pagan nation when Ezekiel prophesied, better days were assured. God would establish His universal rule among His people through a descendant of David (37:24–25). This is a clear reference to the Messiah, a prophecy fulfilled when Jesus was born in Bethlehem more than 500 years later. The followers of Jesus became the "new Israel," or the church—those who seek to follow God and carry out His purpose in the world.

SPECIAL CONSIDERATIONS

In his use of parables, symbolic behavior, and object lessons to drive home his messages, the prophet Ezekiel reminds us of the great prophet Jeremiah. Through the use of parables, Ezekiel portrayed God's Covenant People as a helpless newborn child (16:12), as a lioness who cared carefully for her cubs (19:1–9), as a sturdy cedar (17:1–10), and as a doomed and useless vine (chap. 15). He also used a clay tablet to portray the Babylonian siege against the city of Jerusalem (4:1–2), ate his bread "with quaking" and drank his water "with trembling and anxiety" (12:17) to symbolize God's wrath, and carried his belongings about to show that God would allow His people to be carried into exile by the Babylonians (12:1–16).

Ezekiel may have picked up this technique of acting out his messages from Jeremiah himself. For about 40 years before Jerusalem's fall in 587 B.C., Jeremiah prophesied in the capital city. As a young resident of Jerusalem, Ezekiel probably heard and saw this great prophet at work. When he was called to prophesy to the exiles in Babylon beginning about 593 B.C., he may have used Jeremiah's method as a way to get attention and to win a hearing for God's message.

Imagine the patience needed to press out the oil in a primitive olive press, such as this one in the foreground at Qatzrin, in the Golan Heights. (Todd Bolen, bibleplaces.com)

The Book of Daniel

In this major prophetic book Daniel emphasizes the truth that God is in control of world history. The book is named for Daniel, its author and central personality, who was rescued miraculously from a den of lions after he refused to bow down and worship a pagan king.

Seleucus I of Syria founded Seleucia, this ancient city on the coast of the Mediterranean, to serve as a port for his capital in Antioch. (Todd Bolen, bibleplaces.com)

STRUCTURE OF THE BOOK

Daniel's 12 chapters may be divided naturally into three major sections:

- introductory information about Daniel (chap. 1);
- narratives about Daniel and his friends during their days of captivity among the Babylonians and the Persians (chaps. 2—7); and
- Daniel's dreams and visions concerning the future of Israel and the end of time (chaps. 8—12).

The first chapter sets the stage for the rest of the book by introducing Daniel and his three friends, Hananiah, Mishael, and Azariah. These four young Hebrew men were taken captive in one of the Babylonian raids against Judah in 605 B.C. Intelligent and promising, they were placed in special training as servants in the court of King Nebuchadnezzar; then their names and diets were changed to reflect Babylonian culture in an attempt to take away their Jewish identity. But Daniel and his friends rose to the challenge, proving their Jewish food was superior to the diet of the Babylonians. The young men increased in wisdom and knowledge, gaining favor in the king's court.

In the second major section of the book (chaps. 2—7), Daniel and his friends met several additional tests to prove that although they were being held captive by a pagan people, the God whom they worshiped was still in control. Daniel's three friends (renamed Shadrach, Meshach, and Abed-Nego) refused to worship the pagan Babylonian gods. Cast into the fiery furnace, they emerged unharmed because of God's miraculous protection. Daniel, refusing to bow down and worship Darius, the king of Persia, was also thrown into a den of lions. But he was also saved by God's direct intervention. These tests proved that the God whom they served was superior to the pagan gods of their captors.

Daniel's skill as an interpreter of dreams is also well established in this second section of his book. He interpreted several visions and dreams for King Nebuchadnezzar of Babylon and his successor, Belshazzar. As he revealed the meaning of the mysterious "handwriting on the wall," he made it plain that the Babylonian Empire would be defeated by the Medes and the Persians. This happened exactly as Daniel predicted (5:13–31), and he continued as a servant in the court of the conquering Persian king.

The final section of Daniel's book (chaps. 8—12) consists of a series of visions about succeeding kingdoms and the end of time. These visions came to the prophet during his years in captivity. Standing by the Tigris River in one of these visions, he saw a goat attack a ram. The goat symbolized the Persians, who would defeat the Babylonians. This goat had several different horns, representing the Greek Empire that would rise after the decline of the Persians and the subsequent division of the Greek Empire among the four generals of Alexander the Great.

Daniel had another unusual look into the future known as the Seventy Weeks Prophecy. In this vision, the angel Gabriel revealed to Daniel that the nation of Israel would be restored to its homeland after their period of captivity. This would be followed many years later by the coming of the Messiah and then, finally, the final judgment and the end of time.

Daniel's spectacular book closes with a vision of the final judgment, when the righteous will receive everlasting life and the wicked will receive God's condemnation. But not even Daniel was blessed with perfect understanding of this mystery of the ages. "My Lord, what shall be the end of these things?" (12:8), he asked. To this God replied, "Go your way, Daniel, for the words are closed up and sealed till the time of the end" (12:9).

A Concise Outline of

Daniel

I. The Personal History of Daniel

1. Daniel Carried Away to Babylon   1:1–7
2. The Faithfulness of Daniel in Babylon   1:8–16
3. Daniel's Reputation in Babylon   1:17–21

II. The Prophetic Plan for the Gentiles

1. Nebuchadnezzar's First Dream   2:1–49
2. Nebuchadnezzar's Image of Gold   3:1–30
3. Nebuchadnezzar's Vision of a Great Tree   4:1–37
4. Belshazzar and the Handwriting on
   the Wall   5:1–31
5. Darius' Foolish Decree   6:1–28
6. Daniel's Vision of the Four Beasts   7:1–28

III. The Prophetic Plan for Israel

1. Daniel's Vision of the Ram and Male Goat   8:1–27
2. Daniel's Vision of the Seventy Weeks   9:1–27
3. Daniel's Vision of Israel's Future   10:1—12:13

AUTHORSHIP AND DATE

Most conservative scholars believe the Book of Daniel was written by the prophet and statesman of that name who lived as a captive of Babylon and Persia for more than 50 years after he was taken into captivity in 605 B.C. But this theory is rejected by some scholars, who object to the specific details of the prophetic visions that Daniel records.

Daniel predicted that the empires of Babylon and Persia, for example, would be succeeded by the Greeks under Alexander the Great. He also foresaw that the Greek Empire would be divided among the four generals of Alexander upon his death. Daniel also predicted that the Jewish people would suffer great persecution under an official who would come into power some time after Alexander's death.

Most interpreters identify this ruler, who would "destroy the mighty, and also the holy people" (8:24) as Antiochus Epiphanes, the Greek ruler of Syria. Antiochus persecuted the Jewish people unmercifully from 176 to 164 B.C. because of their refusal to adopt heathen religious practices. According to this line of thinking about Daniel and his prophecies, the book was written not by Daniel the prophet but by an unknown author about 400 years later than Daniel's time. This anonymous writer, according to this theory, wrote the book during the persecution of Antiochus Epiphanes to give the Jewish people renewed hope and religious zeal as they stood against their oppressors. Daniel's prophecies, according to these critics, are not "prophecies" at all, but were written after these events and were attributed to Daniel to show that these great events of world history would eventually happen.

Those who attack the authenticity of the Book of Daniel do not have enough evidence to support their charge. The speculation that it was written by zealous Jews to mobilize their countrymen in opposition to Antiochus Epiphanes is far-fetched and unconvincing. There is no valid reason to abandon the traditional view that it was written by the prophet Daniel. According to evidence in the book itself, Daniel's captivity lasted from the time of Nebuchadnezzar's reign in Babylon (1:1–6) into the reign of Cyrus of Persia (10:1), about 536 B.C. He must have written his book some time during this period or shortly thereafter.

HISTORICAL SETTING

The Book of Daniel clearly belongs to that period among God's Covenant People known as the Babylonian Captivity. Nebuchadnezzar took captives from Judah on three separate occasions, beginning in 605 B.C. Among this first group taken were Daniel and his companions. Their courageous acts must have been a great encouragement to the other captives.

Daniel's own interest in the forthcoming close of the Captivity is supported by his prophecy in chapter 9. His prayer to God is dated at 538 B.C., the very year that Cyrus of Persia issued his decree making it possible for some of the captives to return to Jerusalem to restore their land and rebuild the Temple (Ezra 1:1–4). The fact that some did choose to return may be a tribute to the effectiveness of Daniel's book. He wrote it to show that God was in charge of world history and that He had not yet finished with His Covenant People.

THEOLOGICAL CONTRIBUTION

The major contribution of the Book of Daniel arises from its nature as apocalyptic prophecy. Highly symbolic in language, the prophecy was related to the events of Daniel's near future, but even today it contains a message for the future.

In apocalyptic prophecy, these close-at-hand and further-removed dimensions of the future often blend into each other. An example of this is the figure of Antiochus Epiphanes, prominent in chapters

8 and 11 of the book. In these passages the prophet Daniel moves from the nearer figure , who was to desecrate the Jewish Temple in 168 B.C., to his appearance at a remote time in the future as the Antichrist (8:23–26; 11:36–45; Rev. 13:1–10). This interplay between the near future and the distant future makes it difficult to interpret the book correctly.

In addition to its prophetic contribution, the Book of Daniel portrays a time in biblical history when miracles were abundant. Other periods when miracles were commonplace include the times of Moses, Elijah, Elisha, Jesus Christ, and the early church. In each of these periods, God was working in a spectacular manner to show His power and bring about a new era in His saving relationship to mankind.

SPECIAL CONSIDERATIONS

Chapter 9 of Daniel is a fascinating passage; it combines the best of biblical piety and biblical prophecy. Daniel's study of the prophecy of the 70 years of captivity from the prophet Jeremiah (Jer. 25) led him to pray for God's intervention on behalf of His people. He called on God to shorten the time of their grief (9:1–19). The Lord's answer came through the angel Gabriel, who gave Daniel the prophecy of the Seventy Weeks, or 70 sevens (9:20–27). The 70 sevens as envisioned by the prophet are usually interpreted as years. Thus, the prophecy deals with the next 490 years in the future of God's Covenant People. These 490 years are divided into three groups: 7 weeks (49 years), 62 weeks (434 years), and 1 week (7 years).

Various methods have been used to calculate these periods of years in this prophecy. Here is a general scheme of how it may be done:

During the first seven weeks (49 years), the returned exiles will complete construction of the city of Jerusalem.

The passing of the next 62 weeks (434 years) will mark the time for the cutting off of the Messiah (9:26).

The final or 70th week will bring the making and breaking of a covenant by a mysterious prince and the time of the abomination of desolation (9:27).

These verses contain a full scheme for the history of Israel from Daniel's time to the age of the Messiah. During the first period, the city of Jerusalem will be rebuilt. Then the Messiah will come, but He is destined to be cut off by a mysterious "people of the prince who is to come" (9:26). This prince will have authority during the final period; but his rule will then end, and God's purposes for His people will be realized.

Some scholars believe the 70 weeks or 490 years of this prophecy began with the decree of Ezra 7:11–26, in 458 B.C., when some of the exiles returned to rebuild the city of Jerusalem. They also believe the first 69 weeks (483 years) of this prophecy end roughly at the time of the beginning of the ministry of Christ, in A.D. 26. Others follow a more complex scheme and argue that the beginning point is the order of King Artaxerxes to Nehemiah in Nehemiah 2:5–8, which placed the return of some of the exiles at 445 B.C. In this view, the first 69 weeks, or 483 years, of Daniel's prophecy end at the time of the triumphal entry of Jesus into Jerusalem.

Perhaps the round numbers in this prophecy (70 sevens) should be our clue that it is dangerous to try to pin its fulfillment to a specific day or year. But we can say for sure that the end of the 483 years spoken of by Daniel would bring us to the general period of the ministry of the Lord Jesus Christ. The final week in the prophecy is symbolic of the age between the ascension of Jesus and His second coming. This part of Daniel's prophecy is yet to be fulfilled in the future tribulation described so graphically in the Book of Revelation.

CHAPTER 5

BOOKS OF THE MINOR PROPHETS

The last twelve books of the Old Testament became known as the books of the minor prophets late in the fourth century A.D. not because they were considered less important or less inspired, but because they are generally shorter and they were placed after the five major prophets. The messages are more succinct than those of the major prophets, but they are just as powerful.

Before the time of Christ these twelve books were joined together in one scroll known as "The Twelve." Their combined length of 67 chapters is about equal to that of Isaiah. They were written across a period of about 400 years in the history of the nations of Judah and Israel.

This 400-year span of history moves through the Assyrian, Babylonian, and Persian Empires. Two were prophets to the Northern Kingdom (Amos, Hosea); six were prophets to the Southern Kingdom (Obadiah, Joel, Micah, Nahum, Zephaniah, Habakkuk); one delivered God's message to a pagan nation (Jonah); and three were post-exilic prophets (Haggai, Zechariah, Malachi). Although all the minor prophets are named, very little is known about most of them. Their personalities, backgrounds, interests, and writing styles vary widely, but they shared a common conviction, courage, and commitment.

The chart on page 112 gives an overview of the books of the minor prophets by showing the individual books that make up this section of the Old Testament. These books are then discussed in detail in their appropriate order to give you a better understanding of this major division of God's Word.

Books of the Minor Prophets

Book	Summary
Hosea	A message of Israel's condemnation followed by God's forgiveness
Joel	A prediction of foreign invasion as a form of judgment by God
Amos	A prophecy of eight pronouncements of judgment against Israel
Obadiah	A book prophesying the total destruction of Edom
Jonah	A reluctant prophet who led Nineveh to repentance
Micah	A prediction of judgment and a promise of Messianic restoration
Nahum	A prophecy of the destruction of Nineveh
Habakkuk	A prophet who questioned God and praised His approaching judgment against Judah
Zephaniah	A prediction of destructive judgment followed by tremendous blessing
Haggai	After the return from Babylon, a call to rebuild the Temple
Zechariah	A Messianic prophecy calling for the completion of construction on the Temple
Malachi	A prophecy of destruction followed by Messianic blessing

The Book of Hosea

This prophetic book emphasizes God's steadfast love for His Covenant People in spite of their continuing sin and rebellion. The book is named for its author, the prophet Hosea, who demonstrated God's steadfast love in dramatic fashion through his devotion to his own unfaithful wife.

The modern city of Arbel—with the Sea of Galilee in the background—might be the site of ancient Beth-Arbel, mentioned by Hosea. But no one is certain. (Todd Bolen, bibleplaces.com)

STRUCTURE OF THE BOOK

Hosea contains 14 chapters that are filled with some of the most powerful truths in the Bible. After a brief introduction of himself as God's prophet, Hosea tells about his unusual family situation. God appeared to Hosea, instructing him, "Go, take yourself a wife of harlotry and children of harlotry" (1:2). The reason for this unusual request was to demonstrate that God's Covenant People, the nation of Israel, had been unfaithful to God because of their worship of false gods.

Hosea did as the Lord commanded, taking a prostitute named Gomer as his wife. The first three chapters of the book report their stormy relationship as husband and wife. Soon after their marriage, Gomer bore three children. Hosea gave them symbolic names—Jezreel (God Scatters), Lo-Ruhamah (Not Pitied), and Lo-Ammi (Not My People)—to show that God was about to bring His judgment upon the nation of Israel because the people had fallen into worship of false gods. Just as the nation rejected God, Gomer eventually left Hosea and the children to return to her life of prostitution. But Hosea's love for his wife refused to die.

He searched until he found her at the slave market. Then he brought her back and restored her as his wife. This tender picture showed clearly that God had not given up on Israel, although the people had "played the harlot" many times by returning to their old life of pagan worship and enslavement to sin.

The second major division of Hosea's book, chapters 4—14, contains the prophet's messages of judgment against the nations of Israel and Judah. The northern kingdom of Israel, Hosea's homeland, is singled out for strong rebuke because of its gross sin and immorality. But the book ends on a positive note. In tender language, the prophet reminds the nation of God's undying love. In spite of their unfaithfulness, He is determined to redeem them and restore them to their favored place as His Covenant People.

AUTHORSHIP AND DATE

The undisputed author of this book is the prophet Hosea, who identifies himself in the book as "the son of Beeri" (1:1). His name, a variant form of Joshua and Jesus, means "salvation." The prophet also says that he lived and prophesied during the reign of King Jeroboam II of Israel while four successive kings—Uzziah, Jotham, Ahaz, and Hezekiah—were ruling in Judah. This means his prophetic ministry covered a period of about 40 years, from about 755 B.C. to about 715 B.C. His book was written some time during these years.

HISTORICAL SETTING

Hosea prophesied during the twilight years of the northern kingdom of Israel, a time of rapid moral decline. Worship of false gods was mixed with worship of the one true God. Ritualism rather than righteousness was the order of the day as even the priests lost sight of the real meaning of worship. Although King Jeroboam II was the instigator of many of these policies, at least his 40-year reign (793–753 B.C.) brought a measure of political stability to the nation. This stability came to an end when he died. In rapid succession, six different kings ruled Israel during the next 25 years; four were eliminated by assassination. Weakened by internal strife, Israel collapsed in 722 B.C. when the nation of Assyria destroyed Samaria, Israel's capital city. Hosea was probably an eyewitness to many of these events as his prophecy about God's judgment on Israel was fulfilled.

THEOLOGICAL CONTRIBUTION

Through his marriage and prophetic message, Hosea presents a vivid picture of the steadfast love of God for His people. Because they have sinned and broken the covenant, God's people deserved His

A Concise Outline of

Hosea

I. The Adulterous Wife and Faithful Husband

1. The Introduction of the Book of Hosea   1:1
2. The Prophetic Marriage of Hosea to
   Gomer   1:2—2:1
3. The Application of the Adultery of Gomer   2:2–23
4. The Restoration of Gomer to Hosea   3:1–5

II. The Adulterous Israel and Faithful Lord

1. The Spiritual Adultery of Israel   4:1—6:3
2. The Refusal of Israel to Repent of its
   Adultery   6:4—8:14
3. The Judgment of Israel by God   9:1—10:15
4. The Restoration of Israel to the Lord   11:1—14:9

certain judgment. But because of His undying love for them, His mercy and loving kindness will prevail. Many people believe the Old Testament portrays God's wrath, while the New Testament pictures His love. But the Book of Hosea includes tender expressions of deep love among this prophet's descriptions of judgment. Hosea ranks with Deuteronomy and the Gospel of John as major biblical treatises on the love of God. This love is not mere sentiment; it is rooted in compassion and bound in holiness. God's love makes demands, but it is also willing to forgive.

SPECIAL CONSIDERATIONS

The Book of Hosea is noted for its many references to the history of Israel as well as its vivid poetic images. Throughout the book the prophet speaks tenderly of the nation of Israel as "Ephraim." This is a reference to the largest of the ten northern tribes of Palestine that made up the nation of Israel. Because of their superior numbers, Ephraim was a symbol of power and strength. This tribal name also reminded the nation of its history and tradition. Ephraim, after whom the tribe was named (Gen. 48:17–22), was the son of Joseph.

Few events in the Bible have been debated as strongly as Hosea's marriage. The command for a man of God to marry a harlot is so startling that interpreters have offered many different explanations. Some suggest that the story is meant to be read only as an allegory. Others believe Gomer was faithful at first but went astray after their marriage. Still others believe she was a prostitute from the very beginning, but that Hosea did not learn this until later.

All of these approaches to the passage issue from our offended sense of right and wrong. The plain meaning of the text is that Hosea married a prostitute at God's direct command. In this way, through his own tormented life, Hosea could present a striking picture of the pain in God's heart because of the harlotries of His Covenant People.

The Book of Joel

This brief book predicted the outpouring of the Spirit of God on all people—a prophecy fulfilled several centuries later on the Day of Pentecost (Joel 2:28–32; Acts 2:14–21). The title of the book comes from its author, the prophet Joel, whose name means "Jehovah is God."

The Kidron Valley, looking southward from the Tomb of Zechariah. Some scholars believe this is the "Valley of Jehosophat" mentioned often in the Bible. (Todd Bolen, bibleplaces.com)

STRUCTURE OF THE BOOK

The three brief chapters of this book are divided into two major sections of about equal length. In the first section (1:1—2:11) the prophet Joel introduces himself and speaks to his readers about their need to turn from their sins. The speaker in the second part of the book (2:12—3:21) is the all-powerful God, who warns His people about the approaching day of judgment and assures them of His abiding presence, in spite of their unworthiness.

In the first section of the book, Joel calls attention to a devastating swarm of locusts that had recently swept through the land (1:4). These destructive locusts stripped the foliage from all trees, shrubs, and crops (1:7). The people and livestock of Judah were facing the threat of starvation because of the famine that followed this invasion (1:15–18). As bad as this natural catastrophe had been, the prophet declares it will be as nothing in comparison to the coming day of the Lord. This is the day of judgment, when God will vent His wrath upon His sinful and disobedient people. Joel also informs the people that this terrible day can be avoided. The way of escape is to turn to God "with all your heart, with fasting, and with mourning" (2:12).

After Joel delivers his pleas for repentance, God Himself speaks to His wayward people. In spite of the famine, He declares that there will be plenty to eat in the days of blessing to come (2:18–19). This day of renewal will be marked by the outpouring of His spirit on all people (2:28–29). All the nations of the world will take notice as God gathers His people together in the holy city of Jerusalem to serve as their ruler: "Judah shall abide forever, and Jerusalem from generation to generation" (3:20).

AUTHORSHIP AND DATE

The author of this book was the prophet Joel, who identifies himself in the introduction as "the son of Pethuel" (1:1). This is all we know about this spokesman for the Lord. From evidence in the book itself, we can assume that he knew a great deal about Jerusalem, Judah's capital city, and the rituals associated with Temple worship (2:15). But he probably was not a priest, since he called upon the priests to go into mourning because of the sins of the nation (1:13). Indeed, Joel's many references to agriculture (1:7, 10–12) may indicate he was a farmer or a herdsman, although this is not certain.

It is difficult to determine the exact date of this book's writing. Unlike most of the other Old Testament prophets, Joel mentions no kings of Judah or Israel and no historical events that might give us some indication about when he wrote his prophecy. The one strong clue is the similarity of Joel's concept of the Day of the Lord to the language of the prophet Zephaniah (Joel 2:2; Zeph. 1:14–16). Zephaniah prophesied shortly before the fall of Jerusalem and the nation of Judah in 587 B.C. This also seems the most likely time for the writing of the Book of Joel.

HISTORICAL SETTING

If Joel did write his book about 600 B.C., he would have lived in the frantic final years of the nation of Judah. After the Babylonian army destroyed Jerusalem in 587/586 B.C. the leading citizens of Judah were carried into captivity in Babylon. This invasion of the Babylonians must have given special significance to the terrible "day of the Lord" about which Joel warned his countrymen.

THEOLOGICAL CONTRIBUTION

The Book of Joel is remarkable because it shows that a message from God can often come packaged in the form of a natural disaster. The truth of the book is rooted in the disastrous invasion of locusts, which Joel describes in such vivid language. This prophet teaches us that the Lord may use a natural

A Concise Outline of

Joel

I. The Day of the Lord in the Past

1. The Past Day of the Locust	1:1–12
2. The Past Day of the Drought	1:13–20

II. The Day of the Lord in the Future

1. The Coming Day of the Lord	2:1–27
2. The Ultimate Day of the Lord	2:28—3:21

disaster to stir in His people a renewed awareness of His will. Any traumatic event of nature—flood, fire, storm, or earthquake—should motivate the sensitive ear to listen again to the words of the Lord.

SPECIAL CONSIDERATIONS

Readers of Joel are always impressed with the prediction of the future outpouring of the Holy Spirit (2:28–32). The apostle Peter used this passage to explain the exciting events of Pentecost to his hearers (Acts 2:16–21). Just as Joel predicted, the Holy Spirit was poured out on all these early followers of Jesus who were gathered in Jerusalem seeking God's will and praying for His divine guidance.

But there is still a future dimension to Joel's prediction. The gifts of the Spirit that began to flow through the people of God on Pentecost were not exhausted on that day. They are still available to all who believe in the Lord Jesus Christ and who anxiously await His return and the final establishment of His kingdom.

The Book of Amos

Afiery denunciation of the northern kingdom of Israel during a time of widespread idol worship and indulgent living is prophesied in the Book of Amos. The book is named for its author, the prophet Amos, whose name means "burden bearer." Amos lived up to his name as he declared God's message of judgment in dramatic fashion to a sinful and disobedient people.

Amos himself was a shepherd of Tekoa and might well have looked much like this modern-day Israelite, with his small flock. (Todd Bolen, bibleplaces.com)

STRUCTURE OF THE BOOK

The nine chapters of the Book of Amos emphasize one central theme: The people of the nation of Israel have broken their covenant with God, and His judgment against their sin will be severe. After a brief introduction of Amos as the prophet (1:1–2), the book falls naturally into three major sections:

- judgment against the nations, including Judah and Israel (1:3—2:16);
- sermons of judgment against Israel (3:1—6:14); and
- visions of God's judgment (7:1—9:10). The book concludes with a promise of Israel's restoration (9:11–15).

In the first major section of the book Amos begins with biting words of judgment against the six nations surrounding the lands of Judah and Israel. These nations are Damascus (1:3–5), Gaza (1:6–8), Tyre (1:9–10), Edom (1:11–12), Ammon (1:13–15), and Moab (2:1–3). Next he announces God's judgment against Judah, Israel's sister nation to the south (2:4–5). Because of Israel's bitterness toward Judah, Amos' listeners must have greeted this cry of doom with pleasant agreement.

But Amos was only warming up to the main part of his sermon. Suddenly he launched into a vivid description of God's judgment against the nation of Israel. With biting sarcasm, Amos condemned the citizens of Israel for their oppression of the poor (2:7), worship of idols (2:8), rejection of God's salvation (2:9, 12), and defilement of the Lord's holy name (2:7). Hypocrisy, greed, and injustice prevailed throughout the land. True worship had been replaced by empty ritualism and dependence on pagan gods. And Amos made it plain that Israel would be judged severely unless the people turned from their sin and looked to the one true God for strength and guidance.

In the second major section of his book (3:1—6:14), Amos preached three biting sermons of judgment against the nation of Israel. He referred to the wealthy, luxury seeking women of Samaria—the capital city of Israel—as "cows of Bashan" (4:1). He also attacked the system of idol worship which King Jeroboam had established in the cities of Bethel and Gilgal (4:4; 5:5).

Following these sermons of judgment, Amos moved on in the third major section of his book (7:1—9:10) to present five visions of God's approaching judgment. The prophet's vision of a basket of fruit is particularly graphic. He described the nation of Israel as a basket of summer fruit, implying that it would soon spoil and rot in the blistering sun of God's judgment (8:1–14).

Following these messages of judgment, the Book of Amos ends on a positive, optimistic note. Amos predicted that the people of Israel would be restored to their special place in God's service after their season of judgment had come to an end (9:11–15). This note of hope is characteristic of the Hebrew prophets. They pointed to a glorious future for God's people, even in the midst of dark times. This positive spirit, which issued from Amos' deep faith in God, sustained the prophet and gave him hope for the future.

AUTHORSHIP AND DATE

The author of this book was the prophet Amos, since it is clearly identified in the introduction as "the words of Amos" (1:1). Amos was a humble herdsman, or shepherd, of Tekoa (1:1), a village near Jerusalem in the southern kingdom of Judah. But God called him to deliver His message of judgment to the people who lived in Israel, Judah's sister nation to the north. Amos indicated in his book that he prophesied during the reigns of King Uzziah (Azariah) in Judah and King Jerobaom II in Israel (1:1). This places his prophecy at about 760 B.C. He must have written the book some time after this date, perhaps after returning to his home in Tekoa.

In one revealing passage in his book, Amos indicates that he was "no prophet, nor was I a son of a

A Concise Outline of Amos

prophet, but I was a herdsman and a tender of sycamore fruit" (7:14). In spite of this humble background, he was called by God to preach His message of repentance and judgment to a rebellious nation (7:15–16). His unquestioning obedience and his clear proclamation of God's message show that he was committed to the Lord and His principles of holiness and righteousness. Amos' keen sense of justice and fairness also comes through clearly in the book.

HISTORICAL SETTING

Amos prophesied during the reign of Jeroboam II of Israel (793–753 B.C.), a time of peace and prosperity. The prophet speaks of the excessive luxury of the wealthy (6:3–7), who had no concern for the needs of the poor. Religiously, the nation had departed from the worship of the one true God. Jeroboam encouraged the practice of fertility cults, mixing an element of Baal worship with Israel's faith in their Lord of the Covenant. The situation clearly called for a courageous prophet who could call the nation back to authentic faith as well as a policy of fairness and justice in their dealings with their fellow citizens.

THEOLOGICAL CONTRIBUTION

Amos is known as the great "prophet of righteousness" of the Old Testament. His book underlines the principle that religion demands righteous behavior. True religion is not a matter of observing all the right feast days, offering burnt offerings, and worshiping at the sanctuary. Authentic worship results in changed behavior—seeking God's will, treating others with justice, and following God's commands. This great insight is summarized by these famous words from the prophet: "Let justice run down like water, and righteousness like a mighty stream" (5:24).

SPECIAL CONSIDERATIONS

Although Amos was a shepherd by occupation, his book gives evidence of careful literary craftsmanship. One technique he used was puns or plays on words to drive home his message. Unfortunately, they do not translate easily into English. In his vision of the summer fruit, for example, Amos spoke of the coming of God's judgment with a word that sounds very similar to the Hebrew words for fruit (8:1–2). The summer fruit (*qayits*) suggested the end (*qets*) of the kingdom of Israel (RSV). Like ripe summer fruit, Israel was ripe for God's judgment.

Another literary device which Amos used in his sermons of judgment against the nations is known as numerical parallelism: "For three transgressions . . . and for four . . ." (1:3). He repeated this phrase seven times as he covered the sins of the various nations around Israel (1:3, 6, 9, 11, 13; 2:1, 4). The reader can almost feel the suspense building until the prophet reaches the dramatic climax of his sermon: "For three transgressions of Israel, and for four, I will not turn away its punishment, because they sell the righteous for silver and the poor for a pair of sandals" (2:6).

The Book of Amos is one of the most eloquent cries for justice and righteousness to be found in the Bible. And it came through a humble shepherd who dared to deliver God's message to the wealthy and influential people of his day. His message is just as timely for our world, since God still places a higher value on justice and righteousness than on silver and gold and the things that money will buy.

The Book of Obadiah

This brief prophetic book pronounces God's judgment against the Edomites, ancient enemies of the nation of Israel. The book is the shortest in the Old Testament, containing one chapter of only 21 verses.

These were the mountains in which the Edomites once lived, with the dessert of Arabah stretching out beyond. (Todd Bolen, bibleplaces.com)

STRUCTURE OF THE BOOK

In a brief introduction, the author reveals himself as the prophet Obadiah, a name meaning "servant of the Lord" or "worshiper of Jehovah." He makes it clear he has received this message directly from God. The Lord has announced that He will destroy the Edomites because they have sinned against Israel. They mocked God's Covenant People in their hour of misfortune and even participated in the destruction and looting of the capital city, Jerusalem, when it fell to a foreign power. Because of this great sin, Edom will be destroyed. But Israel, the prophet declares, will be blessed by God and restored to its native land.

AUTHORSHIP AND DATE

The author clearly identifies himself as the prophet Obadiah, but this is all we know about him. Several Obadiahs are mentioned in the Old Testament (1 Kin. 18:3; Ezra 8:9; Neh. 12:25), but none of these can be identified for sure as the author of this book. But at least his prophecy can be dated with greater certainty. Most scholars believe the great humiliation of Israel which the prophet mentions was the siege of Jerusalem by the Babylonians, beginning in 605 B.C. and ending with its final destruction in 587 B.C. Thus, the book must have been written shortly after the fall of the city, perhaps while the Israelites were still in captivity in Babylon.

HISTORICAL SETTING

This book's condemnation of the Edomites is understandable when we consider the bitter feelings that had always existed between these two nations. It began centuries earlier when the twin brothers, Jacob and Esau, went their separate ways (Gen. 27:36). Esau's descendants settled south of the Dead Sea and became known as the Edomites. Jacob's descendants settled farther north, eventually developing into the Covenant People known as the nation of Israel. The Bible reports many clashes between these two factions.

One notable example was the refusal of the Edomites to let the Israelites cross their land as they traveled toward the land of Canaan (Num. 20:14–21). But the final insult to Israel must have been Edom's participation in the looting of Jerusalem after the city fell to the Babylonians. This led the prophet Obadiah to declare, "For your violence against your brother Jacob, shame shall cover you, and you shall be cut off forever" (v. 10).

THEOLOGICAL CONTRIBUTION

The Book of Obadiah makes it clear that God takes His promises to His Covenant People seriously. He declared in the Book of Genesis that He would bless the rest of the world through Abraham and his descendants. He also promised to protect His special people against any who would try to do them harm (Gen. 12:1–3). This promise is affirmed in the Book of Obadiah. God is determined to keep faith with His people, in spite of their unworthiness and disobedience.

SPECIAL CONSIDERATIONS

Verses 1–9 of Obadiah and Jeremiah 49:7–22 express essentially the same idea. Many of the words and phrases in these two passages are exactly alike. Some scholars believe Jeremiah drew from the Obadiah passages to emphasize God's impending judgment on Edom. If this is true, it indicates the little Book of Obadiah was taken seriously by Jeremiah, one of the great prophetic figures in Israel's history.

A Concise Outline of

Obadiah

The Book of Jonah

God's love for all people—pagans and Gentiles as well as His Chosen People, the Israelites—is emphasized in Jonah. The book is named for its central figure, the prophet Jonah, who learned about God's universal love as he struggled with God's call to service.

This ancient carving, of a fish swallowing a man, now rests in the Iconium Museum. Iconium (now Konya) is one of Turkey's oldest continuously inhabited cities. (Todd Bolen, bibleplaces.com)

STRUCTURE OF THE BOOK

The book begins with God's call to Jonah to preach in the great city of Nineveh, capital of the Assyrian empire. As staunch political enemies of the Israelites and as worshipers of false gods, the Assyrians also were shunned as pagans and outcasts. But God's call to Jonah showed clearly He had not given up on Assyria. The prophet was to call Nineveh to repentance, warning the nation of its approaching doom unless it turned to God.

Instead of obeying God's command and heading to Nineveh, Jonah caught a ship traveling in the opposite direction. At sea a great storm arose, and Jonah was tossed overboard by the superstitious sailors in an attempt to appease the prophet's God. Jonah escaped unharmed when he was swallowed by a great fish and was miraculously deposited on shore. This time he obeyed God's command and traveled to Nineveh to carry out his preaching assignment.

But the reluctant prophet was not prepared for the results of his message. The entire city repented, and Jonah sulked in anger because Nineveh escaped God's punishment.

To teach the prophet a lesson, God raised up a plant, perhaps a gourd vine, to shade Jonah from the sun, then allowed a worm to cut it down. A hot wind from the east added to Jonah's misery, and he whined and complained about the missing plant. Then God reminded Jonah that he was a God of compassion who had the right to love and forgive the pagan Assyrians or any other people who turned to Him in obedience and faith. Jonah had been fretting about a plant, while God had turned His attention to a much more important matter—the worth and salvation of people.

AUTHORSHIP AND DATE

The traditional view is that the prophet Jonah wrote this book. This would place its writing at about 760 B.C., since this prophet—"the son of Amittai" (1:1)—is the same Jonah who prophesied during the reign of Jeroboam II of Israel, from 793 to 753 B.C. (2 Kin. 14:25). The only other thing we know about Jonah is that he was a native of the village of Gath Hepher in Israel.

Some scholars insist the book was not written until about three centuries later by an unknown author. According to this theory, the writer composed the story of Jonah and his prophecy to combat the narrow-minded views of the Jewish people after their return to Jerusalem following their years of captivity in Babylon. It is true that the Israelites went to extremes during these years as they tried to cast off all foreign influences and preserve the unique heritage of their faith. And Jonah certainly is a book that emphasizes the universal love of God. But the evidence put forth to support this theory is weak and inconclusive. There is no real reason to reject the traditional view that the prophet Jonah himself wrote the book after his visit to Nineveh about 760 B.C.

HISTORICAL SETTING

The prophet Jonah visited Nineveh during the glorious days of the Assyrian empire. From about 885 to 625 B.C., the Assyrians dominated the ancient world. Numerous passages in the Old Testament report advances of Assyrian military forces against the neighboring kingdoms of Judah and Israel during these years. As early as 841 B.C., Jehu, king of Israel, was forced to pay tribute to the dominating Assyrian ruler, Shalmaneser III. This kind of harassment continued for over a century until Israel finally fell to Assyrian forces about 722 B.C. No wonder Jonah was reluctant to go to Nineveh; God had called him to visit the very heartland of enemy territory and to give the hated Assyrians a chance to repent! It was a radical order that would have taxed the obedience of any prophet. Jonah's grudging attitude should not blind us to the fact that he did carry out God's command.

A Concise Outline of
Jonah

I. The First Commission of Jonah

1. The Disobedience to the First Call	1:1–3
2. The Judgment on Jonah	1:4–17
3. The Prayer of Jonah	2:1–9
4. The Deliverance of Jonah	2:10

II. The Second Commission of Jonah

1. The Obedience to the Second Call	3:1–4
2. The Repentance of Nineveh	3:5–10
3. The Prayer of Jonah	4:1–3
4. The Rebuke of Jonah by God	4:4–11

THEOLOGICAL CONTRIBUTION

One of the great truths emphasized by this book is that God can use people who do not want to be used by Him. Jonah was practically driven to Nineveh against his will, but his grudging message still struck a responsive chord in the Assyrians. This shows that revival and repentance are works of God's Spirit. Our task is to proclaim His message.

But the greatest insight of the book is that God desires to show mercy and grace to all the peoples of the world. No one nation or group can claim exclusive rights to His love. The task of the nation of Israel was to preach this message about God's universal love to all the world (Gen. 12:1–3). But they forgot this missionary purpose and eventually claimed God and His blessings as theirs alone. The Book of Jonah cries out against this narrow-minded interpretation of God and his purpose. In the last verse of the book, God makes it plain to Jonah that His mercy and compassion are as wide as the world itself: "And should I not pity Nineveh, that great city, in which are more than one hundred and twenty thousand persons who cannot discern between their right hand and their left, and also much livestock?" (4:11).

SPECIAL CONSIDERATIONS

Too much attention has been focused on the "great fish" (1:17) that swallowed Jonah and then spat him out on the shore. We solve nothing by debating whether a fish could swallow a man or whether a person could remain alive for three days in the stomach of such a creature. The point of this part of the story is that God worked a miracle to preserve the life of His prophet so he could get to Nineveh to carry out God's orders. The text states that God "prepared" this fish specifically for that purpose (1:17). Other miracles God "prepared" to teach Jonah His purpose for the city of Nineveh were the plant (4:6), the worm that cut the plant down (4:7), and the hot east wind that added to Jonah's misery (4:8).

Some Bible readers insist on interpreting this book as an allegory or a parable. But these approaches ignore Jesus's own literal interpretations of Jonah. In speaking of His death and resurrection, Jesus declared, "For as Jonah was three days and three nights in the belly of the great fish, so will the Son of Man be three days and three nights in the heart of the earth" (Matt. 12:40; also Luke 11:29–32). Thus, the Book of Jonah is much more than a fish story. It is a beautiful account of God's grace that lifts our sights to the greatest love story of all—the death of His Son Jesus Christ for the sins of the world.

The Book of Micah

The rich are condemned in this brief prophetic book because of their exploitation of the poor. Micah also contains a clear prediction of the Messiah's birth in Bethlehem, centuries before Jesus was actually born in this humble little village. The book takes its title from its author, the prophet Micah, whose name means, "Who is like Jehovah?"

Moresheth/Gath, the area in which the prophet Micah was born, is about 25 miles southwest of Jerusalem. (Todd Bolen, bibleplaces.com)

STRUCTURE OF THE BOOK

Micah is a short book of only seven chapters, but it stands as a classic example of the work to which the Old Testament prophets were called. Over and over again, Micah sounds the theme of God's judgment against his homeland, Judah, as well as his sister nation, Israel, because of their moral decline. Micah watched as the Assyrians grew in strength and marched their armies throughout the ancient world. It was clear to him that this pagan nation would serve as the instrument of God's judgment unless Judah and Israel turned back to God.

Micah is also known as the champion of the oppressed. He condemns wealthy landowners for taking the land of the poor (2:2). He also attacks dishonest merchants for using false weights, bribing judges, and charging excessive interest rates. Even the priests and prophets seemed to be caught up in this tidal wave of greed and dishonesty that swept his country. To a people more concerned about observing rituals than living a life of righteousness, Micah thundered, "He has shown you, O man, what is good; and what does the Lord require of you but to do justly, to love mercy, and to walk humbly with your God?" (6:8). This is one of the greatest passages in the Old Testament. It expresses the timeless truth that authentic worship consists of following God's will and dealing justly with other people.

In addition to the theme of judgment, Micah also emphasizes the reality of God's love. Practically every passage about God's wrath is balanced with a promise of God's blessing. The greatest promise in the book is a prophecy of the birth of the Messiah: "But you, Bethlehem Ephrathah, through you are little among the thousands of Judah, yet out of you shall come forth to Me the One to be ruler in Israel" (5:2). This messianic verse is stunning in its accuracy because it names the specific town where the Messiah was born—the village of Bethlehem in the territory of the tribe of Judah. This prophecy was fulfilled about 700 years after Micah's time with the birth of Jesus in Bethlehem.

The final two chapters of Micah's book are presented in the form of a debate between God and His people. God invites the nations of Israel and Judah to reason with Him on the subject of their conduct. He convinces them that their sin is deep and grievous, but He assures them of His presence in spite of their unworthiness.

AUTHORSHIP AND DATE

This book was written by the prophet Micah, a native of the village of Moresheth (1:1) in southern Judah near the Philistine city of Gath. Since Micah championed the rights of the poor, he was probably a humble farmer or herdsman himself. Although he shows a remarkable knowledge of Jerusalem and Samaria, the capital cities of the nations of Judah and Israel. Micah also tells us that he prophesied "in the days of Jotham, Ahaz, and Hezekiah, kings of Judah" (1:1). The reigns of these three kings stretched from about 750 B.C. to 687 B.C.; so his book was probably written some time during this period.

HISTORICAL SETTING

The Book of Micah belongs to that turbulent period during which the Assyrians launched their drive for supremacy throughout the ancient world. Micah probably saw his prophecy of judgment against Israel fulfilled, since the Assyrians defeated this nation in 722 B.C. The fall of Israel to the north must have stunned the citizens of Judah. Would they be the next to fall before the conquering armies of this pagan nation? Still, the religious leaders retreated into a false confidence that no evil would befall them because the Temple was situated in their capital city of Jerusalem (3:11). Micah warned there was no magical saving power in their Temple or their rituals (3:12). They needed to turn back to God as their source of strength and power.

A Concise Outline of
Micah

I. The Prediction of Judgment

1. Introduction to the Book of Micah	1:1
2. The Judgment on the People	1:2—2:13
3. The Judgment on the Leadership	3:1–12

II. The Prediction of Restoration

1. The Promise of the Coming Kingdom	4:1–5
2. The Promise of the Coming Captivities	4:6—5:1
3. The Promise of the Coming King	5:2–15

III. The Plea for Repentance

1. The First Plea of God	6:1–8
2. The Second Plea of God	6:9—7:6
3. The Promise of Final Salvation	7:7–20

THEOLOGICAL CONTRIBUTION

The mixture of judgment and promise in the Book of Micah is striking characteristic of the Old Testament prophets. These contrasting passages give real insight into the character of God. In His wrath He remembers mercy; He cannot maintain His anger forever. Judgment with love is the ironic, but essential, work of the Lord. In the darkest days of impending judgment on Israel and Judah, there always was the possibility that a remnant would be spared. God was determined to maintain His holiness, and so He acted in judgment on those who had broken His covenant. But he was just as determined to fulfill the promises He had made to Abraham centuries earlier. This compelled Him to point to the fulfillment of the covenant in the kingdom to come.

Perhaps the greatest contribution of the Book of Micah is its clear prediction of a coming Savior. The future Messiah is referred to indirectly in some of the prophetic books of the Old Testament. But He is mentioned directly in the Book of Micah.

This prophecy of the Messiah's birth is remarkable when we think of the circumstances that were necessary to bring it to fulfillment. Although they were residents of Nazareth, Mary and Joseph happened to be in Bethlehem at the right time when the Messiah was born about 700 years after Micah's prediction. This is a valuable lesson on the providence of God. He always manages to work His will through a unique combination of forces and events.

SPECIAL CONSIDERATIONS

Micah begins his words of judgment with calls for the people to come to court. God is portrayed as the prosecuting attorney, the witness for the prosecution, and the sentencing judge. God is a witness against His people (1:2); He demands justice (3:1); He even calls upon the elements of creation to be His witnesses, since He had a legal dispute against His people (6:1–2). This type of language is also found in the Book of Isaiah (Is. 1:2). It is likely that Isaiah and Micah drew this terminology from the Book of Deuteronomy (Deut. 31:28). The clear implication is that God has the right to hold His people accountable for their behavior.

God insists that His people keep their part of the covenant agreement. But even while making His demands, He holds out the possibility of grace and forgiveness. This leads His Covenant People to declare: "You will cast all our sins into the depths of the sea. You will give truth to Jacob and mercy to Abraham, which You have sworn to our fathers from days of old" (7:19–20).

The Book of Nahum

This short prophetic book foretells the destruction of the nation of Assyria and its capital city, Nineveh.

A remarkably clear relief carving from Nineveh, showing Sennacherib, the Assyrian king from Nineveh, in a posture of prayer. Nahum prophesied against Nineveh, warning of destruction to come. (Todd Bolen, bibleplaces.com)

STRUCTURE OF THE BOOK

The book opens with a brief identification of the prophet Nahum. Then it launches into a psalm of praise that celebrates the power and goodness of God. This comforting picture is contrasted with the evil deeds of the Assyrians. With graphic language, Nahum presents a prophetic picture of the coming judgment of God. He informs the nation of Assyria that its days as a world power are drawing to a close. In an oracle of woe, the prophet describes Nineveh as a "bloody city, full of lies and robbery" (3:1). But soon the city of Nineveh will be laid waste, and Assyria will crumble before the judgment of God.

AUTHORSHIP AND DATE

This book was written by a prophet known as "Nahum the Elkoshite" (1:1). This brief identification tells us all we know about this spokesman for the Lord. Even the location of his home, Elkosh, is uncertain, although some scholars believe he may have lived in northern Judah. The book can be dated with reasonable accuracy. Nineveh fell, as Nahum predicted, about 612 B.C. Therefore, the book was probably written shortly before this time.

HISTORICAL SETTING

For more than 100 years before Nahum's day, Assyria had been one of the dominant powers of the ancient world. The northern kingdom of Israel fell to Assyrian forces in 722 B.C. Some prophets taught that this pagan nation was used as an instrument of God's judgment against His wayward people. But now it was Assyria's turn to feel the force of God's wrath. The armies of Nabopolassar of Babylon stormed Nineveh in 612 B.C. The entire Assyrian Empire crumbled three years later under the relentless assault of this aggressive Babylonian ruler. Thus, as Nahum prophesied, Assyria's day of dominance ended with their humiliation by a foreign power.

THEOLOGICAL CONTRIBUTION

This book teaches the sure judgment of God against those who oppose His will and abuse His people. Acts of inhumanity are acts against God, and He will serve as the ultimate and final judge. God sometimes uses a pagan nation as an instrument of His judgment, just as He used the Assyrians against the nation of Israel. But this does not excuse the pagan nation from God's laws and requirements. It will be judged by the same standards of righteousness and holiness which God applies to all the other people of the world.

SPECIAL CONSIDERATIONS

By a strange irony, the city in Galilee most closely associated with the ministry of Jesus was Capernaum. The name Capernaum in the Hebrew language means "the village of Nahum."

Some people wonder about the gloomy, pessimistic tone of the Book of Nahum. How can this picture of God's wrath and judgment be reconciled with the God of grace and love whom we meet in the New Testament? As the sovereign, all-powerful God, He has the right to work His purpose in the world. Judgment against sin is a part of the work which He must do in order to remain a just and holy God.

Nahum's announcement of God's approaching judgment also carries a call for holy living and faith proclamation by God's Covenant People. Our work is to carry the message of His salvation to those who are surely doomed unless they turn to God in repentance and faith.

A Concise Outline of
Nahum

The Book of Habakkuk

The age-old problems of evil and human suffering are dealt with in this prophecy. The book is named for the prophet Habakkuk, who received this message from God in the form of a vision.

Lions from the Ishtar gate of Babylon. The prophet Habakkuk warned against the apostasies of Babylon's Baal and Ashtoreth (Ishtar) worship. (Rachel Smith, bibleplaces.com)

STRUCTURE OF THE BOOK

Habakkuk's book contains only three short chapters, but they represent a striking contrast. In the first two, Habakkuk protests, complains, and questions God. But the final chapter is a beautiful psalm of praise. Habakkuk apparently used this complaining and questioning technique to drive home his powerful message about the approaching judgment of God.

Habakkuk begins his book with a cry of woe. Injustice is rampant, the righteous are surrounded by the wicked, the law is powerless, and God doesn't seem to care about the plight of His people (1:1–4). Habakkuk's prophecy is even introduced as a "burden" which the prophet saw (1:1). He wonders why God is allowing these things to happen.

God's reply brings little comfort to the prophet. He explains that the armies of Babylon are moving throughout the ancient world on a campaign of death and destruction. At the time when Habakkuk received this vision, the Babylonians had already defeated Assyria and Egypt. The implication is that Habakkuk's nation, Judah, will be the next to fall.

The prophet was shocked at the news. He reminded God of His justice and holiness (1:12–13). How could He use the wicked Babylonians to destroy His Chosen People? Surely He realized the sins of His people were as nothing, when compared to the pagan Babylonians (1:13). "Why do you . . . hold your tongue when the wicked devours one more righteous than he?" he asks (1:13). This direct question indicates Habakkuk's great faith. Only a person very close to God would dare question the purposes of the Almighty so boldly. God assures Habakkuk that the Babylonians will prevail not because they are righteous but because they are temporary instruments of judgment in His hands (2:6, 9, 12, 15, 19). God will not be mocked; the end of the Babylonians is as certain as the judgment they will bring on Judah. In all of this, God will vindicate His righteous character: "For the earth will be filled with the knowledge of the glory of the Lord, as the waters cover the sea" (2:14).

After this assurance, Habakkuk breaks out with the beautiful psalm of praise to God contained in chapter 3. This is one of the greatest testimonies of faith in the Bible.

AUTHORSHIP AND DATE

Nothing is known about the prophet Habakkuk except his name. But he was surely a sensitive poet as well as a courageous spokesman for God. His little book is a literary masterpiece that points people of all ages to faith in God and His eternal purpose. Since the book speaks of the coming destruction of Judah, it had to be written some time before Jerusalem was destroyed by the Babylonians in 587 B.C. The most likely time for its composition is probably about 600 B.C.

HISTORICAL SETTING

The Book of Habakkuk belongs to that turbulent era in ancient history when the balance of power was shifting from the Assyrians to the Babylonians. Assyria's domination came to an end with the destruction of its capital city, Nineveh, by the invading Babylonians in 612 B.C. Less than 20 years after Habakkuk wrote his book, the Babylonians also destroyed Jerusalem and carried the leading citizens of Judah into captivity. God used this pagan nation to punish His Covenant People for their unfaithfulness and worship of false gods.

THEOLOGICAL CONTRIBUTION

The question-and-answer technique of the prophet Habakkuk teaches a valuable lesson about the nature of God. That God allows Himself to be questioned by one of His followers is an indication of His long-suffering mercy and grace.

A Concise Outline of
Habakkuk

The theme of God's judgment against unrighteousness also is woven throughout the book. God will soon punish His wayward people for their transgression, but He also will punish the pagan Babylonians because of their great sin. God always acts in justice. He will not forget mercy while pouring out His wrath (3:2). His judgment will fall on the proud, but the just will live in His faithfulness (2:4). God's acts of judgment are in accord with His holiness, righteousness, and mercy.

SPECIAL CONSIDERATIONS

The Protestant Reformation under Martin Luther was influenced by the Book of Habakkuk. Luther's discovery of the biblical doctrine that the just shall live by faith came from his study of the apostle Paul's beliefs in the Books of Romans and Galatians. But Paul's famous declaration, "The just shall live by faith" (Rom. 1:17), is a direct quotation from Habakkuk 2:4. Thus, in this brief prophetic book, we find the seeds of the glorious gospel of our Lord and Savior Jesus Christ.

The Book of Zephaniah

This book emphasizes the certainty of God's judgment and the preservation of a remnant, a small group of people who will continue to serve as God's faithful servants in the world. The book takes its title from its author, the prophet Zephaniah, whose name means "the Lord has hidden."

Most scholars believe that Zephaniah prophesied from Jerusalem. This close-up view shows a portion of its western wall as it might have looked in Zephaniah's time. (Todd Bolen, bibleplaces.com)

STRUCTURE OF THE BOOK

Zephaniah contains only three short chapters, but these chapters are filled with some of the most vivid pictures of God's judgment to be found in the Bible. After a brief introduction of himself as God's spokesman, the prophet launches immediately into a description of God's approaching wrath. He portrays this great "day of the Lord" as a time of "trouble and distress," "darkness and gloominess," "trumpet and alarm" (1:14–15).

Zephaniah's prophecy makes it clear that the nation of Judah, as well as surrounding countries, will feel the sting of God's wrath. Judah's capital city, Jerusalem, is soundly condemned for its wickedness, rebellion, and injustice. The prophet even portrays God with search-lamps as He exposes the corruption of the city and marks it for His certain judgment (1:12).

In spite of its underlying theme of judgment and punishment, the Book of Zephaniah closes on a positive note. After God judges the wayward nations, the prophet announces He will raise up a remnant of the faithful who will continue to serve as His Covenant People in the world. The book ends with a glorious promise for the future, a time when God will "quiet you in His love" and "rejoice over you with singing" (3:17).

AUTHORSHIP AND DATE

Scholars are in general agreement that Zephaniah the prophet wrote this book that bears his name. In his introduction (1:1), the author traces his ancestry back four generations to Hezekiah, a former king of Judah noted for his faithfulness to God. Zephaniah must have been proud that he was the great-great-grandson of this beloved ruler, who had led his people back to worship of the one true God.

The book also tells how Zephaniah the prophet ministered during the days of Josiah, a godly king who reigned over the nation of Judah from about 641 to about 609 B.C. Most scholars place the writing of the book at about 627 B.C.

HISTORICAL SETTING

This book belongs to a dark period in Judah's history. About 100 years before Zephaniah's time, Judah's sister nation, the northern kingdom of Israel, had fallen to a foreign power because of its sin and idolatry. Zephaniah sensed that the same thing was about to happen to the southern kingdom of Judah—and for precisely the same reason.

Under the leadership of two successive evil kings, Manasseh and Amon, the people of Judah had fallen into worship of false gods. Zephaniah delivered his prophecy and wrote this book to warn the people of God's approaching wrath and judgment. As Zephaniah predicted, God punished His people and the surrounding pagan nations through a superior foreign power. Not even a brief religious renewal under the good king Josiah was enough to turn the tide of paganism and false worship that carried Judah toward certain destruction. Judgment came to the nation in 587 B.C., when the invading Babylonians destroyed the city of Jerusalem and carried its leading citizens into captivity in Babylon.

THEOLOGICAL CONTRIBUTION

The judgment of the Lord portrayed by the prophet Zephaniah springs from His nature as a God of holiness. Because God demands holiness and righteousness in His people, He will judge those who continue to sin and rebel (1:17). But the Lord also is merciful and faithful to His promise. To the committed remnant He offers encouragement and protection from the approaching dark day (2:1–3). And to the righteous He promises the final realization of the covenant which He sealed with Abraham hundreds of years earlier. People of all nations will gather to worship the Lord (2:11; 3:9). His own people

A Concise Outline of
Zephaniah

I. The Judgment in the Day of the Lord

1. The Judgment on the Whole Earth   1:1–3
2. The Judgment on the Nation of Judah   1:4—2:3
3. The Judgment on the Nations Surrounding
   Judah   2:4–15
4. The Judgment on Jerusalem   3:1–7
5. The Judgment on the Whole Earth   3:8

II. The Salvation in the Day of the Lord

1. The Promise of Conversion   3:9–13
2. The Promise of Restoration   3:14–20

will be renewed in righteousness (3:11–13). And the King of kings Himself will rule in their midst (3:15).

SPECIAL CONSIDERATIONS

The prophet Zephaniah shows keen familiarity with the city of Jerusalem (1:10–11). Since he was a member of the royal line, he was probably a resident of Jerusalem. It must have troubled him deeply to pronounce God's prophecies of judgment against his beloved city.

One of the most beautiful passages in the book is the description of the joy of the Lord (3:8–20). His song of joy will join the happy singing of His people. The dark day of doom will not last. A happy day is coming for those who, like Zephaniah, are "hidden in the day of the Lord's anger" (2:3).

The Book of Haggai

T his short prophetic book was written to encourage the people of Israel who had returned to their native land after the captivity in Babylon.

This ancient tomb, on the Mount of Olives, is associated by tradition with Haggai and Malachi, although it simply is not possible to determine that it ever held the bones of either prophet. (Todd Bolen, bibleplaces.com)

STRUCTURE OF THE BOOK

The two short chapters of Haggai contain four important messages from the prophet to the people. He called on the people to rebuild the Temple, to remain faithful to God's promises, to be holy and enjoy God's great provisions, and to keep their hope set on the coming of the Messiah and the establishment of His kingdom.

AUTHORSHIP AND DATE

This book was written by the prophet Haggai, whose name means "festive." Like those whom he encouraged, he probably spent many years in captivity in Babylon before returning to his native land. A contemporary of the prophet Zechariah, he must have worked constantly as a prophetic voice among his countrymen in Jerusalem. He delivered these messages of encouragement "in the second year of King Darius" (1:1), a Persian ruler. This dates his book precisely in 520 B.C.

HISTORICAL SETTING

Haggai takes us back to one of the most turbulent periods in Judah's history—their captivity at the hands of a foreign power, followed by their release and resettlement in Jerusalem. For more than 50 years they were held captive by the Babylonians. But they were allowed to return to their native land, beginning about 530 B.C., after Babylon fell to the conquering Persians. At first, the captives who returned worked diligently at rebuilding the Temple, but they soon grew tired of the task and gave it up altogether. Haggai delivered his message to motivate the people to resume the project.

THEOLOGICAL CONTRIBUTION

Haggai urged the people to put rebuilding the Temple at the top of their list of priorities. This shows authentic worship is a very important matter. The rebuilt Temple in Jerusalem was important as a place of worship and sacrifice. Centuries later, at the death of Jesus "the veil of the Temple was torn in two" (Luke 23:45), demonstrating that He had given Himself as the eternal sacrifice on our behalf.

SPECIAL CONSIDERATIONS

The Book of Haggai ends with a beautiful promise of the coming of the Messiah. Meanwhile, God's special servant, Zerubbabel, was to serve as a "signet ring" (2:23), a sign or promise of the glorious days to come. As the Jewish governor of Jerusalem under appointment by the Persians, Zerubbabel showed there was hope for the full restoration of God's Covenant People in their native land.

The Book of Zechariah

A beautiful portrayal of the coming glory of the Messiah is given by Zechariah. Many scholars describe Zechariah as the most Messianic of all the Old Testament books because it contains eight specific references to the Messiah in is brief 14 chapters.

This tomb, in the Kidron Valley, is known as the Tomb of Zechariah, although scholars cannot be absolutely certain that he is the prophet whose book bears his name. (Todd Bolen, bibleplaces.com)

STRUCTURE OF THE BOOK

The 14 chapters of Zechariah fall naturally into two major sections: chapters 1—8, the prophet's encouragement to the people to finish the work of rebuilding the Temple, and chapters 9—14, Zechariah's picture of Israel's glorious future and the coming of the Messiah.

In the first section, Zechariah introduces himself as God's prophet and calls the people to repent and turn from their evil ways. Part of their sin was their failure to finish the work of rebuilding the Temple after returning from the captivity in Babylon. In a series of eight symbolic night visions that came to the prophet (1:7—6:8), Zechariah encourages the people to finish this important task. These visions are followed by a coronation scene (6:9-15), in which a high priest named Joshua is crowned as priest and king, symbolizing the Messiah who is to come. This is considered one of the classic Messianic prophecies of the Old Testament.

Chapters 7 and 8 also continue another important element of the Messianic hope: the One to come will reign in justice from Zion, the city of Jerusalem (8:3, 15-16).

The second major section of Zechariah's book, chapters 9—14, contains God's promises for the new age to come. Chapter 9 has a remarkable description of the manner in which the ruling Messiah will enter the city of Jerusalem: "Behold, your King is coming to you; He is just and having salvation, lowly and riding on a donkey, a colt, the foal of a donkey" (9:9). These were the words used by Matthew to describe Jesus's triumphant entry into Jerusalem about 400 years after Zechariah made this startling prediction (Matt. 21:5; Mark 11:7-10).

Other promises for the future in this section of the book include the restoration of the nation of Israel (chap. 10) and Jerusalem's deliverance from her enemies (chap. 12), as well as her purification as the holy city (chap. 3). Like the Book of Revelation, Zechariah closes on the theme of the universal reign of God. All nations will come to worship Him as He extends His rule throughout the world (chap. 14).

AUTHORSHIP AND DATE

Most conservative scholars agree that the entire book of Zechariah was written by the prophet of that name, who identifies himself in the book's introduction as "the son of Berechiah" (1:1). But some scholars insist the second major section of the book, chapters 9—14, was written by an unknown author. These scholars believe this section was added to the book about 30 or 40 years after Zechariah the prophet wrote chapters 1—8.

It is true that these two sections of the book have their own unique characteristics. In the first section Zechariah encourages the people to finish the Temple, while in the second section he is more concerned about the glorious age of the future. The language and style of these two sections of Zechariah are also quite different. And the prophecies in these two sections seem to be set in different times.

Chapters 1—8, Zechariah tells us, were delivered as prophecies "in the eighth month of the second year of Darius" (1:1), and "in the fourth year of King Darius" (7:1). These references to Darius I of Persia (ruled 521–486 B.C.) date these prophecies clearly from 520 to 518 B.C. But chapters 9—14 contain a reference to Greece (9:13), probably indicating it was written after 480 B.C., when the balance of world power was shifting from the Persians to the Greeks. How can these major differences between these two sections of the book be explained unless we accept the theory that they were written by two different people?

One possible explanation is that Zechariah was a young man when he delivered his prophecies in the first section of the book. The book itself contains a clue that this may have been the case. In one of his visions, two angels speak to one another about the prophet, referring to him as "this young man"

A Concise Outline of
Zechariah

(2:4). Thus, it is quite possible that Zechariah could have encouraged the Jewish captives in Jerusalem in the early part of his ministry and could have delivered the messages about the future, contained in the second section of the book, during his final years as a prophet.

After all the evidence is examined, there is no convincing reason to dispute the traditional view that Zechariah the prophet wrote the entire book that bears his name. These prophecies were first delivered and then reduced to writing over a period of about 45 years—from 520 to 475 B.C.

As for the prophet himself, very little is known about him beyond the few facts he reveals in his book. He was a descendant, perhaps the grandson, of Iddo the priest (1:1)—one of the family leaders who returned from captivity in Babylon (Neh. 12:16). This means that Zechariah probably was a priest as well as a prophet—an unusual circumstance because most of the prophets of Israel spoke out against the priestly class. Since he was a young man when he began to prophesy in 520 B.C., Zechariah was probably born in Babylon while the Jewish people were in captivity. He probably returned with his family with the first wave of captives who reached Jerusalem under Zerubbabel about 530 B.C.

HISTORICAL SETTING

The setting at the beginning of the book is the same the setting of the Book of Haggai. The prophet Haggai spoke directly to the issue of the rebuilding of the Temple, encouraging those who returned from captivity in Babylon to finish the task. Zechariah spoke to that issue as well, according to the Book of Ezra (Ezra 5:1). But Zechariah wished to bring about a complete spiritual renewal through faith and hope in God. He spoke about the nature of God's Law and of the hope which God promised to those who were faithful to Him.

The second portion of Zechariah was written in the period between the times of the prophets Haggai (520 B.C.) and Malachi (450 B.C.). The Persian Empire was ruled by two great kings during these years, Darius I (522–486 B.C.) and Xerxes I (585–465 B.C.). This was a period when the Jewish people in Jerusalem were settled in their new land with a walled city and their beloved Temple. But they were unhappy and dissatisfied. Some of the people had expected that Zerubbabel, governor of Jerusalem, might be the Messiah, but this had proven to be false. The people needed a new word concerning God's future for them. This message from God was given in a most dramatic fashion by the great prophet Zechariah.

THEOLOGICAL CONTRIBUTION

One of the greatest contributions of the Book of Zechariah is the merger of the best from the priestly and prophetic elements in Israel's history. Zechariah realized the need for both these elements in an authentic faith. He called the people to turn from their sins. He also realized that the Temple and religious ritual played an important role in keeping the people close to God. Because he brought these elements together in his own ministry, Zechariah helped prepare the way for the Christian community's understanding of Christ as both priest and prophet.

Zechariah is also noted for his development of an apocalyptic, prophetic style—highly symbolized and visionary language concerning the events of the end-time. In this, his writing resembles the Books of Daniel and Revelation. The visions of lampstands and olive trees, horsemen and chariots, measuring lines, and horns place him and these other two books in a class by themselves. Zechariah also has a great deal to say about the concept of God as warrior. While this was a well-established image among biblical writers, Zechariah ties this idea to the concept of the Day of the Lord (see Joel 2). His description of the return of Christ to earth as the great Warrior in the Day of the Lord (14:1–9) is one of the most stirring prophecies of the Old Testament.

On that day, according to Zechariah, Christ will place His feet on the Mount of Olives, causing violent changes throughout the land (14:3–4). The day will be changed to darkness and the darkness to light (14:5–8). The entire world will worship Him as the Lord spreads His rule as King "over all the earth" (14:9).

SPECIAL CONSIDERATIONS

Zechariah 12:10 is a remarkable verse that speaks of the response of the nation of Israel to Jesus Christ as Savior and Lord. It describes a day in the future when the Jewish people (the house of David and the inhabitants of Jerusalem) will recognize the significance of the death of Jesus. This recognition will lead to mourning, repentance, and salvation (compare Rom. 11:25–27).

But the most startling thing about this verse is the phrase "Then they will look on Me whom they have pierced." In speaking through the prophet Zechariah, the Lord identifies Himself as the one who will be pierced. Along with Psalm 22 and Isaiah 53, these words are a wonder of inspiration as they describe the result of Jesus's death as well as the manner in which He died to deliver us from our sins.

The Book of Malachi

This short prophetic book was written to rebuke the people of Israel for their shallow worship practices. The name comes from the Hebrew word *malachi* (1:1), meaning "my messenger" or "messenger of Jehovah." Three "messengers" of the Lord are mentioned in the book: the priest (2:7), the forerunner (3:1), and the "Messenger of the covenant," the Lord Himself.

This unfinished tomb, just south of the Tomb of Zechariah, would have been a fitting location for the prophet Malachi. (Todd Bolen, bibleplaces.com)

STRUCTURE OF THE BOOK

Portions of Malachi are written in the format of a debate, unlike any other book of the Bible. God first makes a statement of truth that is then denied by the people. God then refutes their argument in great detail, restating and proving the truth of His original statement (1:2–7; 2:10–17; 3:7–10). Malachi also uses questions and answers freely to focus his accusations toward the priesthood as well as the people. These features make Malachi one of the most argumentative books of the Bible.

AUTHORSHIP AND DATE

Some scholars believe the word *malachi* should be interpreted as a description ("my messenger") rather than as the name of a specific person. This line of reasoning concludes that the book was written by an unknown author. But no other book of prophecy in the Old Testament was written anonymously. Although nothing else is known about this person, the weight of tradition has assumed the book was written by a prophet name Malachi. He was God's final messenger to the Covenant People in the Old Testament. This message was given about 1,000 years after the time of Moses, the first prophet and Bible writer. Malachi would have been a contemporary with Ezra who was both a priest and historian. The prophecy can be specifically dated at about 450 B.C.

HISTORICAL SETTING

Malachi was addressed to the nation of Israel about 100 years after its return from captivity in Babylon. At first the people had been enthusiastic about rebuilding Jerusalem and the Temple and restoring their system of worship. But their zeal soon began to wane. The people discontinued their tithes and offerings and, as a result, the crops began to fail. They began to offer defective animals as sacrifices. The priests became careless and indifferent in their temple service. Morals were lax, and intermarriage with the heathen around them had become prevalent.

The Israelites wondered about God's love for them as His Chosen People. Malachi was written to call the people back to authentic worship of their Redeemer God.

THEOLOGICAL CONTRIBUTION

The prophecy of Malachi is noted for its vivid portrayal of the love of God as well as His might and power. Israel needed to be reminded of these truths at a time when widespread doubt had dashed its expectations of the Messiah.

SPECIAL CONSIDERATIONS

Malachi leaves us with the feeling that the story is not yet finished, that God still has promises to fulfill on behalf of His people. After Malachi came 400 long years of silence. But when the time was right, heaven would burst forth in song at the arrival of the Messiah.

PART II

THE NEW TESTAMENT

A street in the city of Bethlehem, as it exists today. Christ's parents, Mary and Joseph, might have traveled a street just as steep as this one. (Todd Bolen, bibleplaces.com)

CHAPTER 6

THE GOSPELS

The early church placed the Gospels of Matthew, Mark, Luke, and John at the beginning of the New Testament canon, not because they were the first books to be written, but because they are the foundation upon which Acts and the Epistles are built. Rooted in the Old Testament, the Gospels also fulfill the old order. They provide the theological backdrop for the rest of the New Testament.

The English word *gospel* is a derivative of the Anglo-Saxon *godspell*, which can mean "God story" or "good story." The present order of the four Gospels goes back at least to the late second century A.D. Most of the inhabitants of Palestine spoke two languages, Aramaic and Greek. Greek was the common language of the entire Roman Empire. Thus it was the most suitable vehicle for the gospel accounts.

Although the four Gospels make up almost one-half of the New Testament, they barely touch upon the more than thirty years of preparation for Christ's public ministry. They concentrate upon the final two or three years of Jesus's life, a period when he ministered in Palestine. These four accounts do provide a composite picture of the person and work of the Savior, working together to give depth and clarity to our understanding of the most unique figure in human history. In them He is seen as divine and human, the sovereign Servant, the God-man.

Matthew, Mark, and Luke are known as the synoptic Gospels. The Greek word *synopsis* means "seeing together." This word is an appropriate description of these Gospels because of their common viewpoint and similar characteristics, especially in contrast to John. The agreements and differences among the synoptics have led to the problem of determining their literary relationship. Many scholars have devoted their lives to this fascinating study.

The four Gospels were written to stir and strengthen faith in Christ and to answer some of the objections and misconceptions about Him during and immediately after His public ministry. They were also designed to guide believers into a fuller understanding of His person and power.

The chart on page 160 gives an overview of the Gospels by showing the individual writing that make up this section of the New Testament. These Gospels are then discussed in detail in their appropriate order to give you a better understanding of this important major division of God's Word.

The Gospels

Book	Summary
Matthew	Christ presented as the teacher who is greater than Moses
Mark	Probably the earliest of the Gospels, focusing on Jesus as the Suffering Servant
Luke	Most complete biography of Christ, focusing on Jesus as the keystone in the history of salvation
John	The most symbolic Gospel, which presents Christ as the divine Son of God who came to earth in human form

Located on the northwest side of the Sea of Galilee, the Arbel Cliffs were used by rebels against Herod in Christ's day. (Todd Bolen, bibleplaces.com)

The Gospel of Matthew

Matthew has had perhaps a greater influence on Christian worship and literature than any other New Testament writing. For 17 centuries the church took its readings for Sundays and Holy Days from Matthew, drawing from the other gospels only where it felt Matthew was insufficient.

Matthew offers the most systematic arrangement of Jesus's teaching in the New Testament, and the early church used it heavily for its instruction of converts. Because of its emphasis on the fulfillment of Old Testament prophecy, Matthew is well suited as the opening book of the New Testament. In it the promises of God are recalled and their fulfillment in Jesus Christ is announced.

The Mount of Beatitudes on which Jesus delivered the Sermon on the Mount, including the Beatitudes. (Todd Bolen, bibleplaces.com)

STRUCTURE OF THE GOSPEL

The Gospel of Matthew contains five main sections. Each section consists of stories of Jesus's life, samples of His preaching and teaching, and a concluding refrain, "When Jesus had ended" (7:28; 11:1; 13:53; 19:1; 26:1). The story of Jesus' birth (chaps. 1—2) and the account of His betrayal, trial, and crucifixion (chaps. 26—28) stand outside this framework; they introduce and conclude the story of Jesus.

Section one begins with Jesus's baptism by John. His temptation, and the beginnings of His Galilean ministry (chaps. 3—4). The Sermon on the Mount (chaps. 5—7) follows; in it Jesus sets forth a new system of ethics, both individual and social, for the kingdom. Throughout the Sermon, Jesus contrasts the law, which was given by Moses, with the kingdom, which is present in Himself—showing the superiority of the kingdom. He highlights the contrast with two recurring phrases, "You have heard that it was said to those of old ... but I say to you."

Section two begins with a series of miracles by Jesus (chaps. 8—9), continues with Jesus's teaching to His disciples concerning mission and suffering (chap.10), and ends with the refrain (11:1). Section three contains stories that emphasize the difference between the ways of the kingdom and the ways of the world (chaps. 11—12) and parables on the nature of the kingdom (chap. 13). The refrain is repeated in 13:53, thus concluding the section.

Section four features further miracles, debates, and conflicts from Jesus's ministry (chaps. 14—17). It concludes with words of counsel directed by Jesus to His disciples about the Christian life (chap. 18). The section ends at 19:1. Section five is set in Jerusalem, and it recounts clashes between Jesus and the religious leaders (chaps. 19—22). In the discourses which follow, Jesus denounces the scribes and Pharisees (chap. 23), teaches of the end times (chap. 24), and tells three parables on judgment (chap. 25). The final refrain occurs in 26:1, and leads into the account of the betrayal, arrest, crucifixion, and resurrection of Jesus (chaps. 26—28).

The Gospel of Matthew concludes with Jesus's command to go into all the world and make disciples, baptizing and teaching them in His name. He leaves His disciples with this assurance: "Lo, I am with you always, even to the end of the age" (28:20).

AUTHORSHIP AND DATE

Matthew is an anonymous gospel. Like other gospel titles, the title was added in the second century A.D. and reflects the tradition of a later time. How, then, did the gospel acquire its name? Writing about A.D. 130, Papias, bishop of Hierapolis in Asia Minor (modern Turkey), records, "Matthew collected the oracles in the Hebrew (that is, Aramaic) language, and each interpreted them as best he could." Until comparative studies of the gospels in modern times, the church understood "oracles" to refer to the first gospel and considered Matthew, the apostle and former tax collector (9:9; 10:3), to be the author.

This conclusion, however, is full of problems. Our Gospel of Matthew is written in Greek, not Aramaic (as Papias records); and no copy of an Aramaic original of the gospel has ever been found. The Greek of the gospel cannot readily be translated back into Aramaic; and this strongly indicates that the gospel is not a Greek translation of the Aramaic original. Moreover, it is now generally agreed that Mark is the earliest of the four gospels and that the author of Matthew substantially used the Gospel of Mark in writing this gospel.

If the apostle Matthew wrote the gospel, one would wonder why he quoted so extensively from Mark (601 of Mark's 661 verses appear in Matthew), who was not a disciple of Jesus. Such observations virtually eliminate the possibility of the apostle Matthew being the author of the gospel.

The most promising way out of this dead-end street is to understand the "oracles" mentioned by Papias, not as the Gospel of Matthew, but as a collection of Jesus's sayings collected by the apostle Matthew.

A Concise Outline of
Matthew

Later these sayings were used by an unknown author as a source for the present gospel. The actual author probably was a Palestinian Jew who used the Gospel of Mark, plus a Greek translation of Matthew's Aramaic "oracles," and composed the gospel in Greek. The name of the gospel, therefore, stems from the apostle Matthew on whom the author draws, in part to compose his work. This interpretation has the benefit of paying Papias's testimony the respect it deserves, as well as honoring the problems mentioned above.

HISTORICAL SETTING

The Gospel of Matthew is full of clues that it was written to convince Jewish readers that Jesus is the Messiah. First, the author makes no attempt to translate or explain Jewish words and practices. Also, the gospel quotes more frequently from the Old Testament than does any other gospel. Most important, however, Jesus is portrayed as a descendant of the three greatest personalities of the Old Testament, although He surpasses them. Matthew traces Jesus's genealogy back to Abraham (1:2), the father of the faith.

In the Sermon on the Mount (chaps. 5—7), Jesus appears as a royal teacher whose authority exceeds that of Moses, the founder of the faith. And Jesus fulfills the hopes of David, the greatest king of Israel. He is born in Bethlehem (mentioned five times in chap. 2), and like David He appears as a king (19:28). He is frequently recognized as "the son of David" (9:27; 12:23; 15:22; 21:9; 21:15), although in truth He is David's "Lord" (22:41–46).

Matthew appealed to a Jewish audience, but not exclusively. The visit of the wise men from the (Gentile) East (2:1–12) hints of the gospel's rejection by the Jews and its acceptance by the Gentiles (21:43; also 4:15–16; 8:5–13; 12:18–21; 13:38). Furthermore, the Great Commission—the command to "make disciples of all the nations" (28:19)—indicates an interest beyond the confines of Judaism. We can conclude that Matthew was written to Jews and Jewish Christians to show that Jesus is the promised Messiah of the Old Testament. It also shows that the gospel does not lead to narrow Jewish concerns (chap. 23), but out into the Gentile world.

THEOLOGICAL CONTRIBUTION

Matthew's main subject is the "kingdom of heaven" or "kingdom of God." This kingdom is mentioned 51 times in the Gospel of Matthew, twice as often as in any other gospel. The kingdom is already here in Jesus (12:28), but it is not yet fulfilled (13:43; 25:34). The kingdom cannot be earned (19:23); it can be received only by those who recognize that they do not deserve it (5:3; 21:31). The kingdom extends like a fishing net, gathering people from every part of society (13:47), offering new life in the life-changing presence of God (8:11). The kingdom is more valuable than a precious gem (13:45–46), and it excludes any and all competitors for its allegiance (6:33).

The kingdom of God means the rule or reign of God—in the entire universe, in the world, and in our hearts. The primary indication of the presence of the kingdom in the world is the transformation of life, both individually and socially. A person enters the kingdom not by saying the right words, but by doing "the will of My father in heaven" (7:21).

SPECIAL CONSIDERATIONS

The Gospel of Matthew has at least five special considerations that will be mentioned briefly here:

1. Matthew sought to prove to the Jews that Jesus was the Christ, the fulfillment of Old Testament prophecy. A recurring statement that occurs in this gospel is, "All this was done that it might be fulfilled which was spoken by the Lord through the prophet" (1:22; also 2:15, 17, 23).

2. Matthew has a special interest in the church, which by the time this gospel was written had become the dominant factor in the lives of Christians. Indeed, Matthew is the only gospel to mention the word *church* (16:18; 18:17).

3. Matthew has a strong interest in eschatology (the doctrine of last things)—that is, in the second coming of Jesus, the end of the age, and the final judgment (chap. 25).

4. Matthew has a great interest in the teachings of Jesus, especially concerning the kingdom of God (chaps. 5—7; 10; 13; 18; 24—25).

5. Matthew writes to show that Jesus is the King to whom God has given power and authority to redeem and to judge mankind (1:1–17; 2:2; 21:1–11; 27:11, 37; 28:18).

Rough-surfaced basalt millstones, found at Capernaum—so plentiful they might have been manufactured here. (bibleplaces.com)

The Gospel of Mark

A ccording to most New Testament scholars Mark is the earliest of the four gospels. The Gospel of Mark portrays the person of Jesus more by what He does than by what He says. It is characterized by a vivid, direct style that leaves the impression of familiarity with the original events.

Although Mark is the shortest of the four gospels, it pays close attention to matters of human interest. Mark is fond of linking the episodes of Jesus's ministry together with catchwords (for example, "immediately," "then"), rather than editorial comment; and frequently he interrupts a longer story by inserting a smaller one within it (Mark 5:21–43; 6:6–30; 11:12–25; 14:1–11).

The Holy Sepulcher Tomb of Christ, believed to be the very ledge on which Christ's body was laid after his crucifixion. (Todd Bolen, bibleplaces.com)

STRUCTURE OF THE GOSPEL

The Gospel of Mark can be divided roughly into two parts: Jesus's ministry in Galilee (chaps. 1—9) and Jesus's ministry in Judea and Jerusalem (chaps. 10—16). Mark begins his gospel with the appearance of John the Baptist (1:2–8), followed by the baptism of Jesus (1:9–11). He comments on the temptation of Jesus only briefly (1:12–13) and concludes his introduction by a capsule of Jesus's message, "The time is fulfilled, and the kingdom of God is at hand. Repent, and believe in the gospel" (1:15). Then follows a series of 14 brief stories depicting Jesus as a teacher, healer, and exorcist in and around His hometown of Capernaum. In these stories Jesus often is in conflict with the Jewish authorities of His day.

In chapter 4 Mark assembles a number of Jesus's parables. In each parable Jesus uses common experiences to tell who God is and what man can become. Mark then resumes the activities of Jesus as an open-air preacher and healer with a series of 17 more episodes (4:35—8:26).

The first half of the gospel reaches a climax when Jesus is enroute to Caesarea Philippi and asks His disciples, "Who do men say that I am?" (8:27). Peter responds, "You are the Christ" (8:29); and Jesus then shocks the disciples by explaining that the Christ must suffer and die, and whoever desires to be His disciple must be prepared for the same (8:31—9:1). A glorious transfiguration of Jesus immediately follows this pronouncement; it shows that the Father in heaven confirms Jesus's role as a suffering Messiah (9:2–13). Then follows another series of 23 stories as Jesus journeys to Jerusalem for the Passover.

In the various encounters included in the Gospel of Mark, Jesus tries to drive home the truth He taught at Peter's confession—that messiahship and discipleship involve suffering: "Whoever desires to become great among you shall be your servant . . . For even the Son of Man did not come to be served, but to serve, and to give His life a ransom for many" (10:43, 45).

Chapter 13 contains a discourse of Jesus on the end of the age. Chapters 14—15 conclude the passion story, with accounts of Jesus's betrayal (14:1–11), His last supper with His disciples (14:12–31), His arrest (14:32–52), trial (14:53—15:20), and crucifixion (15:21–41). At the end, Jesus suffers passively "as a sheep before its shearers is silent" (Is. 53:7). In the oldest manuscripts the gospel ends with an angel announcing the resurrection of Jesus (16:1–8).

AUTHORSHIP AND DATE

The Gospel of Mark never mentions the name of its author. The earliest witness to identify the author was Papias (A.D. 60–130), a bishop of Hierapolis in Asia Minor (Turkey). Papias called him Mark, an interpreter of Peter. Papias then added that Mark had not followed Jesus during His lifetime, but later had written down Peter's recollections accurately, although not always in their proper order. Subsequent tradition unanimously agrees with Papias in ascribing this gospel to Mark.

The Mark believed to have written this gospel is John Mark of the New Testament. He was a native of Jerusalem (Acts 12:12), and later became an associate of both Peter (1 Pet. 5:13) and Paul (2 Tim. 4:11). Eusebius tells us that Mark composed his gospel in Rome while in the services of Peter. There are good reasons to accept this report. The gospel has many characteristics of an eyewitness account, for which Peter would have been responsible (1:29–31). Moreover, it is unlikely that the early church would have assigned a gospel to a minor figure like John Mark unless he in fact were its author, since the books of the New Testament normally required authorship by an apostle to qualify for acceptance in the Canon.

It may be that as a youth Mark was present at the arrest of Jesus and that he has left an "anonymous

A Concise Outline of
Mark

I. Presentation of the Servant

1. The Forerunner of the Servant	1:1–8
2. The Baptism of the Servant	1:9–11
3. The Temptation of the Servant	1:12–13
4. The Mission of the Servant	1:14—2:12

II. Opposition to the Servant

1. The Initial Opposition to the Servant	2:13—3:35
2. The Parables of the Servant	4:1–34
3. The Miracles of the Servant	4:35—5:43
4. The Growing Opposition to the Servant	6:1—8:26

III. Instruction by the Servant

1. Peter's Confession of Christ	8:27–33
2. Cost of Discipleship	8:34—9:1
3. The Transfiguration	9:2–13
4. Demon-possessed Son Is Delivered	9:14–29
5. Jesus Foretells His Death	9:30–32
6. Jesus Teaches to Prepare the Disciples	9:33—10:45
7. Blind Bartimaeus Is Healed	10:46–52

IV. Rejection of the Servant

1. The Formal Presentation of the Servant	11:1–19
2. The Instruction on Prayer	11:20–26
3. The Opposition by the Leaders	11:27—12:44
4. The Instruction on the Future	13:1–37
5. The Passion of the Servant	14:1—15:47

V. Resurrection of the Servant

1. The Resurrection of Jesus	16:1–8
2. The Appearance of Jesus	16:9–18
3. The Ascension of Jesus	16:19–20

signature" in the story of the young man who fled naked (14:51–52). If Mark composed his gospel while in the services of Peter, and Peter died in Rome between A.D. 64 and A.D. 68, then the gospel would have been written in Italy in the late 60's.

HISTORICAL SETTING

The Gospel of Mark is evidently written for Gentiles, and for Romans in particular. Mark translates Aramaic and Hebrew phrases (3:17; 5:41; 7:34; 14:36); he transliterates familiar Latin expressions into Greek; for example, *legio* (5:9), *quadrans* (12:42), *praetorium* (15:16), *centurio* (15:39). Moreover, Mark presents Romans in a neutral (12:17; 15:1–10), and sometimes favorable (15:39) light. The emphasis on suffering in the gospel may indicate that Mark composed his gospel in order to strengthen Christians in Rome who were undergoing persecutions under Nero.

THEOLOGICAL CONTRIBUTION

Mark begins his gospel with the statement, "The beginning of the gospel [good news] of Jesus Christ, the Son of God" (1:1); and the last human to speak in the gospel is the centurion who confesses at the cross, "Truly this Man was the Son of God!" (15:39). One of Mark's key objectives is to portray Jesus as God's Son. At decisive points in his story, he reveals the mystery of Jesus's person. At the baptism (1:11) and transfiguration (9:7) the Father in heaven calls Jesus "My beloved Son," thus indicating that Jesus shares a unique relationship with the Father. Demons recognize Jesus as God's Son, too (1:24; 3:11; 5:7), testifying that Jesus is equipped with God's authority and power.

Mark, however, is careful to avoid portraying Jesus as an unrealistic superstar whose feet do not touch the ground. The Son of God is not immune from the problems of life, but enters fully into them. He must be obedient to the will of the Father, even to death on a cross. Mark portrays Jesus according to the model of the Suffering Servant of Isaiah. Thus, Jesus tells a parable, which ultimately reflects His own fate: the only son of the owners of a vineyard suffers rejection and death at the hands of rebellious tenant farmers (12:1–12).

Furthermore, Mark does not emphasize Jesus's deity at the expense of His humanity. Jesus appears sorrowful (14:34), disappointed (8:12), displeased (10:14), angry (11:15–17), amazed (6:6), and fatigued (4:38). In no other gospel is Jesus's humanity presented as strongly as in the Gospel of Mark.

For Mark, faith and discipleship have no meaning apart from following the suffering Son of God. Faith is not a magic that works independently of the believer's participation (6:1–6); rather, it draws the believer into intimate union with Jesus as Lord (9:14–29). Jesus's disciples are to be with Him as He is with the Father, and they are given the same tasks of proclamation and power over the forces of evil as He had (3:13–15; 6:7).

As the Son of Man serves in self-abasement, so too, must His disciples serve (10:42–45). Discipleship with Christ leads to self-denial and suffering: "Whoever desires to come after Me, let him deny himself, and take up his cross, and follow Me" (8:34). This, however, is not a matter of a religious desire to suffer; rather, when one loses his life, he finds it in Christ (8:35). Thus, one can only know and confess Jesus as God's Son from the vantage point of the cross (15:39). It is only through the Son of God who suffers and dies that we may see into the heart of God (symbolized by the tearing of the Temple curtain, thus exposing the Holy of Holies) and enter into fellowship with the Father.

SPECIAL CONSIDERATIONS

The ending of the Gospel of Mark poses a problem. The two oldest and most important manuscripts of the Greek New Testament (Sinaiticus and Vaticanus) end with the words, "For they were afraid" (16:8).

Other manuscripts add, in whole or in part, the material making up verses 9–20. This longer ending, however, is unlike Mark 1:1—16:8 in style and content; it contains material presented exactly as it is in Matthew and Luke. It has long been debated whether Mark intended to end his gospel at 16:8, or whether the original ending was lost and a secondary ending (vv. 9–20) was later added.

The following observations suggest that Mark originally did not end at 16:8, and that the original ending was either lost (for example, the final section of a scroll or codex misplaced or destroyed) or left unfinished (for example, due to Mark's death).

First, it seems unlikely, having begun the gospel with a bold introduction (1:10), Mark would end it on a note of fear (16:8). Considering the centrality of Jesus throughout the gospel, one would expect an appearance of the resurrected Christ rather than just an announcement of His resurrection.

Second, Mark's Gospel conforms in broad outline to the preaching pattern of the early church—except for the shorter ending at 16:8. It would seen logical that one who drafted a gospel along the lines of the early Christian preaching would not have omitted a central feature like the resurrection (1 Cor. 15:3–26).

Third, the longer, later ending (vv. 9–20) testifies that the early tradition was dissatisfied with the shorter ending of Mark.

Finally, why would Matthew and Luke, both of whom normally follow Mark's report, depart from him at the resurrection appearances unless the ending of Mark was somehow defective? These reasons suggest that the shorter ending of Mark (at 16:8) is not the original (or intended) ending—for whatever reason—and that verses 9–20 are a later addition supplied to compensate for the omission.

Another special feature of Mark's Gospel concerns the "messianic secret." Often following a miracle, Jesus commands people healed, onlookers, disciples, and even demons to silence (1:34; 1:44; 3:12; 5:43; 7:36; 8:26; 8:30; 9:9). It has long puzzled readers why Jesus, who came into the world to make Himself known, would work at cross-purposes with His mission by trying to remain hidden.

The puzzle can be explained in part by realizing that Jesus's command to silence was intended to protect Himself from false expectations of the Messiah that were current at that time. For most of the Jesus's contemporaries, "messiah" brought up pictures of a military hero overthrowing the Roman rule of Palestine. Jesus had no intention to take up the warrior's sword; rather, He took up the servant's towel.

Another reason why Jesus tried to conceal His miraculous power was because He realized that faith could not be forced upon people by a spectacle (Matt. 4:5–7). No sight but insight into Jesus's life and purpose could evoke true faith.

Finally, Jesus demanded silence because no title or label could convey Him adequately. Saving knowledge of Jesus needed to come through personal experience with Him. Indeed, until Jesus died on the cross He could not rightly be known as God incognito who reveals Himself to those who are willing to deny self and follow Him in costly discipleship.

The Gospel of Luke

The third gospel is one in which the great truths of Jesus are communicated primarily through vivid stories. Luke is the first of a two-part work. In this work, the history of the gospel is traced from its beginnings in the life of Jesus (the Gospel of Luke) to the founding of the early church (the Acts of the Apostles).

The author of the Gospel of Luke is more interested in persons, especially those in trouble, than in ideas. He also is a skilled writer, and the literary quality of the Gospel of Luke is the highest of all four gospels. Luke often is the most interesting gospel to read. But he is also a serious historian who places Jesus within the context of world history. He presents Jesus and the church as the fulfillment of the history of salvation.

This glorious panoramic view shows the Sea of Galilee from Mount Arbel, highlighting the area in which Jesus ministered. (Todd Bolen, bibleplaces.com)

STRUCTURE OF THE GOSPEL

The literary structure of the Gospel of Luke is constructed primarily around Jesus's ministry in Galilee and in Jerusalem.

The first part of the gospel could be entitled Introduction and Infancy (chaps. 1—2). Here Luke declares his purpose in writing (1:1–4), and he tells the immortal stories of the births of John the Baptist and Jesus. The ministry of Jesus begins with a note of expectation in chapter 3. The rulers of the Roman world at that time are named. Next, accounts are given of the preaching of John the Baptist and of Jesus's baptism, genealogy, and temptation (3:1—4:13).

Between His Temptation and Transfiguration (4:14—9:28), Jesus conducted His ministry in Galilee. Convinced of His approaching death (9:21–27, 43–45), Jesus steadfastly set His face to go to Jerusalem (9:51) where, like the prophets before Him, He would accept His fate. This journey occupies the central part of Luke (9:51—19:27). The reader is kept in dramatic tensions as Jesus moves to Jerusalem and the shadow of the cross darkens His pathway. The cross, however, is not simply unlucky fate; on the contrary, "the Son of Man goes as it has been determined" (22:22) to fulfill the divine plan for which He came (note the use of *must* in 2:49; 4:43; 9:22; 17:25; 22:37; 24:7, 44).

Like Moses, Jesus accomplished for His people a deliverance—a deliverance from sin to salvation. The events of Jesus's final week in Jerusalem (19:28—24:53) conclude the gospel, and the Ascension serves as a transition from the end of Luke to the beginning of Acts.

AUTHORSHIP AND DATE

The author does not identify himself by name, but he does tell us a good deal about himself. Although not an eyewitness of the events he reports, he has followed them closely enough to write an orderly, reliable narrative (1:1–4). He is an educated man with the best command of Greek of any New Testament writer. He counts among his acquaintances a person of high social standing, the "most excellent" Theophilus, to whom he addresses both Luke (1:3) and Acts (1:1). As a Gentile, the author is interested in Gentiles; he is equally disinterested in matters purely Jewish. At some point in his life, he joined the apostle Paul. His experiences with Paul served as a firsthand source for his sequel to the Gospel of Luke.

For the author's name we are dependent on later tradition. Writing about A.D. 175, Irenaeus, bishop of Lyon, identified the author as Luke, the companion of Paul. Eusebius agreed, adding that Luke was a native of Antioch. The importance of Antioch in Acts (13:1–3) lends credibility to Eusebius' statement. The few glimpses we get of Luke from Paul's epistles—a physician, both beloved and compassionate (Col. 4:14) who was with Paul during his Roman imprisonment (Philem. 24; 2 Tim. 4:11)—parallels what we gather from him in Luke-Acts. The logical conclusion is that Luke wrote Luke-Acts.

The date of Luke's writing can only be guessed from inferences. Luke tells us that he drew upon earlier accounts, some of which were written (1:2). It is likely that two such accounts were (about A.D. 50) and the Gospel of Mark (about A.D. 60). The Gospel of Luke probably was written sometime shortly after A.D. 70. Two possible references to the fall of Jerusalem in A.D. 70 (21:20, 24) may indicate that Luke wrote after that event.

HISTORICAL SETTING

Luke is written by a Gentile for Gentiles. The author substitutes Greek expressions for nearly all Jewish expressions (*amen* is one of the few exceptions), and he seldom appeals to Old Testament prophecy. When Luke occasionally quotes from the Old Testament, he usually uses quotations which show that "all flesh [Gentiles as well as Jews] shall see the salvation of God" (3:6). Furthermore, we know that

A Concise Outline of
Luke

The approximate point at which Jesus—on the way to the cross—turned to the women around Him and admonished them not to weep for Him, but for themselves. (Daniel Gebhardt, bibleplaces.com)

Christianity encountered increasingly hostile opposition in the 50s and 60s. One ancient writer referred to "a class hatred for their abominations, called Christians." It appears that Luke intended to supply influential Romans, like Theophilus, with the solid truth about Christians. Luke shows that in every instance where Christians were suspected of sedition against Rome they were judged innocent (Luke 23:4, 14, 22; Acts 16:39; 17:9; 18:15–16; 19:37; 23:29; 25:25; 26:31).

Although Christianity was regarded by many pagans as a "mischievous superstition" which thrived on secrecy, Luke shows that Jesus associated with all sorts of people and that the early church openly proclaimed the gospel (Acts 2:14; 17:22). The truths of the Christian message did not happen in a corner (Acts 26:26), argued the apostle Paul. An implicit argument of Luke-Acts is that if Judaism had earned the toleration of the Roman Empire, then Christianity, which was the fulfillment of the Old Testament, should be granted the same status. It is reasonably certain that one of Luke's reasons for writing his gospel was to show that Christianity was neither superstitious nor subversive.

THEOLOGICAL CONTRIBUTION

Luke has the most universal outlook of all the gospels: Luke portrays Jesus as a man with compassion for all peoples. Whereas Matthew traces Jesus's genealogy back to Abraham, the father of the Jews (1:2), Luke traces it back to Adam, the father of the human race (3:38). In Matthew, Jesus sends His disciples "to the lost sheep of the house of Israel" (10:6) only, but Luke omits this limitation.

Luke is also the most socially-minded of the gospels. When He was in the synagogue at Nazareth, Jesus gave the keynote of His ministry by reading from Isaiah:

The Spirit of the Lord is upon Me,
Because He has anointed Me to preach the gospel to the poor.
He has sent me to heal the brokenhearted.
To preach deliverance to the captives
And recovery of sight to the blind,
To set at liberty those who are oppressed,
To preach the acceptable year of the Lord (Is. 61:1–2).

In Luke, Jesus's life is presented as a commentary on this passage of Scripture. He blesses the poor, the hungry, those who weep, and the excluded (6:20–23). In one parable He takes the side of a beggar who sits outside the gate of a rich man (16:19–31); and in another parable He celebrates a tax collector who shies away from the Temple because of his sinfulness (18:9–14). Jesus reaches out to a widowed mother who had lost her only son (7:11–17) and to a sinful woman (7:36–50). In another parable the hero of mercy is a despised Samaritan (10:25–37); and after a healing, a Samaritan is praised for his gratitude (17:11–19). The open arms of the Father, as in the parable of the Prodigal Son (15:11–32), await all who return to Him. Jesus' identification with sinners leads Him to open His arms to them on the cross, where "He was numbered with the transgressors" (22:37).

Jesus also criticizes the rich. "Woe to you who are rich" (6:24), He says; for the tables will turn. The rich are fools because they think life consists of possessing things (12:13–21). Those wealthy enough to throw dinner parties ought to invite those who cannot repay—"the poor, the maimed, the lame, the blind"—for God will repay "at the resurrection of the just" (14:13–14).

SPECIAL CONSIDERATIONS

For Luke the coming of Christ is good news; and his gospel is one of joy. The births of John and Jesus are echoed by songs of praise from Mary (1:46–55), Zacharias (1:67–79), the angels (2:14), and

Simeon (2:29–32). Even the unborn leap for joy (1:44). Sad and cruel scenes will follow, but the note of joy that rings from Gabriel at the Annunciation (1:32–33) is repeated by the apostles at the end of the gospel (24:52–53).

Second, Luke is a gospel of the Holy Spirit. Unlike the other evangelists, Luke emphasizes the activity of the Spirit in the ministry of Jesus. John the Baptist and his parents are filled with the Spirit (1:15, 41, 67), as is Simeon (2:25–35). Jesus begins His ministry "in the power of the Spirit" (4:14; also 4:1, 18; 10:21), and He promises the Spirit to His disciples in their hour of need (12:12). Jesus is not alone; the Spirit is always with Him, within Him, empowering Him to accomplish God's purpose.

Third, Luke is a gospel of prayer. The multitude prays as Zacharias serves at the altar (1:10). Mary prays at the news of salvation (1:46–55). Jesus prays at His baptism (3:21), when He chooses His disciples (6:12), at Peter's confession (9:18), and at His transfiguration (9:29). In the solitude of prayer Jesus takes the first steps of ministry (5:16) and falls to His knees on the Mount of Olives (22:39–46). He gives His final breath back to God in prayer, "Father, into Your hands I commend My spirit" (23:46).

The Mount of Precipitation, near Nazareth, is the traditional height from which Jesus was nearly thrown by an angry mob of Nazarites. (Todd Bolen, bibleplaces.com)

The Gospel of John

The fourth gospel is the most conceptual of the gospels of the New Testament. The first three gospels portray mainly what Jesus did and how He taught, but the Gospel of John is different. It moves beyond the obvious facts of Jesus's life to deeper, more profound meanings. Events and miracles are kept to a minimum in the Gospel of John. They are used as springboards or "signs" for lengthy discussions that reveal important truths about Christ. On the other hand, John uses a host of key words that symbolize who Jesus is and how we may know God. John is a "spiritual" gospel—not because it is more spiritual than the other three—but because it expresses spiritual ideas in spiritual language. Among the gospels, therefore, John offers a unique portrait of Christ that has been cherished by believers through the centuries.

This is the traditional place where Jesus met with His disciples for the "last breakfast" after His resurrection. (Todd Bolen, bibleplaces.com)

STRUCTURE OF THE GOSPEL

The fourth gospel consists basically of two parts: a book of "signs" and a book of "glory." The signs reveal Jesus's person (chaps. 1—12), and the glory results from Jesus's passion (chaps. 13—20). A prologue (1:1–18) and epilogue (chap. 21) serve as an introduction and conclusion to the gospel. Within this two-part structure, the gospel follows a pattern already presented in the prologue: revelation (1:1f), rejection (1:6–11), and reception (1:12–18). The corresponding divisions of the gospel are: revelation (1:19—6:71), rejection (chaps. 7—12), and reception (chaps. 13—21).

AUTHORSHIP AND DATE

Like the other gospels, John comes to us as an anonymous book. The question of authorship can be resolved only by observing clues within the gospel and by the tradition of the early church. Tradition agrees that the author was John the apostle, who was exiled to the island of Patmos in the Aegean Sea and who later died in Ephesus sometime after Trajan became emperor of Rome in A.D. 98. The gospel claims to come from an eyewitness (1:14; 1 John 1:1–4), and the author is familiar with the geography of Palestine. These external and internal evidences suggest that "the beloved disciple" (13:23; 19:26; 20:2; 21:7; 20), which appears as a title or nickname for John the apostle, composed the fourth gospel.

Other clues within the gospel and epistles of John, however, point beyond the apostle to another author. In 2 and 3 John, verses 1, the author identifies himself as "the elder." The similarities between the gospel and the epistles of John are too strong for us to conclude that the gospel was written by John the apostle and the epistles by John the elder. Early church tradition referred to an elder who was a disciple of John. Moreover, certain passages in the gospel of John tend to suggest that the writer was not the beloved disciple (19:35; 21:24).

Taking the evidence as a whole, it appears that the gospel was composed by a John the elder (*presbyter*), who was a disciple of John the apostle and who depended directly on the apostle's testimony for the content of the gospel. Both Johns are reputed to have lived in Ephesus. Some scholars, on the other hand, identify John the elder with John the apostle and view the gospel as composed by the apostle. Ephesus, therefore, becomes the most likely place for the gospel's origin, sometime around the close of the first century.

HISTORICAL SETTING

It is difficult to say with certainty to whom this gospel was addressed. Unlike Luke (1:1–4), the author mentions no addressee. Unlike Matthew and Mark, he gives few hints of his intended audience. The gospel uses both Jewish and Greek thought forms in its presentation of Christ.

For John, Jesus goes beyond the bounds of Judaism. This gospel reports a fiercer conflict between Jesus and the Jews than the other gospels do. The gospel begins before time (1:1), and it shows that Jesus is timeless. Jesus speaks not to any one nation or ethnic group, but to the human condition. John portrays Jesus for the widest possible readership. This is one reason why the fourth gospel has spoken so deeply to Christians in all ages.

If there is doubt to whom John writes, there can be little doubt about why John writes. The gospel contains a clear statement of purpose: "These [signs] are written that you may believe that Jesus is the Christ, the Son of God, and that believing you may have life in His name" (20:31).

For John, the sole purpose of life is that "you may know and believe that the Father is in me and I in Him" (10:38). Thus, John writes that we might know the Father and experience life eternal through faith in the Son.

A Concise Outline of
John

I. The Incarnation of the Son of God

1. The Deity of Christ	1:1–2
2. The Preincarnate Work of Christ	1:3–5
3. The Forerunner of Christ	1:6–8
4. The Rejection of Christ	1:9–11
5. The Acceptance of Christ	1:12–13
6. The Incarnation of Christ	1:14–18

II. Presentation of the Son of God

1. The Presentation of Christ by John the Baptist	1:19–34
2. The Presentation of Christ to John's Disciples	1:35–51
3. The Presentation of Christ in Galilee	2:1–12
4. The Presentation of Christ in Judea	2:13—3:36
5. The Presentation of Christ in Samaria	4:1–42
6. The Presentation of Christ in Galilee	4:43–54

III. Opposition to the Son of God

1. The Opposition at the Feast in Jerusalem	5:1–47
2. The Opposition During Passover Time in Galilee	6:1–71
3. The Opposition at the Feast of Tabernacles in Jerusalem	7:1—10:21
4. The Opposition at the Feast of Dedication in Jerusalem	10:22–42
5. The Opposition at Bethany	11:1—12:11
6. The Opposition at Jerusalem	12:12–50

IV. Preparation of the Disciples

1. The Preparation in the Upper Room	13:1—14:31
2. The Preparation on the Way to the Garden	15:1—17:26

V. Crucifixion and Resurrection

1. The Rejection of Christ	18:1—19:16
2. The Crucifixion of Christ	19:17–37
3. The Burial of Christ	19:38–42
4. The Resurrection of Christ	20:1–10
5. The Appearance of Christ	20:11—21:25

THEOLOGICAL CONTRIBUTION

John writes with a modest vocabulary, but his words are charged with symbolism. Terms like *believe, love, truth, world, light and darkness, above and below, name, witness, sin, judgment, (eternal) life, glory, bread, water*, and *hour* are the key words of this gospel. In John 3:16–21, a passage of less than 150 words in Greek, seven of these terms occur.

The world is where God reveals truth (8:32), light (8:12), and life (14:6) in His Son Jesus Christ. The world is also where person must decide for or against the witness of Christ, and the decision in judgment (3:18). Sin is to misjudge Jesus—to fail to receive Him as the bread of life (6:35), or not to walk in Him as the light of the world (8:12). The Son has come from above to glorify the Father (17:1), and He does so in His "hour" (12:23; 13:1)—through His suffering on the cross.

In the synoptic gospels—Matthew, Mark, and Luke—Jesus utters short sayings. Longer discourses, such as the Sermon on the Mount (Matthew 5—7), are either collections of saying on various themes, or, like Matthew 13, mostly parables. John, on the other hand, records no parables and few of the brief sayings so common to the synoptics. Rather, he expands upon an incident; for example, Nicodemus (chap. 3), the woman at the well (chap. 4), the man born blind (chap. 9), Lazarus (chap. 11), or footwashing (chap. 13). Or he takes up an image; for example, bread (chap. 6), water (chap. 7), light (chap. 8), or shepherd (chap. 10). John then uses these words as symbols to reveal a fuller revelation of Christ. These discourses are blended so completely with John's own style that frequently the reader cannot tell whether it is John or Jesus speaking (3:16).

Why does John present such a different picture of Jesus? John may reveal Jesus as He taught in private, while the other three gospels may recall His public method of address (Mark 4:34). This may be a partial answer. A fuller explanation may be that the other gospels retain the actual form of Jesus's teaching, while John uncovers the essence of Jesus as a person.

This does not imply that John disregards historical truth. At some points his gospel probably preserves the facts of Jesus's life more accurately than the other gospels do. For example, Matthew, Mark, and Luke leave the impression that Jesus ministered mainly in Galilee, making only one Passover journey to Jerusalem. This leads one to assume that Jesus's ministry lasted less than one year. John, however, mentions at least three Passover journeys (2:13, 23; 6:4; 12:1) and longer periods of ministry in Judea. The other three gospels do hint of previous visits by Jesus to Jerusalem (Matt. 23:37; Luke 13:34). A longer ministry, therefore, as presented by John, is probably closer to the events of Jesus's life.

Nevertheless, it is clear that John is guided more by theological than historical interests. The gospels of Matthew, Mark, and Luke begin by showing Jesus's role as the fulfiller of the Old Testament promises of salvation. But John begins with the pre-existence of Jesus: "In the beginning was the Word" (1:1). Jesus is divine ("the Word was God," 1:1), but He is also human ("the Word became flesh," 1:14). Only as such as He is the revealer of the Father.

In the first chapter, John introduces Jesus by seven key titles: Word, Lamb of God, Rabbi, Messiah, King of Israel, Son of God, and Son of Man. Only in John do we find the "I am" sayings: "I am the bread of life" (6:35), "I am the light of the world" (8:12), "before Abraham was, I AM" (8:58), "I am the door of the sheep" (10:7), I am the good shepherd" (10:11), "I and My Father are one" (10:30), "I am the way, the truth, and the life" (14:6), and "I am the vine" (15:5). In each of these sayings the "I" is emphatic in Greek. It recalls the name of God, "I AM," in the Old Testament (Ex. 3:14).

In the Old Testament God's words were to be reverently received. So it is with Jesus. In John He begins His messages by saying, "Truly, truly I say to you." Just as in the Old Testament God alone was to be worshiped, in John people are to believe in Jesus alone. Here John stresses his concept of "believing." The verb "to believe" is found nearly a hundred times in the gospel, though the noun "belief/faith" does not occur. For John, saving faith is a verb, carrying the sense of active trust in Jesus; it is not a static noun.

When one considers Jesus's moral teaching, another key word emerges. In John, Jesus does not enter into questions of prayer, fasting, almsgiving, swearing, marriage, or wealth as He does in the other gospels. Rather, one's relationships to God, others, and the world are summed up in love. The love which God has for His beloved Son (3:35; 15:9) is passed on by the Beloved to "His own" (13:1). As recipients of God's love, Christians are to love God by loving one another (13:34). This love, which unites believers (17:1f.), is also a testimony to the world. The key verse of John expresses the basic theological truth of the gospel: "For God so loved the world that He gave His only begotten Son, that whoever believes in Him should not perish but have everlasting life" (3:16).

The Gospel of John expresses the uniqueness of the Son's relationship with the Father. The Son existed before the world with the Father; He was sent into the world by the Father; and He goes out of the world to the Father.

SPECIAL CONSIDERATIONS

Our present Gospel of John contains a story that probably was not written by the original author. The account of the woman caught in adultery (7:53—8:11) differs markedly in style from the rest of John. It is not found in the earlier and better manuscripts of the book. It was probably added at a later date by an unknown author under God's inspiration to express an important truth about Jesus and His attitude toward sinful people.

By tradition, this is the stone on which Jesus body was wrapped in linen and spices before being placed in the tomb. (Todd Bolen, bibleplaces.com)

CHAPTER 7

ACTS: A HISTORY OF THE EARLY CHURCH

The Acts of the Apostles begins where Luke concluded his gospel. In it is recorded the initial fulfillment of the Great Commission of Matthew 28:19–20 as it traces the beginning of the church in Jerusalem and its rapid growth throughout the Roman Empire.

Acts is the historical link between the gospels and the epistles. It is the only book that carries on the story from the ascension of Jesus to the period of the epistles. Because of Luke's strong emphasis on the ministry of the Holy Spirit, this book should really be regarded as the Acts of the Spirit of Christ working in and through the apostles. Luke's interest in the progressive spread of the gospel is reflected in this apostolic history.

From a theological standpoint, Acts was written to trace the development of the church over the one-generation transition from a primarily Jewish to a predominantly Gentile membership. In this way Christianity is seen as distinct from Judaism but also as its fulfillment.

The title of Acts is somewhat misleading, for only a few of the apostles of Jesus are mentioned in the book. In reality, Acts relates some acts of some of the apostles, primarily Peter and Paul, and involves a time-span of about 30 years—from the ascension of Jesus (about A.D. 30) to Paul's imprisonment in Rome (about A.D. 62).

This is the Gangitis River, near Philippi, where Paul preached the gospel to a group of women, one of whom (Lydia) believed his message and was baptized. (Todd Bolen, bibleplaces.com)

STRUCTURE OF THE BOOK

The Acts of the Apostles is like a drama with two main characters, Peter and Paul. This drama portrays the spread of the gospel from Jerusalem to Rome in six divisions:

- The founding of the church in Jerusalem (1:1—6:7);
- the extension of the gospel through Judea and Samaria (6:8—9:31);
- the church in Antioch of Syria (9:32—12:24);
- the first missionary journey of Paul to Asia Minor (12:25—16:5);
- the second and third missionary journeys to Macedonia and Achaia (Greece) (16:6—19:20); and
- the events leading to Rome (19:21—28:31).

AUTHORSHIP AND DATE

There can be little doubt that the Book of Acts and the Gospel of Luke come from the same author. Each book is the length of a scroll (about 35 feet), and each is addressed to the same individual, Theophilus. The similiarities between the Gospel of Luke and the Book of Acts in literary style, vocabulary, and theological ideas are unmistakable. Although the author does not identify himself by name, scholars have ascribed the authorship of both books to Luke, the companion of Paul.

It is difficult to say when Acts was written. We know only that it follows the gospel: "The former account [Gospel of Luke] I made, O Theophilus" (Acts 1:1). If the gospel were written in the early 70's, Acts would have been composed shortly thereafter. Other scholars date Acts as early as A.D. 62 because it ends abruptly with Paul's imprisonment in Rome.

Luke is a reliable historian, in part because of the sources he used. He was closely associated with many events of Paul's mission, and this results in greater vividness in the latter half of Acts. At three places in Acts (16:10–17; 20:5—21:18; and 27:1—28:16) the narrative changes to the first person ("we"), indicating that Luke was personally present. Luke also may have had access to written documents (for example, the decree of the Council of Jerusalem, Acts 15:23; or letters from early Christian leaders).

Above all, Luke had the benefit of a wide circle of contacts. In the Book of Acts he mentions 95 different persons from 32 countries, 54 cities, and 9 Mediterranean islands. From these he gathered information for the first part of Acts (especially chapters 1—12) and for his gospel. Luke, however, writes selective history, focusing only on the course of the gospel from Jerusalem to Rome.

HISTORICAL SETTING

As in the Gospel of Luke, Luke writes to Gentiles. He wants his audience to know the truthful and triumphant course of the gospel, beginning in Jesus and continuing in the church (Acts 1:1).

This is his primary motive for writing the Book of Acts. In addition, Luke defends, where possible, the Christian faith from suspicion on sedition or superstition. The "Way" (9:2) is not a secret, subversive cult (26:26). On the contrary, it is proclaimed in the city squares for all to hear and judge. This is one reason the many public speeches were included in Acts. Neither is Christianity politically dangerous. If Christians are suspected of sedition against Rome, Luke shows that in each instance where they are brought before Roman authorities they are acquitted (Acts 16:39; 17:6; 18:12; 19:37; 23:29; 25:25; 26:31). Luke devotes nearly one-third of Acts (chaps. 21—28) to Paul's imprisonment. He does this not only to show that the gospel reaches its destination in spite of insurmountable obstacles, but also to show that Paul and his message are not politically subversive.

THEOLOGICAL CONTRIBUTION

The Acts of the Apostles could be justly entitled, "The Acts of the Holy Spirit," for the Spirit is mentioned nearly 60 times in the book. In His parting words, Jesus reminds the disciples of the promise of the Father (1:4–8); ten days later the power of the Spirit descends at Pentecost (2:1–4). Persons "from every nation under heaven" (2:5) are enabled by the Holy Spirit to hear "the wonderful works of God" (2:11), and so the church was born.

Pentecost was a reversal of the Tower of Babel, where language became confused and nations were separated by misunderstanding (Gen. 11:1–9). At Pentecost, the Holy Spirit gathered persons from every nation into one united fellowship. From Pentecost onward, the Holy Spirit directs the unfolding drama of the growth of the church.

Acts contains portraits of many outstanding Christians of the early church. Barnabas exemplifies generosity (4:36–37), Stephen forgiveness (7:60), Philip and Paul obedience (8:26; 26:19), Cornelius piety (10:2), and the witness of the early church vibrates with boldness (2:29; 4:13, 29, 31; 28:31). Ordinary people are empowered to perform extraordinary feats. A faltering apostle is empowered to address multitudes (2:14) or make a defense before rulers (4:8). A prayer fellowship is shaken (4:31); a deacon defends his faith by martyrdom (7:58). The despised Samaritans receive the Spirit (8:4–8), as does a Gentile soldier (10:1–48). A staunch persecutor of the gospel is converted (9:1–19), and through him the gospel reaches the capital of the world!

Paul reaches Rome in chains. Circumstances, too, may be adverse: persecutions (8:3–4; 11:19), famines (11:27–30), opposition (13:45), or violent storms (27:1–44). Through it all, however, the Holy Spirit directs the drama so that "all things work together for good" (Rom. 8:28) to further the cause of Christ.

SPECIAL CONSIDERATIONS

Nearly one-fifth of Acts consists of speeches, primarily from Peter, Stephen, and Paul. Common to each of the speeches is a basic framework of gospel proclamation. This proclamation can be outlined as follows:

1. The promises of God in the Old Testament are now fulfilled.
2. The Messiah has come in Jesus of Nazareth.
   a. He did good and mighty works by the power of God.
   b. He was crucified according to the purpose of God.
   c. He was raised from the dead by the power of God.
   d. He now reigns by the power of God.
   e. He will come again to judge and restore all things for the purpose of God.
3. All who hear should repent and be baptized.

This outline is our earliest example of the gospel proclaimed by the early church. It is the "foundation of the apostles and prophets, Jesus Christ Himself being the chief cornerstone" (Eph. 2:20), upon which the church is built. In this sense, the Book of Acts is not yet completed, for each generation is enabled by Holy Spirit to add its chapters by proclaiming the "wonderful works of God" (2:11).

A Concise Outline of **Acts**	**I. The Witness in Jerusalem**	
	1. The Power of the Church	1:1—2:47
	2. The Progress of the Church	3:1—8:3
	II. The Witness in Judea and Samaria	
	1. The Witness of Philip	8:4–40
	2. The Conversion of Saul	9:1–31
	3. The Witness of Peter	9:32—11:18
	4. The Witness of the Early Church	11:19—12:24
	III. The Witness to the End of the Earth	
	1. The First Missionary Journey	12:25—14:28
	2. The Jerusalem Council	15:1–35
	3. The Second Missionary Journey	15:36—18:22
	4. The Third Missionary Journey	18:23—21:14
	5. The Trip to Rome	21:15—28:31

To encourage their soldiers the Israelites brought the Ark of the Covenant to their camp, but it was captured and taken by the Philistines to Aphek—and perhaps to a fortress like this one. (Todd Bolen, bibleplaces.com)

CHAPTER 8

THE EPISTLES (LETTERS) OF THE APOSTLE PAUL

Paul, under the inspiration of the Holy Spirit, was able to address specific problems and issues of his time with perspectives that are universal and timeless. Even the most mundane matters stimulated lofty thoughts in the mind of the apostle. He adapted his style to the changing situations. Paul could be logical, personal, rhetorical, lyrical, formal, practical, or emotional.

Paul's writings are properly called letters because of their form and personal character. They generally follow the standard form of letters in Paul's day: the sender's name and office, the name of the recipient, a greeting or wish for prosperity, the main body, a farewell with closing greetings, and the signature.

The use of the epistle as a medium of divine revelation was unheard of until the time of Paul and his contemporaries. This very personal form of communication was appropriate to the message that believers have been made adopted children in the household of God by His grace. Paul's epistles contain an abundance of doctrine, but these theological instructions are designed for practical application, not theoretical speculation.

Nine Pauline letters were addressed to churches and four to individuals. It is evident, however, that Paul wrote letters that are now lost (see 1 Cor. 5:9; 2 Cor. 10:9–10; Col. 4:16; 2 Thess. 3:17). Paul's thirteen epistles are arranged so that the first nine (to churches) and the last four (to individuals) are in order of decreasing length. The probable chronological order is: Galatians, 1 Thessalonians, 2 Thessalonians, 1 Corinthians, 2 Corinthians, Romans, Colossians, Philemon, Ephesians, Philippians, 1 Timothy, Titus, and 2 Timothy.

Paul's Christian life was characterized by unflagging dedication to the cause of Christ in the face of suffering. This comes through clearly in his thirteen epistles in the New Testament. The chart on page 186 gives an overview of Paul's letters by showing the individual books that make up this section of the New Testament. These books are then discussed in detail in their appropriate order to give you a better understanding of this important major division of God's Word.

A modern replica of an ancient quill and inkwell, as used by a biblical scribe. (Kim Guess, bibleplaces.com)

Epistles (Letters) of the Apostle Paul

Book	Summary
Romans	An explanation of the Christian faith for both Jews and Gentiles, Addressed to the church at Rome
1 Corinthians	Instructions to the church at Corinth dealing with problems among Christians
2 Corinthians	Paul's defense and explanation of his apostleship
Galatians	An account of the necessity of salvation by divine grace rather than the law
Ephesians	A letter to the church at Ephesus explaining the believer's position in Christ
Philippians	A joyful letter to the church at Philippi, telling of Paul's conquering faith during imprisonment
Colossians	An account of the supremacy of Christ, written to the church of Colossae
1 and 2 Thessalonians	Instructions to the church at Thessalonica about the coming of the Lord
1 and 2 Timothy	Manuals of leadership for the young pastor at Ephesus
Titus	A manual of Christian conduct for church leaders, written to a young pastor at Crete
Philemon	An appeal for Christian unity and forgiveness for a runaway slave

The Epistle to the Romans

The main theme of Romans is that righteousness comes as a free gift of God and is receivable by faith alone. Romans stands at the head of the Pauline epistles because it is the longest of his letters, but it is also Paul's most important epistle.

Repeatedly in its history, the church has found in this epistle a catalyst for reform and new life. In the fourth century a troubled young man, sensing divine command to open the Bible and read the first passage he came to, read these words: "Not in revelry and drunkenness, not in licentiousness and lewdness, not in strife and envy. But put on the Lord Jesus Christ, and make no provision for the flesh, to fulfill its lusts" (13:13–14).

"In an instant," says St. Augustine, "the light of confidence flooded into my heart and all the darkness of doubt was dispelled." In the 16th century a young monk found release from his struggles with God by claiming salvation by grace through faith (Rom. 1:17; 3:24). This truth caused Martin Luther to launch the greatest reform the church has ever known. Romans, perhaps more than any single book of the Bible, has exerted a powerful influence on the history of Christianity.

Paul mentions the city of Centhrea in Romans 16:1, as the home of Phoebe. It was about nine miles from Corinth, on the Saronic Bay, as shown in this photograph. (Todd Bolen, bibleplaces.com)

STRUCTURE OF THE EPISTLE

The Epistle to the Romans consists of two halves, a doctrinal section (chaps. 1—8) and a practical section (chaps. 12—16), separated by three chapters on the place of Israel in the history of salvation (chaps. 9—11).

Paul declares his main theme in the first chapter—that the gospel is the power of salvation to everyone who believes (1:16–17). This declaration is then held in suspension to show that all people are in need of salvation: the Gentiles have broken the law of conscience, and the Jews the law of Moses (1:18—3:20).

Paul then returns to his opening theme. In a classic statement of the Christian gospel, he explains that righteousness comes by the grace of God through man's trust in the saving work of Christ (3:21–31). The example of Abraham testifies through faith (4:1–25). The benefits of justification are peace and confidence before God (5:1–11). Thus, Christ's ability to save is greater than Adam's ability to corrupt (5:12–21).

Paul then takes up the problem of sin in the Christian life. Rather than acting as a stimulus to sin, grace draws us into a loyal union with Christ (6:1–14). Christ has freed us from slavery to sin so that we may become slaves of righteousness (6:15—7:6). Paul admits that the law brings sin to light, but sin convinces us of our need for a Savior (7:7–25). Paul concludes the doctrinal section by one of the most triumphant chapters in all the Bible: believers are not condemned by God, but are raised by the power of the Holy Spirit to face all adversity through the redeeming love of God (8:1–39).

In chapters 9—11 Paul discusses the question of why Israel rejected the Savior sent to it.

Paul then discusses a number of practical consequences of the gospel. A proper response involves the sacrifice of one's entire life to the gospel (12:1–2). The gifts of grace to the church are complementary, not competitive or uniform (12:3–8). He lists insights for Christian conduct (12:9–21). Christians are instructed on the attitudes they should have toward the government (13:1–7), neighbors (13:8–10), the Second Coming (13:11–14), and judging (14:1–12) and cooperating with others (14:13—15:13). Paul closes with his travel plans (15:14–33) and a long list of greetings (16:1–27).

AUTHORSHIP AND DATE

There can be no doubt that Romans is an exposition of the content of the gospel by the strongest thinker in the early church—the apostle Paul. The epistle bears Paul's name as author (1:1). Throughout, it reflects Paul's deep involvement with the gospel. Paul most likely wrote the epistle during his third missionary journey as he finalized plans to visit Rome (Acts 19:21). His three-month stay in Corinth, probably in the spring of A.D. 56 or 57, would have provided the extended, uninterrupted time needed to compose such a reasoned commentary on the Christian faith.

HISTORICAL SETTING

Romans was written to a church that Paul did not found and had not visited. He wrote the letter to give an account of his gospel in preparation for a personal visit (1:11). Paul wrote most probably from Corinth, where he was completing the collection of money from the Macedonian and Achaian Christians for the "poor saints" in Jerusalem. After delivering the money, he planned to visit Rome and, with the Roman's support, to travel to Spain. The epistle, therefore, served as an advanced good-will ambassador for Paul's visit to Rome and his later mission to Spain (15:22–33).

THEOLOGICAL CONTRIBUTION

The great theme of Romans is God's power to save. The Romans understood power; when Paul wrote this epistle to the capital of the ancient world, Rome ruled supreme. The gospel, however, is nothing to

A Concise Outline of
Romans

The Roman pantheon dates back almost 2000 years. This photo shows the interior of the rotunda, with several built-in alcoves. (Todd Bolen, bibleplaces.com)

be ashamed of in comparison; for it, too, is power—indeed the "power of God to salvation for everyone" (1:16). In the gospel both Jews and Gentiles find access to God, not on the basis of human achievement, but because of God's free grace bestowed on those who accept it in faith.

Paul emphasizes that everyone stands in need of God's grace. This was apparent in the case of the Gentiles, who, instead of worshiping the Creator, worshiped the things created (1:25). But the Jews, in spite of their belief that they were superior to Gentiles, were also bankrupt. The Jews knew the revealed will of God and they judged others by it; but they failed to see they were condemned by the very law under which they passed judgments (2:1—3:8). Thus, "there is no difference, for all have sinned and fall short of the glory of God" (3:22–23).

But the "good news" is that God's love is so great that it reaches humankind even in their sin. The form it took was the death of the beloved Son of God on the cross. The righteous one, Jesus, died on behalf of the unrighteous. Therefore, God pronounces persons justified, not when they have attained a certain level of goodness—thus excluding justification by works—but in the midst of their sin and rebellion (5:8–10). Such grace can be received only by grateful and trusting surrender, which is faith.

In light of this magnificent salvation, Paul urged the Romans not to return to their old human nature, which always stands under condemnation of the law. Rather, he called on them to live free from sin and death through the power of the indwelling presence of the Holy Spirit (8:10–11).

SPECIAL CONSIDERATIONS

Romans reflects Paul's deep concern with the relation between Jew and Gentile (chaps. 9—11). The Jews are indeed God's Chosen People, although their history is one of rebellion against God. Their rejection of Christ is consistent with their history, although a remnant does remain faithful. The rejection of the Jews, ironically, has increased the truly faithful because the cutting off of the native olive branch (Israel) has allowed a wild branch (Gentiles) to be grafted onto the tree (11:13).

Paul also declared that the inclusion of the Gentiles in the household of God aroused the Jews to jealousy, moving them to claim God's promised blessings. Thus, the hardened response of the Jews to the gospel is only temporary, until the Gentiles are fully included into the faith. At some future time the Jews will change and, like the remnant, "all Israel will be saved" (11:26).

Paul's wrestling with this problem caused him not to doubt or condemn God, but to marvel at God's wisdom (11:33). This marvelous epistle has kindled the same response in Christians of all generations.

The "Erastus" referred to in this ancient inscription was almost certainly the same Erastus mentioned by Paul in Romans 16:23. (bibleplaces.com)

The First and Second Epistles to the Corinthians

First Corinthians is unique among the Pauline letters because of the variety of its practical concerns. Second Corinthians is one of Paul's most personal letters, containing a wealth of insights into the heart of Paul the pastor. Both letters reveal the degree to which Paul identified with his churches, suffering in their shortcomings and celebrating in their victories. The Corinthian correspondence draws us into a world much like our own. Paul, the anxious pastor, wrote to young Christians who were concerned with problems involved in living the Christian life in a non-Christian environment.

This scene of the Corinth excavations was shot from the northwest. In Paul's day, Corinth was a center of commerce, pagan religions, and worldly pleasures. (Todd Bolen, bibleplaces.com)

STRUCTURE OF THE EPISTLES

Following the introduction (1 Cor. 1:1–9), Paul appeared to the Corinthians to mend the divisions within the church (chaps. 1—4). Paul reminded the Corinthians that they all were united by the simple, but life-changing, preaching of the cross (1 Cor. 1:18—2:16). Indeed, each church leader builds on the one foundation of Jesus (chap. 3), and consequently labors in behalf of Christ (chap. 4). In chapters 5 and 6 Paul took up two moral abuses in Corinth. He judged a man who had sexual intercourse with his father's wife (chap. 5), and he reproved the believers for generating arguments that wound up in court before non-believing judges (1 Cor. 6:1–11).

Paul then addressed certain questions which were brought to him by the Corinthians: about sexuality (6:12–19), marriage (chap. 7), and eating food offered previously to idols (chap. 8). On such matters Paul appealed for a responsible use of Christian freedom—not for self-gain, but in consideration for the other. He reminded them that he conducted his own ministry in this way (chap. 9), and he warned against becoming fixed on anything that could lead to idolatry (chap. 10).

Paul then returned to other abuses, especially involving church order. In chapter 11 he developed the correct teaching on the Lord's Supper; in chapter 12 on spiritual gifts; in chapter 13 on love; in chapter 14 on the charismatic gifts of tongues and prophecy, and in chapter 15 on the resurrection. Finally, he reminded the Corinthians of the weekly collection for the saints in Jerusalem. He concluded with travel plans and greetings (chap. 16).

Second Corinthians is closely related to the circumstances that occasioned its writing. The letter begins with reference to a painful experience of rejection at Corinth (Paul's third visit). Paul gave thanks that the Corinthians were now reconciled to him (chap. 1), but he recalled his torment over their stubbornness (chap. 2). Chapters 3 and 4 are theological reflections on ministry, and chapters 5 and 6 on reconciliation. In chapter 7 Paul shared his joy at the church's repentance. Paul changed perspective in chapters 8 and 9 by turning to the matter of the collection for the church in Jerusalem.

The tone of 2 Corinthians changes in chapters 10—13. These chapters are laced with warnings to the Corinthians and Paul's opponents, defenses of his apostleship, and a rehearsal of Paul's sufferings as an apostle. If chapters 1—9 reveal Paul's joy and relief, chapters 10—13 let us see the wounds, both physical and emotional, which he bore as an apostle. The letter closes with the only trinitarian benediction in the Bible (2 Cor. 13:14).

AUTHORSHIP AND DATE

First and Second Corinthians bear the unmistakable marks of Pauline authorship (1 Cor. 1:1; 2 Cor. 2:1). This first epistle was written from Ephesus (1 Cor. 16:8) during Paul's third missionary journey, perhaps in A.D. 56. The second letter followed some 12 to 15 months later from Macedonia, where Paul met Titus and received news of the church's repentance (2 Cor. 2:12–17).

HISTORICAL SETTING

Acts 18:1–8 records the founding of the Corinthian church. During his second missionary journey, Paul went alone from Athens to Corinth in about A.D. 51. There he labored with a Jewish-Christian couple, Aquila and Priscilla, who recently had been expelled from Rome by the emperor Claudius because they were Jews. Silas and Timothy also joined Paul in Corinth. When Paul left Corinth 18 months later, a Christian congregation flourished. The congregation was composed primarily of former pagans (1 Cor. 12:2), most of them apparently from the lower classes (1 Cor. 1:26f.). Some were slaves (1 Cor. 7:21). A few wealthier persons (1 Cor. 11:22–32) and Jews (8:1–13), however, were among the believers.

A Concise Outline of
First Corinthians

A Concise Outline of
Second Corinthians

A bit of detective work enables us to reconstruct the circumstances of the Corinthian correspondence. It is reasonably certain that Paul wrote four letters and paid perhaps three visits to the church in Corinth.

During his third missionary journey, Paul received word about immorality in the young congregation at Corinth. He wrote a letter (which has since been lost) against mixing with fornicators (1 Cor. 5:9). The letter apparently failed to achieve its purpose. Some time later Paul learned (1 Cor. 1:11, 16:17) that the sexual problems persisted, along with many others. Paul responded by writing a second letter (1 Corinthians), in which he referred to various points raised by the Corinthians (see the sections beginning, "Now concerning," 1 Cor. 7:1, 25; 8:1; 12:1; 16:1). In addition, he condemned the Corinthians for their divisions (1 Cor. 1:10) and their gross sexual violations (1 Cor. 5:1).

This letter also failed to correct the abuses at Corinth. Paul then apparently made a visit to Corinth, during which he was rebuffed (2 Cor. 2:1). From Ephesus Paul then wrote a third letter in which he spared no punches in his contest with the willful Corinthians. This letter, which he sent by Titus, has also been lost. Many scholars believe it has been attached to 2 Corinthians and preserved as chapters 10—13 of his epistle.

In anxiety over the possible effect of this drastic letter, and impatient over Titus' delay in returning, Paul traveled north from Ephesus to Macedonia. There Titus met him and, to Paul's relief and joy, reported that the Corinthians has punished the ring leader of the opposition and repented (2 Cor. 2:5–11). Paul then wrote a fourth letter (2 Corinthians), recounting his former anxiety and expressing his joy over the reform in Corinth.

THEOLOGICAL CONTRIBUTION

The problems which Paul faced in the church at Corinth were complex and explosive. The correspondence which resulted is rich and profound in theological insight. While addressing the problems in Corinth, the apostle reaches some of the most sublime heights in all New Testament literature.

Corinth, like its neighboring city of Athens, symbolized Greek culture in its desire for wisdom and power. Paul must have been tempted to write to the Greeks as a Christian philosopher (1 Cor. 2:4). He was rejected on the irony of the cross, "to the Jews a stumbling block and to the Greeks foolishness" (1 Cor. 1:23). The foolishness of the gospel—indeed, its offensiveness to cultured Greeks—was indication of its power to save. To those who respond, "Christ is the power of God and the wisdom of God" (1 Cor. 1:24). According to Paul, the preaching of the cross is not a human teaching but a revelation of the Spirit, who makes known the mind of Christ (1 Cor. 2:10–16). The centrality of the cross overcomes all divisions within the church.

Since many of the problems arising in Corinth concerned behavior and morals, Paul majored on ethical advice in his correspondence. The leading principle he uses is that "all things are lawful for me, but not all things are helpful" (1 Cor. 6:12; 10:23). Christians ought to use their freedom not for self-advantage, but for the glory of God and the good of their neighbors. This principle goes beyond legislating simple "do's and don'ts." Instead, it cultivates a mature and responsible faith which will provide guidance for every moral problem.

First Corinthians is also important because of its teaching on the gifts of the Spirit (chap. 12) and the resurrection of the dead (chap. 15). Paul recognized a variety of gifts (12:4–10), but insisted that "one and the same Spirit" gives them. The body consists of different parts, but remains one organism. Likewise, Christ's body of believers consists of members with different gifts, each given by the one Spirit.

First Corinthians 15 is our earliest record of the resurrection in the New Testament. Unless Christ has been resurrected, Paul maintained, the faith of Christians is empty (15:12–19). As death came through Adam, so new life comes through Christ (15:21, 45). The resurrection of Jesus is a "firstfruits" (15:20) of the victory to come. Because of the resurrection the believer can confess, "O death, where is your sting?" (15:55).

Second Corinthians is probably best known for its teaching on Christian ministry. Chapters 4 and 5 are unrivaled for their beauty of expression and grandeur of thought. Paul marvels at the treasure of the gospel which God entrusts to human servants. Indeed, the weakness of the servant only highlights the message of salvation (4:1–15). This message finds its most famous expression in 2 Corinthians 5:17: "If anyone is in Christ, he is a new creation; old things have passed away; behold, all things have become new." The voltage of this truth transforms Christian messengers into ambassadors for Christ.

SPECIAL CONSIDERATIONS

As in the case with the resurrection, Corinthians also contains the earliest record of the Lord's Supper (1 Cor. 11:23–26). The immortal last words of Christ, "This cup is the new covenant in my blood" (11:24–25), recall His past death and anticipate His future return.

First Corinthians also contains one of the best-known chapters in the New Testament. In poetic cadence Paul proclaims "the more excellent way" of *agape* (chap. 13). Love is not merely a feeling, but an attitude committed to patience, hope, and stability in the face of problems. Such love will outlast the world itself. Agape love is the greatest characteristic of the Christian life.

An ancient carving, from Capernaum, showing a cup surrounded by clusters of grapes—perfect imagery for a miracle involving wine. (Todd Bolen, bibleplaces.com)

The Epistle to the Galatians

This is a brief but energetic letter from the apostle Paul to the Christians of Galatia. Galatians is one of Paul's most commanding epistles; its importance far exceeds its size. It provides valuable information about Paul's life between his conversion and missionary journeys (1:11—2:14). Beyond its autobiographical value, however, Galatians ranks as one of Paul's great epistles; in it he forcefully proclaims the doctrine of justification by faith alone. Martin Luther, the Reformer, claimed Galatians as "my epistle." So wedded was Luther to Galatians, both in interest and temperament, that, together they shaped the course of the Reformation. Galatians has been called the "Magna Carta of Christian Liberty." The peals of its liberating truth have thundered down through the centuries, calling men and women to new life by the grace of God.

STRUCTURE OF THE EPISTLE

Galatians falls into three sections, each two chapters long. The first third of the letter is a defense of Paul's apostleship and gospel (chaps. 1—2). The middle section (chaps. 3—4) is devoted to the question of salvation. In it Paul uses a variety of means—logic (3:15–20), quotations from the Old Testament (3:7–14), metaphor (4:1–6), personal authority (4:12–20), and allegory (4:21–31)—to argue that salvation comes not through obeying the Mosaic law, but by receiving the grace of God through faith. The third section of Galatians concerns the consequences of saving faith (chaps. 5—6). The Christian is free to love (5:1–15); the Holy Spirit produces fruit in his life (5:16–26); and the needs of others lay a rightful claim on his life (6:1–10). Paul concludes by summing up the main points of the letter (6:11–16), along with a closing admonition that he bears the marks of Jesus in his body (6:17), and a blessing (6:18).

AUTHORSHIP AND DATE

No epistle in the New Testament has better claim to come from Paul than does Galatians. The epistle bears his name (1:1), tells his story (1:11—2:14), and expounds the truth that occupied his life—justification by faith in Jesus Christ (2:16).

The date of the epistle is less certain. It depends on another question: To whom is the epistle addressed? This question is difficult because the word *Galatia* (1:2) is ambiguous. Ethnically, the word refers to a people of Celtic stock living in northern Asia Minor. Politically, however, it refers to the region throughout central Asia Minor, including various districts in the south, that were annexed to Galatia when it was made a province by the Romans in 25 B.C. It is impossible to say for sure which use of the term Paul intended, although the broader political usage seems more probable.

Paul was well-acquainted with southern Galatia (Acts 13–14; 16:1–5), and we have no certain evidence that he ever visited northern Galatia (unless Acts 16:6 and 18:23 refer to that area).

Moreover, it seems unlikely that Paul would have addressed the Galatians in such a direct way unless he enjoyed a close relationship with them. These reasons indicate that the people to whom the letter was addressed probably lived in southern Galatia. If this is so, it probably was written before the Council of Jerusalem (Acts 15). If it had already occurred (about A.D. 49), Paul would undoubtedly have cited that decision of that council since it agreed with the thrust of his argument in the epistle. If this is so, Galatians may be Paul's earliest (surviving) epistle, written perhaps in A.D. 48.

If, on the other hand, "Galatia" refers to the northern ethnic region, which Paul could not have visited before his second (Acts 16:6) or third (Acts 18:23) missionary journeys, the letter could not have been written before the mid-fifties. But this viewpoint seems less likely to be true.

HISTORICAL SETTING

After Paul had evangelized the churches of Galatia, he received disturbing news that they were falling away from the gospel he had taught them (1:6). Certain religious activists had visited Galatia after Paul's departure, persuading the Christians there that the gospel presented by Paul was insufficient for salvation (1:7). In addition to faith in Jesus Christ, they insisted that a person must be circumcised according to the law of Moses (5:12) and must keep the Sabbath and other Jewish holy days (4:10), including the Jewish ceremonial law (5:3). These "troublers" (1:7), as Paul calls them, may have included some Gnostic ideas (4:3, 9) in their teachings. These teachers are sometimes referred to as Judaizers, since they taught that both faith and works—belief in Jesus and obedience to the Law—are necessary for salvation.

A Concise Outline of
Galatians

Iconium was a major city in South Galatia. Paul and Barnabus preached here; now, the modern city of Konya rests on the same site. (Todd Bolen, bibleplaces.com)

THEOLOGICAL CONTRIBUTION

News of the troublers' "perversion of the gospel" (1:7) was distressing to Paul. Paul quickly rose to the Judaizers' challenge and produced this letter. From the outset he was ready for battle; he abandoned his customary introduction and plunged immediately into the battle with the Judaizers. The Judaizers had suggested that Paul was an inferior apostle, if one at all, and that his gospel was not authoritative (1:10). Paul countered with an impassioned defense of his conversion (1:11–17) and of his approval by the leaders of the church at Jerusalem (1:18—2:10). Indeed, the gospel that Paul had delivered to the Galatians was not his own, nor was he taught it; but it came "through the revelation of Jesus Christ" (1:11–12). Those who presumed to change it were meddling with the very plan of God (1:7–8).

God's plan is that Jews and Gentiles are justified before God by faith alone. This plan can be traced to the beginning of Israel's history, for Abraham, "believed God, and it was accounted to him for righteousness" (3:6; Gen. 15:6). The Law, which did not come until 430 years after Abraham (3:17), was never intended to replace justification by faith. Rather, the law was to teach us of our need for Christ (3:24–25). Christ, therefore, is the fulfillment of the promise to Abraham.

The result of justification by grace through faith is freedom. Paul appealed to the Galatians to stand fast in their freedom, and not get "entangled again with a yoke of bondage [that is, the Mosaic law]" (5:1). Christian freedom is not an excuse to gratify one's lower nature; rather, it is an opportunity to love one another (5:13; 6:7–10). Such freedom does not insulate one from life's struggles. Indeed, it may intensify the battle between the Spirit and the flesh. Nevertheless, the flesh (the lower nature) has been crucified with Christ (2:20); and, as a consequence, the Spirit will bear its fruit—such as love, joy and peace—in the life of the believer (5:22–23).

SPECIAL CONSIDERATIONS

The letter to the Galatians was written in a spirit of inspired agitation. For Paul, the issue was not whether a person was circumcised, but whether he had become "a new creation" (6:15). If Paul had not been successful in his argument for justification by faith alone, Christianity would have remained a sect within Judaism, rather than becoming the universal way of salvation. Galatians, therefore, is not only Luther's epistle; it is the epistle of every believer who confesses with Paul:

"I have been crucified with Christ; it is no longer I who live, but Christ lives in me; and the life which I now live in the flesh I live by faith in the Son of God, who love me and gave Himself for me" (Gal. 2:20).

The Epistle to the Ephesians

Ephesians is one of four shorter epistles written by the apostle Paul while he was in prison, the others being Philippians, Colossians, and Philemon. Ephesians shares many similarities in style and content with Colossians; it may have been written about the same time and delivered by the same person.

In the Epistle to the Ephesians, Paul is transported to the limits of language in order to describe the enthroned Christ who is Lord of the church, the world, and the entire created order. As the ascended Lord, Christ is completing what He began in His earthly ministry, by means of His now "extended body," the church. Christ's goal is to fill all things with Himself and bring all things to Himself.

This statue shows Paul with a real sword—not quite what he referred to in Ephesians 6:17 as the "sword of the Spirit, which is the word of God" (NKJV).
(William L. Krewson, bibleplaces.com)

STRUCTURE OF THE EPISTLE

Ephesians divides naturally into two halves: a lofty theological section (chaps. 1—3), and a section of ethical appeal and application (chaps. 4—6).

Paul begins by greeting his readers and assuring them that they have been blessed with God's gracious favor—redemption in Christ—from before the foundation of the world (1:1–14). Paul then prays that God may grant them an even greater measure of spiritual wisdom and revelation (1:15–23). Chapter 2 begins with perhaps the clearest statement of salvation by grace through faith in all the Bible (2:1–10). Although the Ephesians were once alienated from God, now they are reconciled both to God and to one another by Christ, who is "our peace" (2:11–22). Paul was made an apostle to proclaim the "mystery of Christ"—the inexhaustible riches of the gospel to the Gentiles (3:1–13). Paul brings the first half of the epistle to a close with a prayer that the Ephesians may understand the depth of Christ's love (3:14–19). A benediction concludes the doctrinal section (3:20–21).

An appeal to adapt one's life to one's faith (4:1) marks the transition to the second half of the epistle. The Christian fellowship should pattern itself after the unity of the Godhead (4:1–16), and the Christian should pattern himself after the example of Christ (4:17—5:20): as a new person in Christ he should walk in love, light, and wisdom. Paul cites Christ's relationship with the church as a model for wives and husbands (5:22–33), children and parents (6:1–4), and servants and masters (6:5–9). The epistle ends with an appeal to put on the whole armor of God and to stand against the forces of evil (6:10–20), followed by final greetings (6:21–24).

AUTHORSHIP AND DATE

Ephesians bears the name of Paul (1:1; 3:1), and it sets forth many of the great Pauline themes, such as justification by faith (2:1–10) and the body of Christ (4:15–16). Nevertheless, Ephesians has a number of notable differences from the undisputed letters of Paul. We know, for instance, that Paul spent three years in Ephesus (Acts 19:1–40), and it is clear that the Ephesians cherished his ministry among them (Acts 20:17–38). Strangely, however, Paul writes to the Ephesians as though they knew of his ministry only by hearsay (3:2). Moreover, with the exception of Tychicus (6:21), Paul mentions no one by name in Ephesians. Because of the impersonal nature of the epistle, plus the fact that it contains a number of words and phrases not characteristic of Paul, some scholars suspect that Ephesians was written by someone other than the apostle Paul.

Although this is possible, it is not likely. If Ephesians were not written by Paul, then it was written by someone who understood Paul's thinking as well as the apostle himself. Moreover, it is unlikely that a person capable of writing Ephesians could have remained unknown to the church. Many scholars have resolved the problems of authorship by suggesting that while Ephesians was indeed written by Paul, it was intended as a circular letter, or "open letter," to a number of communities surrounding Ephesus.

In the oldest manuscripts of the epistle, the phrase "in Ephesus" (1:1) is absent. Perhaps this phrase was omitted to leave space in copies of the letter for the insertion of different place names. Paul is known to have used circular letters on occasion (Col. 4:16), and the circular theory would account for the general tone of the letter.

If Paul was the author of Ephesians, then he probably wrote it about the same time as the Epistle to the Colossians. Both Ephesians and Colossians agree to a large extent in style and content. Both these letters were also delivered by Tychicus (Eph. 6:21; Col. 4:7). Furthermore, Paul was in prison at the time, presumably in Rome. This would suggest a date in the late 50s or early 60s.

A Concise Outline of
Ephesians

I. The Position of the Christian

II. The Practice of the Christian

A first-century Ephesian statue of Artemis, one of the Olympian gods worshipped by the Ephesians in Paul's day. (Todd Bolen, bibleplaces.com)

HISTORICAL SETTING

The general nature of Ephesians makes it difficult to determine the specific circumstances that gave rise to the epistle. It is clear, however, that the recipients were Gentiles (3:1) who were estranged from citizenship in the kingdom of Israel (2:11). Now, thanks to the gracious gift of God, they enjoy the spiritual blessings that come from Christ.

THEOLOGICAL CONTRIBUTION

The theme of Ephesians is the relationship between the heavenly Lord Jesus Christ and His earthly body, the church. Christ now reigns "far above all principality and power and might and dominion" (1:21) and has "put all things under His feet" (1:22). Exalted though He is, He has not drifted off into the heavens and forgotten His people. Rather, so fully does He identify with the church that He considers it His body, which He fills with His presence (1:23; 3:19; 4:10).

The marriage relationship between husband and wife is a beautiful analogy for expressing Christ's love, sacrifice, and lordship over the church (5:22–32). The enthroned Christ has reinvested Himself in the hearts of believers through faith (3:17) so they can marvel at His love. Absolutely nothing exists beyond His redeeming reach (1:10; 3:18; 4:9).

Christ's bond with His church is also portrayed in the oneness of believers. Those who were once "far off" and separated from God "have been made near by the blood of Christ" (2:13). In fact, believers are now raised with Christ and seated with Him in the heavenly places (2:5–6). Since believers are with Him, they are accordingly to be like Him—"endeavoring to keep the unity of the Spirit in the bond of peace" (4:3). "He [Christ] Himself is our peace" (2:14), says Paul, and He removes the walls and barriers that formerly divided Jews and Gentiles, and draws them together in one Spirit to the Father (2:14–22).

Having spoken of these marvelous spiritual blessings, Paul then appeals to believers "to have a walk worthy of the calling with which you were called" (4:1). This appeal is a helpful insight on Christian ethics. Rather than setting down laws and regulations, Paul says, in effect, *Let your life be a credit to the One who called you.* The Christian is set free by Christ; yet he is responsible for Christ. Paul makes several statements about how believers can honor Christ (4:17—5:9), but the goal is not to earn merit through morality. Instead of looking for nice people, Paul envisions new persons, the "perfect person," remade according to the stature of Christ Himself (4:13). This "mature manhood" (RSV) could refer to the desired, and still unattained, unity of the church.

SPECIAL CONSIDERATIONS

The term *heavenly places* (1:3; 1:20; 2:6; 3:10; 6:12) is not the same as heaven, for in one instance Paul speaks of "spiritual hosts of wickedness in the heavenly places" (6:12). "Heavenly places" implies the unseen, spiritual world beyond our physical sense. It is the region where the most difficult, and yet authentic, Christian discipleship is lived out—the world of decisions, attitudes, temptations, and commitments. It is the battleground of good and evil (6:12).

Christ has raised believers to the heavenly places with the assurance that the One in whom we hope is more powerful, real, and eternal than the forces of chaos and destruction which threaten our world.

The Epistle to the Philippians

This short epistle was written by the apostle Paul while he was in prison. Paul founded the church at Philippi (Acts 16:12–40). Throughout his life the Philippians held a special place in his heart, Paul writes to them with affection, and the epistle breathes a note of joy throughout. When Paul first came to Philippi, he was thrown in jail. In the deep of the night, bound and beaten, he sang a hymn to God (Acts 16:25). A decade later Paul was again in prison, and he still was celebrating the Christian's joy in the midst of suffering, "Rejoice in the Lord always. Again I will say, rejoice!" (Phil. 4:4).

STRUCTURE OF THE EPISTLE

Paul begins the epistle by giving thanks for the love of the Philippians and by praying for its increase (1:1–11). Even though Paul is in prison, the gospel is not confined; on the contrary, it is increasing. Whether Paul lives or dies, "Christ is preached" (1:18); and this results in salvation (1:12–26). Following these reflections, Paul introduces a series of exhortations: to remain faithful in suffering (1:27–30); to remain considerate of others, as Jesus Christ was (2:1–11); and to avoid evil and live blamelessly (2:12–18).

Paul then turns to news of two companions. Once a decision has been reached about his trial, Paul will send Timothy to the Philippians with the news (2:19–24). For the present, he is sending back Epaphroditus, who had brought the Philippians's gift to him and who in the meantime has been critically ill (2:25–30). In chapter 3 Paul discusses the differences between true and false righteousness. Whereas the Judaizers would say, "If you do not live rightly you will not be saved," Paul teaches, "If you do not live rightly you have not been saved."

The final chapter summarizes several miscellaneous matters. Paul exhorts quarrelsome church members to rise above their differences (4:2–5). He also leaves two important lessons, on substituting thankful prayer for anxiety (4:6–7), and on the characteristics of a noble and godly life (4:8–9) he concludes with thanks for the Philippians' gift and includes final greetings (4:10–23).

AUTHORSHIP AND DATE

There can be little doubt that Philippians comes from Paul. The entire epistle bears the stamp of his language and style; the setting pictures Paul's imprisonments; and the recipients correspond with what we know of the church of Philippi.

During his second missionary journey, in A.D. 49, Paul sensed the Lord called him to visit Macedonia (Acts 16:6–10). At Philippi he founded the first Christian congregation on European soil (Acts 16:11–40). A lifelong supportive relationship developed between the Philippians and Paul (Phil. 1:5; 4:15). He visited the church again during his third missionary journey (Acts 20:1, 6).

At the time he wrote Philippians, Paul was in prison awaiting trial (Phil. 1:7). The Philippian Christians came to Paul's aid by sending a gift, perhaps of money, through Epaphroditus (4:18). During his stay with Paul, Epaphroditus fell desperately ill. But he recovered and Paul sent him back to Philippi. Paul sent this letter with Epaphroditus to relieve the anxiety of the Philippians over their beloved fellow worker (2:25–30).

HISTORICAL SETTING

The location of Paul's imprisonment has been long debated. Much can be said for Ephesus or Caesarea but still more for Rome. Paul refers to "the whole palace guard" (1:13), and he even sends greetings from "Caesar's household" (4:22). These references suggest Rome, as does the description of his confinement in 1:12–18. This description is similar to Clement's description of Paul's Roman imprisonment written near the close of the first century. Paul also considers the possibility of his death (1:23). This prospect was more likely toward the end of his life in Rome than earlier. The epistle, therefore, should probably be dated about A.D. 60.

THEOLOGICAL CONTRIBUTION

The focus of Paul's thoughts in this epistle is the Christ-centered life, the hallmark of which is joy. Paul has surrendered everything to Christ and can say, "For to me, to live is Christ" (1:1), "to be a prisoner

A Concise Outline of

Philippians

I. Paul's Account of His Present Circumstances

1. Paul's Prayer of Thanksgiving	1:1–11
2. Paul's Afflictions Promote the Gospel	1:12–18
3. Paul's Afflictions Exalt the Lord	1:19–26
4. Paul's Exhortation to the Afflicted	1:27–30

II. Paul's Appeal to Have the Mind of Christ

1. Paul's Exhortation to Humility	2:1–4
2. Christ's Example of Humility	2:5–16
3. Paul's Example of Humility	2:17–18
4. Timothy's Example of Humility	2:19–24
5. Epaphroditus's Example of Humility	2:25–30

III. Paul's Appeal to Have the Knowledge of Christ

1. Warning Against Confidence in the Flesh	3:1–9
2. Exhortation to Know Christ	3:10–16
3. Warning Against Living for the Flesh	3:17–21

IV. Paul's Appeal to Have the Peace of Christ

1. Peace with the Brethren	4:1–3
2. Peace with the Lord	4:4–9
3. Peace in All Circumstances	4:10–19
4. Conclusion	4:20–23

This primitive prison room in Philippi could be the one in which Paul and Silas were freed by an earthquake, as told in the 23rd chapter of Acts. (Todd Bolen, bibleplaces.com)

for Christ" (1:13), "to live and die in Christ" (1:20), "and to give up all to win Christ" (3:7–8). Christ has laid hold of Paul (3:12), and Paul's sole passion is to glorify Christ (3:8–9). Paul longs for his experience of Christ to be repeated in the lives of the Philippians. He prays that they will abound in the love of Christ (1:9), will lay hold of the mind of Christ (2:5–11) and, like himself, will know the experience of Christ—His sufferings, death, and resurrection (3:10–11).

Because Paul's only motive is to "know Him" (3:10), he shares in the power of Christ and "can do all things through Christ," who is his joy and strength (4:13).

Several times in the epistle Paul exhorts the Philippians to translate their relationship with Christ into daily life by being "like-minded" with Christ or "setting their minds on Christ." In the face of opposition, Paul tells them to "stand fast . . . with one mind striving together for the faith of the gospel" (1:27). Differences between Christians can be overcome when the parties have "the same mind in the Lord" (4:2). Paul exhorts the believers to set their minds on the high calling of God in Jesus Christ (3:14–15) and to meditate on whatever is true, noble, just, pure, lovely, and of good report (4:8). To have the mind of Christ to see life from Christ's perspective and to act toward other people with the intentions of Christ.

SPECIAL CONSIDERATIONS

Nowhere is the mind of Christ presented to the Christian more strongly than in Philippians 2:1–11. Appealing to the Philippians to be of "one mind" (2:2) in pursuing humility, Paul cites the example of the incarnation of God in Jesus Christ. "Let this mind be in you which was also in Christ Jesus" (2:5), urges Paul. Unlike Adam, who sought to be equal with God (Gen. 3:5), Christ did not try to grasp for equality with God. Instead, being God, he poured Himself out and took upon Himself the form of a slave, to the point of dying the death of a common criminal. "Therefore," glories Paul, "God . . . has highly exalted Him, and given Him the name which is above every name" (2:9).

This is the Christ whose attitude and intention all believers must share. To be identified with Christ in humility and obedience is the noblest achievement to which anyone can aspire.

The Epistle to the Colossians

This is another epistle written by Paul while he was in prison. The Epistle to the Colossians focuses on the person and work of Jesus Christ. It reaches heights of expression that rival anything said of Christ elsewhere in Scripture. Colossians shares many similiarities in style and content with Ephesians. Colossians probably was written as a companion to the brief letter to Philemon (compare Col. 4:7–13 and Philem. 12, 24).

Known simply as "carcer" ("prison") in Paul's day, this building is now known as the Mamertine Prison. By tradition it is the one in which Paul wrote the Book of Colossians. (Todd Bolen, bibleplaces.com)

STRUCTURE OF THE EPISTLE

Colossians is neatly divided, as are most of Paul's epistles, into doctrinal (chaps. 1—2) and practical (chaps. 3—4) sections. Following the opening address (1:1–2), Paul expresses his thankfulness for the faith, love, hope, and example of the Colossians (1:3–8). He then develops a majestic hymn to Christ, emphasizing His role in both creation and redemption (1:9–23). In light of the surpassing worth of Christ and His work, Paul willingly accepts the obligation to proclaim Christ and to suffer for Him (1:24—2:5). He also appeals to the Colossians to take root in Christ rather than in confusing speculations (2:6–23).

In the second section, Paul urges the Colossian Christians to mold their behavior to fit their beliefs. Since believers share in Christ's resurrection (3:1–4), Paul encourages them to continue living to please God. He urges them to "put to death" various vices and to "put on" the character of Christ (3:5–17). True Christianity also works itself out in social relationships between wives and husbands (3:18–19), children and parents (3:20–21), and slaves and masters (3:22—4:1). Paul concludes with a note on witnessing to unbelievers (4:2–6) and his customary greetings (3:7–18).

AUTHORSHIP AND DATE

Colossians was written by Paul (and Timothy, 1:1) to a Christian community (perhaps "house churches," 1:2; 4:15) which he had not visited (2:1). Paul had established a resident ministry in Ephesus, 100 miles west of Colossae. For more than two years the influence of his ministry reached "all who dwelt in Asia" (Acts 19:10). Epaphras must have heard Paul in Ephesus and then carried the gospel to Colossae (1:7–8; 4:12–13).

Paul wrote the epistle from prison (4:3, 10, 18), but he did not indicate where he was imprisoned. Caesarea and Ephesus have been suggested, but the most probable place is Rome (Acts 28:30). This would date the epistle in the late 50s or early 60s.

HISTORICAL SETTING

False teaching had taken root in Colossae. This teaching combined Jewish observances (2:16) and pagan speculation (2:8); it is possible this resulted in an early form of Gnosticism. This teaching pretended to add to or improve upon the gospel that, indirectly at least, had come from Paul. Some of the additions Paul mentions are feasts and observances, some of them related to astrology (2:16), plus a list of rules (2:20). These practices were then included within a philosophy in which angels played a leading role (2:18); Paul calls this philosophy "the basic principles of the world" (2:8).

THEOLOGICAL CONTRIBUTION

Paul unmasks the false teaching as "empty deceit . . . of men" (2:8), having the "appearance of wisdom" (2:23), but useless in fact. He declared that the addition of such things dilutes rather than strengthens the faith (2:20).

But Paul does more than denounce false teaching. The best medicine is a firm grip on who Jesus Christ is and what He did for our salvation. In Christ "are hidden all the treasures of wisdom and knowledge" (2:3), and "in Him all fullness" dwells (1:19). In fact, "He is the image of the invisible God" (1:15). He has stripped every power opposed to Him (2:15), wiped out every accusation against us (2:14), and actually "reconciled all things to Himself" (1:20). He is not only head of the church (1:18); but He stands before all time and above every power and at the end of all history (1:16).

This beautiful epistle on the majesty of Jesus Christ speaks to us today as much as to the Colossians. It reminds us that Jesus Christ is sufficient for every need and is still the most powerful force in the world.

A Concise Outline of
Colossians

I. Supremacy of Christ in the Church

1. Introduction	1:1–14
2. The Preeminence of Christ	1:15—2:3
A. Christ Is Preeminent in Creation	1:15–18
B. Christ Is Preeminent in Redemption	1:19–23
C. Christ Is Preeminent in the Church	1:24—2:3
3. The Freedom in Christ	2:4–23
A. Freedom from Enticing Words	2:4–7
B. Freedom from Vain Philosophy	2:8–10
C. Freedom from the Judgment of Men	2:11–17
D. Freedom from Improper Worship	2:18–19
E. Freedom from the Doctrine of Men	2:20–23

II. Submission to Christ in the Church

1. The Position of the Believer	3:1–4
2. The Practice of the Believer	3:5—4:6
A. Put Off the Old Man	3:5–11
B. Put On the New Man	3:12–17
C. Personal Commands for Holiness	3:18—4:6
3. Conclusion	4:7–18

An entrance door leading into the Mamertine Prison, in Rome. Paul would have entered through a door very similar to this, if not the same one. (Todd Bolen, bibleplaces.com)

The First and Second Epistles to the Thessalonians

These two letters are among the first written by Paul. The major theological theme of 1 and 2 Thessalonians is the return of Christ to earth. Important as this theme is, however, the Thessalonian letters leave the reader wide awake to the responsibilities of the present, not gazing into the future. Both epistles aim to establish and strengthen a young church in a stormy setting (1 Thess. 3:2, 13; 2 Thess. 2:17; 3:3). In neither epistle does Paul fight any grave errors in the church. In both epistles, the reader feels the heartbeat of Paul the pastor as he identifies with a young congregation taking its first steps in faith.

Once a proud edifice, the Thessalonica forum still features several surviving arches and the remains of supporting walls. (Todd Bolen, bibleplaces.com)

STRUCTURE OF THE EPISTLES

Paul begins the first epistle by thanking God for the faith, hope, and love of the Thessalonians, and marveling that they have become "examples to all in Macedonia and Achaia" (chap. 1). Paul recalls his sacrificial labor for the gospel (2:1–12) and the suffering the Thessalonians endured (2:13–16). Longing to see them again (2:17—3:5), Paul exposes his relief and encouragement upon hearing Timothy's report of their well-being (3:6–10). He prays for their growth in the gospel (3:11–13).

In chapters 4 and 5 Paul addresses three concerns. He reminds his converts that in sexual matters a Christian must conduct himself differently from a pagan (4:1–8). He adds a gentle reminder to work diligently and thus earn the respect of "those who are outside" (non-Christians, 4:9–12). Paul then devotes extended consideration to the most pressing questions in Thessalonica, the Second Coming of Christ (4:13—5:11).

The first letter concludes with a number of memorable exhortations and a charge to read the epistle "to all the holy brethren" (5:12–28).

Second Thessalonians is both shorter and simpler than 1 Thessalonians. Paul follows a nearly identical opening (1:1) with an assurance that when Christ returns He will punish those who persecute the Thessalonians (chap. 1). Chapter 2 brings Paul to the purpose of the letter—to clarify and expand his teaching on the Second Coming. Certain signs will precede the return of Christ, in particular, an outbreaking of lawlessness, followed by the appearance of "the man of sin," or "lawless one" (Antichrist), who will escort to their doom those who have no love for the truth (2:1–12). In contrast to those who are perishing, believers can give thanks to God for their call to salvation (2:13–17).

Paul concludes by requesting the prayers of the Thessalonians (3:1–3) and encouraging idlers to earn their living rather than live off their neighbors (3:6–15). He ends with a benediction in his own hand (3:16–18).

AUTHORSHIP AND DATE

The vocabulary, style, and thought of the Thessalonian correspondence are genuinely Pauline. In 1 Thessalonians 2:1—3:10, Paul shares his point of view on some of the events described in Acts 16:16—18:7, thus supporting Luke's description of Paul's ministry in Acts. Both letters bear Paul's name as author (1 Thess. 1:1; 2 Thess. 1:1). Paul's co-workers, Silvanus (Silas) and Timothy, are both mentioned along with Paul in the opening greeting of both epistles.

It is possible to date the Thessalonian letters with some precision. Paul wrote both from Corinth (1 Thess. 1:1; 2 Thess. 1:1; Acts 18:5) while Gallio was proconsul (governor of a Roman province) of Achaia. We know from an inscription discovered at Delphi that Gallio ruled in Corinth from May, A.D. 51, to April, A.D. 52. If Paul spent 18 months in Corinth (Acts 18:11), and yet was brought to trial before Gallio (Acts 18:12–17), he must have arrived in Corinth before Gallio become proconsul. If he wrote to the Thessalonians shortly after leaving them, which seems probable, the letters would have to be dated in late A.D. 50 or early A.D. 51.

HISTORICAL SETTING

Paul founded the church at Thessalonica in A.D. 49 or 50 during his second missionary journey (Acts 17:1–9). The church consisted of a few Jewish converts and a larger number of former pagans (1 Thess. 1:9; Acts 17:4). Desiring not to handicap the young church, Paul worked at his own job as a tentmaker—and at some sacrifice to himself, he adds (1 Thess. 2:7–12)—twice receiving aid from the ever-faithful Philippians (Phil. 4:16).

| A Concise Outline of
First
Thessalonians | 1. Paul's Personal Reflections on
   the Thessalonians | 1:1—3:13 |
| | 2. Paul's Instructions to the Thessalonians | 4:1—5:28 |

A Concise Outline of **Second** **Thessalonians**	1. Paul's Encouragement in Persecution	1:1–12
	2. Paul's Explanation of the Day of the Lord	2:1–17
	3. Paul's Exhortation of the Church	3:1–18

Paul's stay in Thessalonica was cut short, however, when the Jews gathered some local troublemakers and accused him before the city fathers of "turning the world upside down" by favoring Jesus as king instead of Caesar (Acts 17:1–7). This accusation was no small matter; it was a matter of treason, which in the Roman Empire was punishable by death. Not surprisingly, an uproar broke out; and Paul was escorted out of town, leaving Timothy to patch up the work (Acts 17:10, 15). Separated so suddenly from the infant church, Paul describes his feelings as one who had been "orphaned" (Greek text, 1 Thess. 2:17).

Once he was safe in Athens, Paul sent Timothy (who apparently had since rejoined him) back to Thessalonica to strengthen and encourage the believers (1 Thess. 3:2). When Timothy returned to Paul, who had since moved on to Corinth (Acts 18:1–5), he brought news of the love and faith of the Thessalonians. Paul was greatly relieved at this news.

In response to Timothy's encouraging report, Paul wrote the first epistle to Thessalonica. Evidently the Thessalonians were unsettled over the Second Coming of Christ, because Paul discusses the issue in both letters. In the first letter he informs them that at Christ's coming the dead in Christ must be raised first, then the living (1 Thess. 4:13–18). Since the time of Christ's coming will be as secretive as a thief's, Paul admonishes the believers to keep alert and be watchful (1 Thess. 5:1–11). Some, however, may have been too watchful, assuming that Christ would come any moment. In his second letter, therefore, Paul reminds the Thessalonians that certain events, namely, a rebellion against faith and the appearance of a "lawless one" (Antichrist), must happen before Christ returns (2 Thess. 2:8–9). In the meantime, Paul tells them to get back to work: "If anyone will not work, neither shall he eat" (2 Thess. 3:10).

THEOLOGICAL CONTRIBUTION

Three themes appear in the Thessalonian correspondence: thanksgiving for their faith and example in the past; encouragement for those undergoing persecution in the present; and exhortation to further work and growth in the future.

Paul writes the epistles in the spirit of a true pastor. He is overjoyed with their enthusiastic response to the gospel (1 Thess. 1). He longs for the day when they will stand with him in the presence of the Lord Jesus (1 Thess. 2:19–20). At the same time, Paul is grieved at unjust charges leveled against him that his gospel is more talk than action (1 Thess. 1:5; 2:1–8). Cut off from his flock, he is anxious for their well-being (1 Thess. 2:17—3:5).

Paul compares himself to a nursing mother caring for her children (1 Thess. 2:7) and to a father working on behalf of his family (1 Thess. 2:9–12). He gives himself body and soul to the Thessalonians (1 Thess. 2:8) and dares to hope that they will give themselves likewise to God (1 Thess. 5:23). Such is the concern of a dedicated pastor.

With pastoral concern, Paul addresses the question of the return of Christ. He reminds them that confidence in Christ's return enables believers to be patient (1 Thess. 1:10), creates hope and joy (1 Thess. 2:19), and spurs them to pursue pure and blameless lives (1 Thess. 3:13; 5:23). Uncertainty as to when Christ will return demands alertness and watchfulness (1 Thess. 5:1–11), but the certainty that he will return makes present trials and sufferings bearable (2 Thess. 1:3–11). His return will come as a surprise, like a thief in the night (1 Thess. 5:4); but it will not be disorderly: those who have died first in Christ will proceed first to Christ, followed by the living, "And thus we shall always be with the Lord" (1 Thess. 4:17).

SPECIAL CONSIDERATIONS

There is no mention in either letter of a Millennium, followed by a battle between Christ and Satan (Rev. 20:1–10). Paul simply states that at His coming Jesus will destroy the "lawless one" and will judge the unrighteous (2 Thess. 2:8–12). The end, however, will follow widespread rebellion and abandonment of the faith. Paul appeals for them to be levelheaded during the time of trouble and warns Christians not to despair when they see the Antichrist pretending to be God (2 Thess. 2:4). The schemes of "the man of sin" or "man of lawlessness" (2 Thess. 2:6, NIV) will be restrained until his treachery is fully disclosed, and then Christ will utterly destroy him (2 Thess. 2:8).

On the subject of the Second Coming, Paul assures the Thessalonians what will happen, but not when it will happen. His discussion throughout is dominated by an emphasis on practical living, rather than on speculation. The best way to prepare for Christ's return is to live faithfully and obediently now.

This huge brick-and-mortar arch was erected in what was then the middle of the city of Thessalonica, in A.D. 305, to celebrate a Roman military victory. (William L. Krewson, bibleplaces.com)

The First and Second Epistles to Timothy

The two letters of the apostle Paul to Timothy along with the Epistle to Titus, form a trilogy called the Pastoral Epistles. These letters are called Pastoral Epistles because they deal with matters affecting pastors and congregations. In these letters to Timothy, Paul's primary concern is to instruct his young associate to guard the spiritual heritage that he has received (1 Tim. 6:20; 2 Tim. 1:12–14; 2:2) by establishing sound doctrine in the church.

Most scholars believe Timothy was living in Lystra when Paul first encountered him. If so, this is the view toward the south that Timothy would have known. (Todd Bolen, bibleplaces.com)

STRUCTURE OF THE EPISTLES

First Timothy begins with a warning against false doctrine (1:1–11) and a reminder of God's mercy, illustrated by Paul's experience of salvation (1:12–20). This is followed by instructions on church practices: on prayer (2:1–7), on public worship (2:8–15), and on the qualifications of bishops (3:1–7) and deacons (3:8–13). A salute to Christ concludes the section (3:14–16).

Continuing with Timothy's responsibilities, Paul warns that false teachers will infiltrate the church (4:1–5). He instructs Timothy on the characteristics of a fit minister of the gospel (4:6–16), as well as his duties toward others (5:1–2), widows (5:3–16), elders (5:17–25), and servants (6:1–2). Following another warning against false teaching (6:3–10), Paul exhorts Timothy to "fight the good fight of faith" (6:11–21).

After a brief greeting (1:1–2), the second Epistle to Timothy begins by recalling Timothy's spiritual heritage (1:3–7), exhorting him to be strong under adversity and to keep the faith (1:8–18). In chapter 2 Paul uses the metaphors of solder (2:3–4), farmer (2:6), experienced worker (2:15), and household utensils (2:20–21) as models for Timothy to imitate as a strong and worthy servant of the gospel. Paul declares what people will be like in the last days (3:1–9), although Timothy can take encouragement in the face of adversity from Paul's example and from the Scriptures (3:10–17).

The final chapter of 2 Timothy takes on a solemn tone as Paul appeals to Timothy to press forward in fulfilling his pastoral calling (4:1–5). Writing in the shadow of his impending death (4:6–8), Paul closes with personal greetings (4:9–22).

AUTHORSHIP AND DATE

The authorship and date of the Pastoral Epistles remain an unresolved question in New Testament studies. On the one hand, the epistles bear the name of Paul as author (1 Tim. 1:1; 2 Tim. 1:1; Titus 1:1) and preserve personal references to him (1 Tim. 1:3; 12–16; 2 Tim. 4:9–22; Titus 1:5; 3:12–13). Other considerations, however, pose problems for Paul's authorship of the Pastorals. These can be listed under the following categories:

Historical—The Book of Acts makes no mention of a situation in which Paul goes to Macedonia, leaving Timothy behind in Ephesus (1 Tim. 1:3) or Titus in Crete (Titus 1:5).

Ecclesiastical—The description of church order in the Pastorals (for example, bishops, elders, deacons, and an enlistment of widows) appears rather advanced for Paul's time.

Theological—Some ideas in the Pastorals differ from Paul's thought. For example, "faith" (Titus 1:13; 2:2) suggests orthodoxy or "sound doctrine," rather than a saving relationship with Christ; "righteousness" (Titus 3:5) suggests "good deeds," rather than a status of being justified before God. Likewise, the understanding of law (1 Tim. 1:8–11) differs from Paul's usual teaching on the subject (compare Rom. 3:19–20).

Literary—The vocabulary and style of the Pastorals differ from Paul's other writings. A significant number of words that appear in the Pastorals are not found in Paul's genuine letters, and the tone of the letters is uncharacteristically harsh at places (for example, Titus 1:12–13).

Each of these objections is not of equal weight, although taken as a whole they are impressive. If one assumes, as church tradition often has, then Paul was released following the Roman imprisonment mentioned in Acts 28 (2 Tim. 4:16) and later went to Spain (1 Clement 5, writing about A.D. 96), or revisited points eastward, many of the problems listed above are lessened. In this view, the circumstances of the Pastorals would fall after the events described in Acts. Thus, confronted by a rise in false teaching and by a need to increase church discipline and order, Paul could have written the Pastorals with

A Concise Outline of **First Timothy**	1. Paul's Charge Concerning Doctrine	1:1–20
	2. Paul's Charge Concerning Public Worship	2:1—3:16
	3. Paul's Charge Concerning False Teachers	4:1–16
	4. Paul's Charge Concerning Church Discipline	5:1–25
	5. Paul's Charge Concerning Pastoral Motives	6:1–21

| A Concise Outline of **Second Timothy** | 1. Persevere in Present Testings | 1:1—2:26 |
| | 2. Endure in Future Testings | 3:1—4:22 |

This is an inscribed stone from Lystra, Timothy's home town. In Timothy's day, Lystra would have been a Roman colony, subject to Roman law. (Todd Bolen, bibleplaces.com)

the help of a secretary who expressed Paul's ideas in somewhat un-Pauline ways. This would date the letters between Paul's first and second Roman imprisonments, or about A.D. 65.

Another theory of authorship dates the letters near the end of the first century. This theory suggests that an admirer of Paul wrote in Paul's style to address the problems of a growing church. This admirer may have even used notes or letters from the apostle.

HISTORICAL SETTING

First and Second Timothy differ in historical context. In the first epistle Paul writes from Macedonia to young Timothy (1 Tim. 4:12), who has been left in Ephesus to oversee the congregation (1 Tim. 1:3). The second epistle, also written to Timothy in Ephesus (2 Tim. 1:18), comes from Rome where Paul is undergoing a second (2 Tim. 4:16) and harsher imprisonment (2 Tim. 1:8, 16; 2:9). Paul is alone (except for Luke, 2 Tim. 4:11), and he knows the end of his life will come soon (2 Tim. 4:6). One can almost hear the plaintive echo of the apostle's voice as he bids Timothy to "come quickly before winter" (2 Tim. 4:9, 21).

The occasion for both epistles is much the same. Paul is deeply troubled by false teaching (1 Tim. 1:3–11; 2 Tim. 2:23) and apostasy (1 Tim. 1:6; 4:1; 2 Tim. 3:1–9) which endanger the church at Ephesus. He warns Timothy to beware of fables and endless genealogies (1 Tim. 1:4; 4:7; 2 Tim. 4:4), idle gossip (1 Tim. 5:13; 2 Tim. 2:16), rigid lifestyles based on the denial of things (1 Tim. 4:3), the snares of wealth (1 Tim. 6:9–10, 17–19), and religious speculations (1 Tim. 6:20). He warns that apostasy, in whatever form, will spread like cancer (2 Tim. 2:17). Paul urges Timothy to combat its malignant growth by teaching sound doctrine, promoting good works, and accepting one's share of suffering for the sake of the gospel (2 Tim. 1:8; 2:3, 11–13).

THEOLOGICAL CONTRIBUTION

The message of 1 and 2 Timothy can be summed up by words like *remember* (2 Tim. 2:8), *guard* (1 Tim. 6:20), *be strong* (2 Tim. 2:1), and *commit* (1 Tim. 1:18; 2:2). For Paul, the best medicine for false teaching and apostasy is "sound doctrine" (1 Tim. 1:10; 4:3). The gospel is a spiritual inheritance to be received from faithful witnesses and passed on to such (2 Tim. 2:2). It brings about wholeness or health (which is the meaning of "sound" in Greek), not only in belief, but also in good deeds. So vital is sound doctrine to the health of the church that it is something to be pursued (1 Tim. 6:11), fought for (1 Tim. 6:12), and even suffered for (2 Tim. 1:8; 2:3, 11–13).

SPECIAL CONSIDERATIONS

The Epistles to Timothy might be considered our earliest manual of church organization. Within them we find guidelines for the selection of church leaders (1 Tim. 3:1–13). They also reveal an awareness of the need for standard forms of expressing the faith. For example, the words, "This is a faithful saying," appear four times in the epistles (1 Tim. 1:15; 3:1; 4:9; 2 Tim. 2:11). Two creeds or perhaps hymns, also appear (1 Tim. 3:16; 2 Tim. 2:11–13). Finally, 2 Timothy presents the first (and only) pronouncement in the New Testament on the Bible as "Scripture" (referring to the Old Testament, 2 Tim. 3:14–17).

In Greek, the word for "inspiration" (2 Tim. 3:16) means "breathed into by God." As God breathed life into the written word, making it useful for teaching, reproof, and correction. Paul leaves us, therefore, not with a theory about Scripture, but with a description of its purpose and its power for salvation (2 Tim. 3:15).

The Epistle to Titus

First and Second Timothy and Titus are called the Pastoral Epistles because they deal with matters concerning pastors and congregations. They are the only letters of Paul addressed to individuals (Philemon is addressed "to the church in your house," 1:2). The purpose of the Epistle to Titus was to warn against false teaching and to provide guidance on sound doctrine and good works for one of Paul's younger associates.

There are 13 references to Titus in the Pauline Epistles. Obviously he was one of Paul's closest and most trusted companions. Paul spoke of this reliable and gifted associate as his "brother" (2 Cor. 2:13), his "partner and fellow worker" (2 Cor. 8:23), and his "son" (1:4). He praised Titus's character and conduct in 2 Corinthians 7:13–15 and 8:16–17.

A view of one of the natural harbors on the Island of Crete, where Paul left Titus behind to work with the Cretan churches. And, where Titus was living when his epistle from Paul arrived. (© 2007 JupiterImages Corporation)

STRUCTURE OF THE EPISTLE

Following an extended greeting (1:1–4), Paul advises Titus on the qualifications for church, elders or bishops (1:5–9) and warns against false teachers (1:10–16). He proceeds to list ideal characteristics of older men (2:1–2), older women (2:3–5), younger men (2:6–8), and slaves (2:9–10) in the church. The grace of God as it is shown in Jesus Christ, provides the foundation for such qualities of life (2:11–15). The final chapters lists ideal characteristics for Christians in society as a whole (3:1–2), again based on the goodness and grace of God (3:3–7); right beliefs thus lead to right actions (3:8–11). The letter closes with personal news and greetings (3:12–15).

AUTHORSHIP AND DATE

The circumstances were the same as those under which the apostle Paul wrote the letters to Timothy. The Pastorals were written during the fourth missionary tour between Paul's two Roman imprisonments. The date would be about A.D. 64–66.

HISTORICAL SETTING

The island of Crete is 156 miles long and up to 30 miles wide. A number of Jews from Crete were present in Jerusalem at the time of Peter's sermon on the Day of Pentecost (Acts 2:11). Some of them may have believed in Christ and introduced the gospel to their countrymen.

According to Titus 1:5, Paul left Titus on the island of Crete to continue establishing churches by appointing "elders in every city." As soon as Artemas or Tychicus relieved him, Titus was to meet Paul in Nicopolis (on the west coast of Greece) where the apostle planned to spend the winter (Titus 3:12).

The occasion for the letter was clear enough—to warn against false teachers (1:10–16). The precise nature of the teaching was less clear, although it included "Jewish fables," legalism, and disputes over genealogies (1:10, 14; 3:9–10). Paul urged Titus to avoid such traps, for anyone associated with them would get caught in his own schemes (3:11).

THEOLOGICAL CONTRIBUTION

Titus emphasizes sound doctrine (1:9; 2:8, 10) and challenges believers to good works (1:16; 2:14; 3:14). Paul summons Titus "to affirm constantly that those who have believed in God should be careful to maintain good works" (3:8). This letter will allow no separation between belief and action. Paul included three doctrinal sections in this letter to emphasize that proper belief gives the basis for proper behavior. We often hear it said that it makes no difference what we believe, as long as we do what is right. The truth, however, is that we become what we think, and all action is shaped by belief.

A Concise Outline of **Titus**		
I. Appoint Elders		
1. Introduction		1:1–4
2. Ordain Qualified Elders		1:5–9
3. Rebuke False Teachers		1:10–16
II. Set Things in Order		
1. Speak Sound Doctrine		2:1–15
2. Maintain Good Works		3:1–11
3. Conclusion		3:12–15

The Epistle to Philemon

Philemon is the shortest and most personal of Paul's epistles. It tells the story of the conversion of a runaway slave, Onesimus, and the appeal to his owner, Philemon, to accept him back. The letter is warm and masterful, reminding us that the presence of Christ drastically changes every relationship in life.

A cold water stream very close to where Philemon lived, in Colossae. Perhaps it even looked exactly like this in the first century A.D. (Todd Bolen, bibleplaces.com)

STRUCTURE OF THE EPISTLE

Philemon consists of one chapter of 25 verses. A greeting, addressed to Philemon and the church which meets in his house (vv. 1–3), is followed by four verses in praise of Philemon's love and faith (vv. 4–7). Paul comes to his point in verses 8–16, where he tells of his affection for Onesimus and entreats Philemon to receive him back as a "beloved brother" (v. 16). Paul is so confident that Philemon will do even more than he asks that he offers to pay any expenses Philemon has incurred and asks him to prepare the guest room for a forthcoming visit (vv. 17–22). Final greetings conclude the letter (vv. 23–25).

AUTHORSHIP, DATE, AND HISTORICAL SETTING

The Epistle to Philemon is a companion to the Epistle to the Colossians. Both were written during Paul's imprisonment, probably in Rome (Col. 4:18; Philem. 9). They contain the names of the same greeters (compare Col. 4:7–17) with Philem. 23–25) and were delivered at the same time by Tychicus and Onesimus (Col. 4:7–9; Philem. 12). The date for the two letters is the late 50s or early 60s. Two other Pauline epistles were also written from prison during this time. They are the Epistles to the Ephesians and Philippians.

Philemon was a resident of Colossae (Philem. 1–2) and a convert of Paul (v. 19), perhaps through an encounter with Paul in Ephesus during Paul's third missionary journey. Philemon's house was large enough to serve as the meeting place for the church there (v. 2). He was benevolent to other believers (vv. 5–7), and his son Archippus evidently held a position of leadership in the church (see Col. 4:17; Philem. 2). Philemon may have had other slaves in addition to Onesimus, and he was not alone as a slave owner among the Colossian believers (Col. 4:1). Thus, this letter and his response would provide guidelines for other master-slave relationships.

THEOLOGICAL CONTRIBUTION

The Epistle to Philemon is a lesson in the art of Christian relationships. No finer example of "speaking the truth in love" (Eph. 4:15) exists than this beautiful letter. While it was Philemon's legal right in the ancient world to punish or even kill a runaway slave, Paul hoped—indeed expected (v. 19)—that Philemon would receive Onesimus back as a brother in the Lord, not as a slave (v. 16). From beginning to end Paul addresses Philemon as a trusted friend rather than as an adversary (v. 22); he appeals to the best in his character (vv. 4–7, 13–14, 17, 21). In spite of Paul's subtle pressures for Philemon to restore Onesimus, he is careful not to force Philemon to do what is right; he helps them choose it for himself (vv. 8–9, 14).

SPECIAL CONSIDERATIONS

Although Paul never, so far as we know, called for an end to slavery; the Epistle to Philemon laid the ax at the root of that cruel and deformed institution—and to every way of treating individuals as property instead of persons. If there is "one God and Father of all" (Eph. 4:6), and if all are debtors to Him (Rom. 3:21–26), then no person can look on another person as something to be used for his own purpose. In Christ that person has become a "beloved brother."

A Concise Outline of **Philemon**	1. The Prayer of Thanksgiving for Philemon	1–7
	2. The Petition of Paul for Onesimus	8–16
	3. The Promise of Paul to Philemon	17–25

A modern view of Colossae, from its acropolis. Philemon certainly would not have recognized the buildings in the background. (Todd Bolen, bibleplaces.com)

CHAPTER 9

GENERAL EPISTLES (LETTERS)

These eight epistles exert an influence out of proportion to their length, which is less than ten percent of the New Testament. They supplement the 13 Pauline Epistles by offering different perspectives on the richness of Christian truth. Each of the five authors—James, Peter, John, Jude, and the author of Hebrews—has a distinctive contribution to make from his own point of view. These writers provide a sweeping portrait of the Christian life in which the total is greater than the sum of the parts.

The problem of heretical teachings reached alarming proportions in the early church. Most of the general epistles deal firmly with these dangerous doctrines. The churches of this time were threatened not only by external opposition and persecution, but also by internal attacks from false prophets.

The term *general epistle* appears in the King James Version titles of James, 1 and 2 Peter, 1 John, and Jude, but it was not used in the oldest manuscripts. These epistles were not addressed to specific churches or individuals, and they came to be known as the general or "catholic" (universal) epistles. The epistles of 2 and 3 John are also included in this group, although they are addressed to specific people. Because of this problem, and because Hebrews is not regarded as a general epistle, it would be safe to designate these eight epistles as the non-Pauline Epistles (assuming that Paul did not write Hebrews; see Hebrews article under Authorship and Date).

These epistles were usually placed before the Pauline Epistles in Greek manuscripts, but early catalogs of the canonical New Testament books generally listed them in the order Christians are familiar with today. This seems preferable because of their date, length, and content. It is also an indication of the delay most of these letters experienced in being admitted into the canon. All but the first epistles of Peter and John were disputed for a period of time for various reasons before being officially recognized as authoritative. This illustrates the great care taken by the early church in distinguishing between false and genuine books.

The Book of Revelation is the culmination of the New Testament as well as the Bible as a whole, since it completes the story begun in Genesis. This is the only New Testament book that concentrates on prophecy.

The chart on page 226 gives an overview of the general epistles by showing the individual books that make up this section of the New Testament. These books are then discussed in detail in their appropriate order to give you a better understanding of this important major division of God's Word.

Books of the Minor Prophets

Book	Summary
Hebrews	A presentation of Jesus Christ as High Priest, addressed to Jewish believers
James	Practical instructions for applied Christianity
1 Peter	Encouragement and comfort from Peter to suffering Christians
2 Peter	Peter's warning against false teachers
1 John	John's reminder of the full humanity of Christ
2 John	John's letter of encouragement and approval
3 John	John's personal note of appreciation to Gaius
Jude	A strong warning against false teachers
Revelation	An encouraging prophecy of the final days and God's ultimate triumph

The Epistle to the Hebrews

Hebrews is a letter written by an unknown Christian to show how Jesus Christ had replaced Judaism as God's perfect revelation of Himself. Hebrews begins with a marvelous tribute to the person of Christ (1:1–3). Throughout the epistle, the author weaves warning with doctrine to encourage his readers to hold fast to Jesus as the great High Priest of God. The author makes extensive use of Old Testament quotations and images to show that Jesus is the supreme Mediator between God and man. Because of its literary style and the careful way it develops its argument, Hebrews reads more like an essay than a personal letter.

The remains of an ancient mosaic floor in Corinth, one of the cities to which its unknown author might have addressed the Book of Hebrews. (Todd Bolen, bibleplaces.com)

STRUCTURE OF THE EPISTLE

The letter begins by showing that Jesus is the Son of God and, therefore, is superior to angels (1:1—2:18) and to Moses (3:1–6). This section contains a warning not to lose the blessings, or "rest," of God because of unbelief, as the Israelites did under Moses (3:7—4:13).

The second section of the letter (4:14—10:18) attempts to show that Christ is the perfect High Priest because of His unmatched compassion for people and complete obedience to God (4:14—5:10). Following a second warning against renouncing the faith (5:11—6:20), the author then describes Jesus as a priest according to the order of Melchizedek (7:1–28). The emphasis of Melchizedek, who is mentioned only twice in the Old Testament (Gen. 14:18–20; Ps. 110:4), may seem far-fetched to modern readers. However, there is a good reason for comparing Christ to Melchizedek; it is to show that Melchizedek, unlike Aaron, was unique. He had no predecessors and no successors. He was, therefore, a priest forever, like the Son of God (7:1–3). As a consequence of His being like Melchizedek, Jesus inaugurated a new and better covenant (8:1–13) because His sacrifice of Himself replaces the sacrifice of "bulls and goats" (9:1—10:18).

The final section of the epistle appeals to the readers not to give up the benefits of Christ's work as High Priest (10:19—13:17). In an attempt to offset spiritual erosion (10:19–39), the author recalls the heroes of faith (11:1–40). Let their example, he says, encourage the readers to "run with endurance the race that is set before us" (12:1). The letter closes with various applications of faith to practical living (13:1–19), a benediction (13:20–21), and greetings (13:22–25).

AUTHORSHIP AND DATE

Other than 1 John, the Epistle to the Hebrews is the only letter in the New Testament with no greeting or identification of its author. Although the King James Version entitles the book "The Epistle of Paul the Apostle to the Hebrews," this title stems from later manuscripts which came to include it. It is highly doubtful, however, that Paul wrote Hebrews. The language, vocabulary, and style of Hebrews differ from Paul's genuine letters. Such typically Pauline expressions as "Christ Jesus," "in Christ," or "the resurrection" are all but absent in Hebrews. When Hebrews and Paul treat the same subjects, they often approach them differently. For example, in Hebrews "law" means the ritual law, whereas for Paul it means the moral law; "faith" in Hebrew is belief in the trustworthiness of God, where for Paul it is a personal commitment to a living Lord. The author of Hebrews sounds more like a Platonic philosopher than Paul when he speaks of the old covenant (8:5) and the law (10:1) as "shadows" of their originals.

There has been no shortage of suggestions concerning who the author may have been. The list includes Luke, Priscilla, Aquila, Clement of Rome, Silvanus, and Philip. Perhaps the two most likely candidates are Apollos and Barnabas. Both have characteristics which commend them, Apollos because he was an eloquent Alexandrian Jew who knew the Scriptures well (Acts 18:24), and Barnabas because he was a Levite (Acts 4:36). As with the others, however, this suggestion is only a possibility. The writer of the epistle remains anonymous.

One can only make an educated guess about the date and place of composition. Since the author's purpose was to show that Christianity had replaced Judaism, to have been able to point to the destruction of the Temple (which occurred in A.D. 70) as an indication that God had no further use for it would have been a decisive argument. Since the author does not make use of this information, it is reasonable to assume the destruction of the Temple had not happened yet, thus dating the letter sometime before A.D. 70. The only clue about where Hebrews was written is found in the closing remark, "Those from Italy greet you" (13:24). This may indicate that the author was writing from Italy, presumably Rome.

A Concise Outline of
Hebrews

I. Superiority of Christ's Person

1. The Superiority of Christ over the Prophets   1:1–3
2. The Superiority of Christ over the Angels   1:4—2:18
3. The Superiority of Christ over Moses   3:1—4:13

II. Superiority of Christ's Work

1. The Superiority of Christ's Priesthood   4:14—7:28
2. The Superiority of Christ's Covenant   8:1–13
3. The Superiority of Christ's Sanctuary
   and Sacrifice   9:1—10:18

III. Superiority of the Christian's Walk of Faith

1. A Call to Full Assurance of Faith   10:19—11:40
2. Endurance of Faith   12:1–29
3. A Call to Love   13:1–17
4. Conclusion   13:18–25

This slightly chipped basalt grindstone comes from Qumran, one of three or four ancient settlements in which the original recipients of the Book of Hebrews might have lived. (Todd Bolen, bibleplaces.com)

HISTORICAL SETTING

The repeated use of Old Testament quotations and images in Hebrews suggests that the people who received this book had a Jewish background. The repeated warnings against spiritual unbelief reveal that the readers of this epistle were on the verge of renouncing the Christian faith and returning to their former Jewish ways (2:1–4; 3:7—4:14; 5:12—6:20; 10:19–39; 12:12–29). Negligence in good deeds and sloppy attendance at worship services (10:23–25) were evidence of a cooling in their faith. In an effort to rekindle the readers's flame of commitment to Christ, the author urges his readers not to retreat from persecution (10:32–39), but to hasten to the front lines. He calls for a new exodus (3:7–19); he holds before them examples of a pilgrim faith (chap. 11); and he tells them not to "draw back" (10:39), but to "go forth to Him, outside the camp, bearing His reproach" (13:13).

THEOLOGICAL CONTRIBUTION

In a spirit similar to Stephen's defense before the Jewish Sanhedrin (Acts 7), Hebrews sets out to show that Christianity is superior to Judaism because of the person of Jesus Christ, who is the Son of God, the Great High Priest, and the Author of salvation. Christ stands as the peak of revelation, superior to angels (1:1—2:9) and to Moses (3:1–6). He is the Son of God, the reflection of God's own glory and, indeed, the very character and essence of God (1:3). Whatever revelations appeared before Jesus were but shadows or outlines of what was to appear in Him.

Christ is also the Great High Priest (4:14). Whereas earthly priests inherited their office, Christ was appointed by the direct call of God (5:5–6). Whereas earthly Christ, who has no successors, is a priest forever, according to the order of Melchizedek (7:17). Whereas earthly priests ministered within temples made with human hands, Christ ministers within the true sanctuary—the eternal house of God (8:2; 9:24). Whereas earthly priests offered animals sacrificed for their sins as well as for those of the people, Christ offered the one perfect sacrifice which never need be offered again—His sinless self (5:3; 10:4–14).

As the unique Son of God who made the supreme sacrifice of Himself to God, Jesus is described by the author of Hebrews as the "author of their salvation" (2:10), the "finisher of our faith" (12:2), and the "great Shepherd of the sheep" (13:20). Christ saves His people *from* sin and death, and He saves them *for* fellowship with God. In Hebrews salvation is called the "rest" of God (4:1), "eternal inheritance" (9:15), the "Most Holy Place" (9:12). These three emphases—Jesus as Son, High Priest, and Savior—are drawn together in one key passage:

"Though He was a *Son*, yet He learned obedience by the things which He suffered. And having been perfected, He became the *author of eternal salvation* to all who obey Him, called by God as *High Priest* 'according to the order of Melchizedek'" (5:8–10).

In light of Christ's preeminence, the author urges his readers to hold fast to the true confession and endure whatever suffering or reproach is necessary on its behalf (4:14; 6:18; 13:13).

SPECIAL CONSIDERATIONS

Two passages in Hebrews often trouble Christians. In 6:4–6 and 10:26 the author warns that if a person willingly turns from fellowship with Christ, he can no longer be forgiven. The intent of these verses is to cause Christians to remember the great cost of God's grace and to take their profession of faith seriously. The intent of these verses is not to cause believers to doubt their salvation. There is no example in the Bible where anyone who desired the forgiveness of Christ was denied it.

The backbone of this epistle is the finality of Christ for salvation. This wonderful truth is no less urgent for us today than it was for the original readers of Hebrews. The rise of cults, with their deceptive claims of security, is but one example of the many things that appeal for our ultimate loyalty. Hebrews reminds us that "Jesus Christ is the same yesterday, today, and forever" (13:8). Because of His perfect sacrifice of Himself, He is still the only Mediator between us and God. Only Jesus is the true Author of our salvation.

A view into the Holy of Holies inside the Tabernacle, showing the golden cherubim, with wings touching, atop the Ark of the Covenant. (Matt Floreen, bibleplaces.com)

The Epistle of James

This book is characterized by its hard-hitting, practical religion. The epistle reads like a sermon and, except for a brief introduction, has none of the traits of an ancient letter. Each of the five chapters is packed with pointed illustrations and reminders designed to motivate the wills and hearts of believers to grasp a truth once taught by Jesus: *A tree is known by its fruit* (Matt. 12:33).

In speaking of the sun in James 1:11, James almost certainly would have remembered a sunset or two like this one, over the Sea of Galilee. (Matt Floreen, bibleplaces.com)

STRUCTURE OF THE EPISTLE

One cannot separate what James says from the way he says it. James believes that his message is better caught than taught. He uses a terse style punctuated with vivid analogies and crisp commands to achieve this purpose. His metaphors and similes come primarily from nature (1:11, 17; 3:3, 11, 12; 4:14; 5:2, 7). James must have been a man of practical bent, for he leaves no doubt in the minds of his readers about the points he wishes to make; every second verse contains an imperative or command. Although he takes up varying themes at random, each can be oriented around his central purpose, that "faith by itself, if it does not have works, is dead" (2:17).

AUTHORSHIP AND DATE

The author identifies himself as "James, a servant of God and of the Lord Jesus Christ" (1:1). At least five personalities named James appear in the New Testament. None has a stronger claim to being the author of this epistle than James, the brother of the Lord. Apparently neither a disciple nor an apostle during Jesus's lifetime, he is first mentioned in Mark 6:3, where he is listed as the first (oldest) of Jesus' four younger brothers. After the ascension of Jesus, James emerged as a leader of the church in Jerusalem (Acts 15:13; 1 Cor. 15:7; Gal. 2:9)—a position he must have occupied for nearly 30 years, until his martyrdom, according to church tradition.

This James is probably the author of the epistle that bears his name. He refers to himself simply as "James," with no explanation added. This indicates he was well-known to his readers. He calls himself a "servant" rather than an apostle; and he begins the epistle with the same "greetings" (1:1) with which he begins the apostolic decree following the Council of Jerusalem (Acts 15:23). These factors suggest one and the same James, the brother of the Lord.

The most important argument against authorship by the Lord's brother is that the Epistle of James was virtually unknown in the ancient church until the third century. It remains an unsolved mystery why it was neglected and then accepted into the New Testament canon at a relatively late date if James, the Lord's brother, were its author. Although this consideration cannot be overlooked, it does not rule out the Lord's brother as the most probable author of the epistle.

The Epistle of James gives few hints by which it might be dated. Estimates range from A.D. 45 to 150, depending on how one regards its authorship. If James, the Lord's brother, is its author, then it must have been written before A.D. 62 (the approximate time of his death). The epistle may have been written after Paul's letters were in circulation, because James's emphasis on works may be intended to offset Paul's emphasis on faith. This would date the epistle around A.D. 60.

HISTORICAL SETTING

James addressed the epistle "to the twelve tribes which are scattered abroad" (1:1). This implies a readership of Jewish Christians living outside Palestine. Elsewhere in the epistle, however, James refers to hired field labor (5:4), and this locates his audience inside Palestine. In James's day, only in Palestine did farmers employ hired rather than slave labor, as was customary elsewhere. The epistle makes frequent references or allusions to the Old Testament. Its style and language are reminiscent of the Old Testament, especially wisdom literature and the prophet Amos. All these factors indicate that James was writing to persons of Jewish-Christian background. His emphasis was on the essentials of obedient living in accordance with the true intent of the law of God.

A Concise Outline of
James

I. The Test of Faith

1. The Purpose of Tests	1:1–12
2. The Source of Temptations	1:13–18

II. The Characteristics of Faith

1. Faith Obeys the Word	1:19–27
2. Faith Removes Discriminations	2:1–13
3. Faith Proves Itself by Works	2:14–26
4. Faith Controls the Tongue	3:1–12
5. Faith Produces Wisdom	3:13–18
6. Faith Produces Humility	4:1–12
7. Faith Produces Dependence on God	4:13—5:6

III. The Triumph of Faith

1. Faith Endures, Awaiting Christ's Return	5:7–12
2. Faith Prays for the Afflicted	5:13–18
3. Faith Confronts the Erring Brother	5:19–20

It is quite possible that James was speaking of Samarian wildflowers exactly like these, in James 1:20. (Todd Bolen, bibleplaces.com)

THEOLOGICAL CONTRIBUTION

The Epistle of James is a sturdy, compact letter on practical religion. For James, the acid test of true religion is in the doing rather than in the hearing, "believing," or speaking. James exalts genuineness of faith, and is quick to encourage the lowly that God gives grace to the humble (4:6), wisdom to the ignorant (1:5), salvation to the sinner (1:21), and the kingdom to the poor (2:5). He is equally quick to condemn counterfeit religion which would substitute theory for practice, and he does so with biting sarcasm. True religion is moral religion and social religion. True religion is *doing* the right thing in one's everyday affairs. In this respect James echoes clearly the ethical teaching of Jesus, especially as it is recorded in the Sermon on the Mount (Matt. 5—7). "Not everyone who says to Me, 'Lord, Lord,' shall enter the kingdom of heaven, but he who does the will of My Father in heaven" (Matt 7:21).

SPECIAL CONSIDERATIONS

Some Bible scholars suggest that James and Paul differ in their views on the saving significance of faith and works. Paul states, "A man is justified by faith apart from the deeds of the law" (Rom. 3:28), and James says, "A man is justified by works, and not by faith only" (James 2:19). A closer reading of the two however, reveals that they differ more in their definition of faith than in its essence. James writes to readers who are inclined to interpret faith as mere intellectual acknowledgement (2:19). As a consequence he stresses that a faith which does not affect life is not saving faith; hence, his emphasis on works. Actually, this is quite close to Paul's understanding. For Paul, faith is the entrusting of one's whole life to God through Christ, with the result that one's life becomes renewed with the "fruit of the Spirit" (Gal. 5:22).

In his discussion of the balance between faith and conduct, James might have been thinking of a first-century scale, such as this. (Todd Bolen, bibleplaces.com)

The First and Second Epistles of Peter

These two epistles bear the name of "Peter, an apostle of Jesus Christ" (1 Pet. 1:1) and "Simon Peter, a servant and apostle of Jesus Christ" (2 Pet. 1:1), though otherwise they have little in common.

First Peter, the longer of the two epistles, is written in fine Greek and refers frequently to the Old Testament. It is an epistle for the down-hearted, written to give encouragement in times of trial and disappointment. First Peter anchors the Christian's hope not on logic or persuasion, but on the matchless sacrifice of Jesus Christ, who "suffered for us, leaving us an example, that you should follow His steps" (2:21).

In contrast to 1 Peter, 2 Peter is briefer and written in a forced style. It rails against false teachers, while reminding believers of their election by God and assuring them of Christ's return.

A bronze statue of Peter, standing in front of the traditional site of his house in Capernaum. (Todd Bolen, bibleplaces.com)

STRUCTURE OF THE EPISTLES

Following a greeting (1:1–2), 1 Peter begins on a positive note, praising God for the blessings of a "living hope" which He has reserved for believers (1:3–12). This doxology of praise sets a triumphant tone for the remainder of the letter, which can be divided into three parts: blessings, duties, and trials. The blessings extend from 1:3 to 2:10. Because of the "inheritance incorruptible and undefiled . . . reserved in heaven for you" (1:4), Peter calls on his readers to live a life holy and blameless, reminding them that they are a "holy nation, His [God's] own special people" (2:9).

The second part of 1 Peter extends from 2:11 to 3:22. This section consists of guidance for social duties. The Christian's lifestyle ought be a testimony to non-believers (2:11–17); slaves ought to obey their masters—even unjust ones—bearing their humiliation as Christ bore His (2:18–25); the silent example of a Christian wife has great effect on a non-Christian husband (3:1–6); Christian husbands are to treat their wives as joint-heirs of the grace of life (3:7). In all things, let a blameless lifestyle bring shame on whoever would show opposition (3:8–22).

The third and final part of 1 Peter addresses the questions of trials (4:1—5:11). In light of the nearness of the end, Christians must be "good stewards of the manifold grace of God" (4:1–11). They can rejoice in sharing Christ's sufferings because of the glory that awaits them (4:12–19). In their pastoral duties, church elders are to follow the example of Jesus, who perfects, establishes, and strengthens the flock (5:1–11). The epistle closes with mention of Silvanus, the secretary who wrote the letter, and with greetings from "Babylon" (5:12–14).

Second Peter begins with a greeting (1:1–2), enjoining believers, because they have been chosen by God, to develop noble characters (1:3–11). Recognizing that his own death is near, the author sees in the transfiguration of Jesus a forecast of the brilliant day when Christ will come again (1:16–21). Chapter 2 is a condensation of material from the Letter of Jude, condemning false teachers and prophets. The final chapter deals with the future coming of the Lord and the reasons for its delay (3:1–18).

AUTHORSHIP AND DATE

First Peter identifies its author as "Peter, an apostle of Jesus Christ" (1:1). His frequent references to Christ's suffering (2:21–24; 3:18; 4:1; 5:1) show that the profile of the Suffering Servant was etched deeply upon his memory. He calls Mark his "son" (5:13), recalling his affection for the young man and family mentioned in Acts 12:12. These facts lead naturally to the assumption that the apostle Peter wrote this letter.

Authorship of the epistle by the apostle Peter has been challenged, however, on the following grounds:

- no official persecutions of the church took place during Peter's lifetime;
- the epistle echoes some of Paul's teachings; and
- the literary quality of the Greek seems too refined for a Galilean fisherman.

Valid as these objections are, they do not seriously challenge Peter's authorship of the epistle. The sufferings mentioned in the epistle need not refer to official persecutions, which did not begin until the time of the Roman emperor Domitian (A.D. 81–96), but to earlier local incidents. The last two questions are neatly resolved by recognizing the role that Silvanus (5:12) played in composing the epistle.

As a former associate of the apostle Paul, and as one who doubtlessly came to the Greek language as a native, Silvanus may have played an important role in bringing this epistle to completion. We might say of 1 Peter, that the idea came from Peter, but the design from Silvanus. The reference to "Babylon"

A Concise Outline of
First Peter

I. Salvation of the Believer

1. Salutation	1:1–2
2. Salvation of the Believer	1:3–12
3. Sanctification of the Believer	1:13—2:12

II. Submission of the Believer

1. Submission to the Government	2:13–17
2. Submission in Business	2:18–25
3. Submission in Marriage	3:1–8
4. Submission in All of Life	3:9–12

III. Suffering of the Believer

1. Conduct in Suffering	3:13–17
2. Christ's Example of Suffering	3:18—4:6
3. Commands in Suffering	4:7–19
4. Minister in Suffering	5:1–9
5. Benediction	5:10–14

A Concise Outline of
Second Peter

I. Cultivation of Christian Character

1. Salutation	1:1–2
2. Growth in Christ	1:3–14
3. Grounds of Belief	1:15–21

II. Condemnation of False Teachers

1. Danger of False Teachers	2:1–3
2. Destruction of False Teachers	2:4–9
3. Description of False Teachers	2:10–22

III. Confidences of Christ's Return

1. Mockery in the Last Days	3:1–7
2. Manifestation of the Day of the Lord	3:8–10
3. Maturity in View of the Day of the Lord	3:11–18

(5:13), a common image for civil power opposed to God, indicates that the epistle was written from Rome.

The question of authorship of 2 Peter is more difficult. Although the epistle claims to come from the apostle Peter (1:1; 3:1–2), who witnessed the transfiguration of Christ (1:18) and at the time of writing was nearing his death (1:14), few scholars believe Peter wrote the letter. Reasons for this judgment stem from a number of factors.

The style of 2 Peter is inferior to that of 1 Peter. Nearly the whole of Jude 4–18 has been reproduced in the second chapter; if Jude were not written until late in the first century, then 2 Peter obviously could not have been written before it. Again, 2 Peter refers to Paul's epistles as a part of "the Scriptures" (3:16). This suggests a date, perhaps early in the second century, when Paul's epistles had reached a level of authority in the early church. Finally, the Epistle of 2 Peter seems to have been unknown to the early church, and it was one of the last books to be included in the New Testament.

These factors suggest that 2 Peter was written by an anonymous author but attributed by someone to the apostle Peter in order to assure a hearing for a message in a time well after Peter's death.

HISTORICAL SETTING

First Peter is addressed to Christians living in "Pontus, Galatia, Cappadocia, Asia, and Bithynia" (1:1)—places in the northern and western parts of Asia Minor (modern Turkey). The readers appear to be have been Gentiles (1:14, 18; 2:10; 4:3), although they probably had not been evangelized by Peter himself (1:12). The letter was obviously written to believers undergoing trials and persecutions, to give them courage in the face of their adversities (5:10).

Since it makes no mention of its audience, 2 Peter was probably intended for a general readership. Its primary purpose was to combat false teachers. Widespread in the ancient world was the view that sparks of eternal light lay trapped within the prisons of human bodies. These sparks of light, which longed to return to their primal home, could be liberated only by *gnosis*, or knowledge. Second Peter uses "knowledge" (1:5–6; 3:18) to show that only in Jesus Christ is the knowledge of God and salvation fully revealed. These false teachers also must have been critical of the delay in Christ's return. To this challenge the author devoted the entire third chapter.

THEOLOGICAL CONTRIBUTION

First Peter was written by one who sensed the triumphant outcome of God's purpose for the world (1:4). The triumph of the future depends in no way on what we have done but on the resurrection of Jesus Christ. Because God has raised Jesus from the dead, God is deserving of praise; for "His abundant mercy has begotten us again to a living hope" (1:3).

The unshakableness of our hope in Jesus Christ, which awaits us in heaven, resounds like a clap of thunder throughout this epistle. Because Christ has been raised from the dead, His suffering and death have meaning. The believer can gain courage in present adversity by looking to the example of Christ in His suffering. We have a sure hope for the future because of Christ's resurrection. This truly is a "living hope," for it is one we can live by, even in the midst of "various trials" (1:6).

If 1 Peter is an epistle of hope, the accent falls not on wishful thinking, but on present help. No biblical writer shows the connection between faith and conduct in a clearer manner than does Peter. "Conduct," in fact, is a key word in this epistle (1:15, 17–18; 2:12; 3:1–2, 16). For Peter, practice is not simply the most important thing; it is the only thing.

Peter's emphasis on behavior, however, is not an appeal to some vague sense of "moral goodness" in people. The conduct Peter describes is the result of a life reclaimed by the perfect power of Jesus Christ.

Christ has redeemed believers (1:18–19); Christ upholds and guides them (1:8; 2:25); and Christ will reward them (5:4). Christ is both the model and goal of the redeemed life. Consequently, believers may move forward on the pilgrim way, confident that the end will rise up to meet them with joy and salvation (2:11; 4:13–14).

Jesus said, "Blessed are those who are persecuted for righteousness's sake, for theirs is the kingdom of heaven" (Matt. 5:10). There is no better commentary on this Beatitude than the Epistle of 1 Peter. Here is no pale, tight-lipped religion. Rather, "living from the end" cultivates an abiding joy even in the trials of the present. Here, too, Jesus is our sole help and our sure Lord, "who for the joy that was set before Him endured the cross" (Heb. 12:2).

Second Peter shifts the emphasis from a hope by which one can live to a hope on which one can count. The epistle speaks to the assurance of salvation in chapter 1 by making the extraordinary claim that Christians are "partakers of the divine nature" (1:4). The second chapter deals with false teachers. The unique contribution of 2 Peter, however, comes in chapter 3.

In chapter 3 the "day of the Lord" (3:10) or the "day of God" (3:12) breaks through the gloom of the doubters who taunt the hopeful: "Where is the promise of His coming? For since the fathers fell asleep, all things continue as they were from the beginning of creation" (3:4). Such persons may be assured that God does not delay in coming because He lacks power or concern. Rather, what the unfaithful interpret as delay, the faithful know to be patience; for God is "not willing that any should perish but that all should come to repentance" (3:9).

A view of the remains of the house Peter actually lived in. Much evidence suggests that this truly is the correct site. (Todd Bolen, bibleplaces.com)

The First, Second, and Third Epistles of John

These epistles read like a love letter from an elderly saint who writes from long years of experience with Christ and His message. Although unnamed, the author addressed his readers intimately as "little children" (1 John 2:1, 18, 28; 3:7, 18; 4:4; 5:21) and "beloved" (1 John 3:2, 21: 4:1, 7, 11). His tone changes, however, when he bears down on his opponents for making light of the bodily existence of Jesus (1 John 2:18–23; 4:1–3, 20).

The "tell" in the background of this photo is the truncated hill, an excavation site for the city of Colossae, to which John is believed to have addressed one or more of his three letters. (Todd Bolen, bibleplaces.com)

STRUCTURE OF THE EPISTLES

None of the three epistles yields naturally to a structural outline. First John begins with an uncompromising testimony to the bodily existence of Jesus (1:1–4). Since God is light, fellowship with God must result in confession of our sin before Christ, our forgiveness, and our "walking in the light" (1:5—2:2). To know Christ is to keep His commandments, or "to walk just as He walked" (2:6). One cannot be in the light and hate his brother or love the world (2:7–17).

The presence of antichrists, who deny that Jesus is the Christ, is a sign of the end times. But true believers rest secure in the "anointing" of the Holy Spirit which they have from Christ (2:18–27). Since God is righteous, believers are to be righteous in their lives. When the Lord returns, His children will be like Him (2:28—3:3). Whoever abides in Christ does not continue to sin habitually or constantly (3:4–10).

Christian love is not something merely to talk about, but to do (3:11–18). Active love gives us confidence before God (3:19–24). A person must examine various spiritual manifestations to determine if they are of God; only teachers who confess that Jesus Christ has come in the flesh are of God (4:1–6). In His love God sent His Son as an atoning sacrifice for sin. As a consequence we are to love one another (4:7–21).

Faith is victory over the world (5:1–5), and there is a threefold witness to faith: the Holy Spirit, the water (baptism), and the blood (Holy Communion) (5:6–12). Christians may be assured that God hears and grants their requests (5:13–15). The letter concludes with assurance that the Son of God is sufficient to save (5:18–21).

Second John identifies its author as "the elder" and those to whom the letter is written as "the elect lady and her children" (v. 1). The "lady" and "children" are personified ways of referring to the church and its believers. Like 3 John, the letter has the character of a note from the elder, reminding his "children" to walk in truth and love (vv. 4–6). The elder also draws attention to false teachers who deny the bodily existence of Jesus Christ, and he warns against receiving them (vv. 7–11). He hopes to visit the church soon (vv. 12–13).

Third John, also from "the elder," is addressed to Gaius (v. 1), who has demonstrated his loyalty by offering hospitality to traveling missionaries (vv. 2–8). A certain Diotrephes had previously ignored a letter from the elder, and he receives some stiff criticism for doing so (vv. 9–11). In contrast to Diotrephes, a certain Demetrius is highly commended (v. 12). The elder expresses his hope to visit the church soon (vv. 13–15).

AUTHORSHIP AND DATE

Although these three epistles were written by an anonymous author, he wrote affectionately to his readers as "little children" and referred to himself as "the elder" (2 John 1; 3 John 1). He must have been well-known and well-loved by those to whom he wrote.

Eusebius, an early church leader, mentions a John the elder (presbyter) who was a disciple and companion of John the apostle in Ephesus. Although we cannot say for sure, it may be that John the elder is the same "elder" mentioned in 2 and 3 John. If so, then he wrote the Gospel of John as well as these three letters; the style and content in each are very similar.

The inclusion of personal testimony (1 John 1:1–4) indicates that John the elder depended directly on the testimony of the apostle John in writing these documents. The epistles were probably written from Ephesus toward the close of the first century A.D.

HISTORICAL SETTING

First John has none of the usual features of an epistle: no salutation or identification of author; no greetings; and no references to persons, places, or events. Ironically, although its format is impersonal, like a

A Concise Outline of
First John

I. The Basis of Fellowship

1. Introduction	1:1–4
2. The Conditions for Fellowship	1:5—2:14
3. The Cautions to Fellowship	2:15–27

II. The Behavior of Fellowship

1. Characteristics of Fellowship	2:28—5:3
2. Consequences of Fellowship	5:4–21

A Concise Outline of
Second John

I. Abide in God's Commandments

1. Salutation	1–3
2. Walk in Truth	4
3. Walk in Love	5–6

II. Abide Not with False Teachers

1. Doctrine of the False Teachers	7–9
2. Avoid the False Teachers	10–11
3. Benediction	12–13

A Concise Outline of
Third John

I. Commendation of Gaius

1. Salutation	1
2. Godliness of Gaius	2–4
3. Generosity of Gaius	5–8

II. The Condemnation of Diotrephes

1. Pride of Diotrephes	9–11
2. Praise for Demetrius	12
3. Benediction	13–14

sermon or treatise, its tone is warm and personal. This suggests that it was written to a broad audience (probably in and around Ephesus) that was very dear to the author.

All three epistles were written to deepen the spiritual life of the churches while guarding against false teaching. False teachers had arisen within the church, although the content of their teaching betrayed that they were not part of the church (1 John 2:19; 4:4). John fears that such a splinter group will lead true believers astray (1 John 2:26–27; 3:7; 2 John 7). He calls them "antichrists" (1 John 2:18, 22; 4:3; 2 John 7) for denying that Jesus had come in the flesh (1 John 4:1–13; 2 John 7; also 1 John 2:18–25; 4:15).

By emphasizing the divine nature of Jesus, the false teachers appeared to be Christians; but they showed their true colors by denying that God became a true human in Jesus. Claiming to have the Spirit of God, they were actually false prophets (1 John 4:1–6).

THEOLOGICAL CONTRIBUTION

Like the Gospel of John, the epistles of John are built on the foundation blocks of love, truth, sin, world, life, light, and the Holy Spirit. The epistles of John emphasize the great themes of knowing, believing, walking, and abiding. These words seem simple on the surface. But in the hands of one who had pondered the mystery and meaning of Jesus' existence in human form, they yield many deep truths.

For John, the keystone in the arch of the gospel is that God has appeared in human form (1 John 1:1–4). The Incarnation is life (1 John 1:2); and this life is available in the Son of God, Jesus Christ (1 John 5:11): "He who has the Son has life, he who does not have the Son of God does not have life" (1 John 5:12). The message of life is the alpha (1 John 1:2) and omega (1 John 5:20), the beginning and the end, of the epistle.

Jesus Christ has transferred us from death to life (1 John 3:14) by destroying the works of the devil (1 John 3:8). God made Jesus a "propitiation" (1 John 2:2; 4:10) in order to forgive sin (1 John 1:7–9; 2:12; 3:5). As a propitiation, Jesus is our "Advocate with the Father" (1 John 2:1) who takes away the guilt of our wrongdoing and gives us confidence to approach the judgment seat of God (1 John 2:28; 4:17). Jesus Christ is both the Son of God and the bearer of sin, the eternal demonstration of the love of God.

For John, love is not a feeling or attitude towards others. God is love (1 John 4:8, 16), and He acts in love on our behalf (1 John 4:9–10). Love, therefore, is something a person does, by keeping God's commandments (1 John 2:2–5; 5:3), "in deed and in truth" (1 John 3:18), and, above all, by loving others (1 John 2:9–11; 3:10). John declares that it is hypocritical to profess love for God and to show hatred toward others (1 John 4:20). The love of God does not take us out of this world. Rather, it draws us into fellowship with God (1 John 1:3) and with others (1 John 1:7).

Fellowship with God is realized by knowing God and abiding in Him. To *know* God (the verb occurs 25 times in the epistles) is not to know about God, but to be joined to Him in righteousness (1 John 2:29), truth (1 John 3:19), and especially love (1 John 4:7–8). The permanence of such knowing is expressed in the word *abide*, which occurs 26 times in these epistles. To abide in God is to share the identity of Jesus Christ and to experience the characteristics of God: light (1 John 2:10), love (1 John 3:17; 4:12), and eternal life (1 John 3:15).

SPECIAL CONSIDERATIONS

Many Christians wonder about John's declaration, "Whoever abides in Him [Jesus Christ] does not sin" (1 John 3:6). This does not mean that if someone sins he is not a Christian. Indeed, in these epistles we are told that Christ came to forgive sins; and we are admonished to confess our sins to Him (1 John 1:6—2:2; 3:5; 4:10). The statement means that Christ has transferred us from death to life and has caused us to share in the nature of God. Consequently, we are no longer confined to darkness, because Jesus Christ has broken the power of sin in our lives (1 John 3:8).

John says that believers may pray to God on behalf of others (1 John 5:16–17), unless their sins "lead to death." The exact meaning of such sin in unclear, although it probably refers to a denial of the bodily existence of Jesus (1 John 2:22; 4:3; 5:12).

The Epistle of Jude

Jude is a brief but hard-hitting epistle written by a man who believed in not allowing negative influences to destroy the church. Jude unmasks false teaching with pointed language and vivid images, while appealing to the faithful to remember the teachings of the apostles.

In verse 12 Jude speaks of "late autumn trees without fruit" (NKJV), perhaps like some of these in the Galilean hills. (Todd Bolen, bibleplaces.com)

STRUCTURE OF THE EPISTLE

A salutation (vv. 1–2) is followed by a warning that "licentiousness" has found its way into the church (vv. 3–4). Such blasphemies will receive the judgment of God, as did sinful Israel (v. 5), rebellious angels (v. 6), and Sodom and Gomorrah (v. 7). Verses 8 through 13 note that the outrage of the blasphemers exceeds that of Satan himself and is similar to the rebellions of Cain (Gen. 4:3–8), Balaam (Num. 22—24), and Korah (Num. 16:19–35). Their schemes are nothing new; Enoch of old prophesied their punishment (vv. 14–16). Christians need not be victimized by such deceivers; their defense lies in remembering the words of the apostles and by working for the salvation of those caught in such errors (vv. 17–23). A famous benediction concludes the epistle (vv. 24–25).

AUTHORSHIP AND DATE

The author of the epistle introduces himself as "Jude, a servant of Jesus Christ, and brother of James" (v. 1). There is no further identification, and the James mentioned is probably the Lord's brother (Gal. 1:19). Jude, therefore, would also be a brother of Jesus (Judas, Mark 6:3; Matt. 13:55), although not an apostle (Jude 17). The emphasis on remembering "the words which were spoken before the apostles" (v. 17) suggests that the epistle was composed some time after the apostles had taught, thus favoring a date near the close of the first century.

HISTORICAL SETTING

The Epistle of Jude has the character of a tract or brief essay written for a general Christian audience (v. 1). The author set out to write about "our common salvation" (v. 3), but the more pressing issue of false teachers launched him into a bitter attack on the "ungodly" (v. 15). Their ungodliness took the form of denying the lordship of Jesus Christ and, in the name of grace (v. 4), justifying a life that included immorality of all sorts (vv. 4, 7, 16), mercenary interests (vv. 11, 16), cheap talk (v. 16), and worldliness (v. 19).

The false teachers attacked by Jude seem to have separated "spiritual" matters from behavior. Apparently they taught that the world is evil, and therefore it makes little difference how one behaves. Like the Nicolaitans (Rev. 2:6, 15), the false teachers deserved the just punishment of God. They refused to recognize the implications of the Incarnation—that if God cared enough to send His Son into the world, then He certainly cares how people behave in it.

THEOLOGICAL CONTRIBUTION

Jude writes as a defender of the faith who is "contending earnestly for the faith which was once for all delivered to the saints" (v. 3). The "ungodly" are not the heathen outside the church; they are the false teachers inside (v. 12). Their association with the faith, however, does not mean they live in the faith: the ungodly have not the Spirit (v. 19), whereas the faithful do (v. 20); the ungodly remain in eternal darkness (v. 13), but the saints have eternal life (v. 21). Condemning his opponents in sharp imagery, Jude calls them "raging waves of the sea, foaming up their own shame; wandering stars for whom is reserved the blackness of darkness forever" (v. 13). The saints, on the other hand, must set their anchor in the teaching of the apostles (v. 17), and in the love of God (v. 21). They must work to retrieve those who have been deceived from certain destruction (vv. 22–23).

SPECIAL CONSIDERATIONS

Jude's last word on the problem of corruption in the church is preserved in a memorable benediction. Only God can keep us from error and bring us to Himself:

"Now to Him who is able to keep you from stumbling, and to present you faultless before the presence of His glory with exceeding joy, to God our Savior, who alone is wise, be glory and majesty, dominion and power, both now and forever. Amen."

A Concise Outline of **Jude**		
I. Purpose of Jude		1–4
II. Description of False Teachers		
1. Past Judgment of False Teachers		5–7
2. Present Characteristics of False Teachers		8–13
3. Future Judgment of False Teachers		14–16
III. Defense against False Teachers		17–23
IV. Doxology of Jude		24–25

The Revelation of Jesus Christ

This is the only book of apocalyptic literature in the New Testament. *Apocalypse*, the title of this book in the original Greek, means "unveiling" or "disclosure" of hidden things known only to God. Other examples of apocalyptic literature can be found in the Old Testament in Daniel (chaps. 7—12), Isaiah (chaps. 24—27), Ezekiel (chaps. 37—41), and Zechariah (chaps. 9—12).

Like the counterparts, the Book of Revelation depicts the end of the present age and the coming of God's future kingdom through symbols, images, and numbers. These symbols include an angel whose legs are pillars of fire, men who ride on horses while smiting the earth with plagues of destruction, and a fiery red dragon with seven heads and ten horns who crouches before a heavenly woman about to deliver a child.

Why was apocalyptic literature written in such imagery? One reason is that these books were written in dangerous times when it was safer to hide one's message in images than to speak plainly. Moreover, the symbolism preserved an element of mystery about details of time and place. The purpose of such symbolism, however, was not to confuse, but to inform and strengthen believers in the face of persecution.

Although the keys to some symbols have been lost, the overall message of this book is clear: God is all-powerful. No counter-moves of the devil, no matter how strong, can frustrate the righteous purposes of God.

STRUCTURE OF THE BOOK

The Book of Revelation contains seven visions.

The first vision (chaps. 1—3) is of Christ Almighty exhorting His earthly church to remain loyal against all hostile attacks.

The second vision (chaps. 4—7) is of Christ the Lamb standing with a sealed scroll before God in heaven. As the Lamb opens each of the seven seals, which symbolize knowledge of the destinies of individuals and nations, a series of disasters befall the earth.

A series of seven angels blowing seven trumpets forms vision three (chaps. 8—11). At the sound of these trumpets more disasters occur.

The fourth vision (chaps. 12—14) consists of the persecution of the church—symbolized by a heavenly woman and by two witnesses (Moses and Elijah)—by Satan and the beast.

Vision five (chaps. 15—16) is another series of seven: seven bowls pouring out God's wrath.

The judgment of Babylon (a symbol for Rome) forms the sixth vision (17:1—19:10).

The final victory, final judgment, and final blessedness form the seventh and final vision (19:11—22).

The consummation of God's eternal kingdom finds expression in the word *new*. Christ comes with the promise to make all things new: a new heaven, a new earth, and a new Jerusalem (chap. 21). The book closes with the sigh and longing of all Christians, "Come, Lord Jesus!" (22:20).

AUTHORSHIP AND DATE

The author identifies himself as John (1:4, 9; 21:2; 22:8), a prophet (1:1–4; 22:6–7). He was familiar enough with his readers to call himself their "brother and companion in tribulation" (1:9). He indicates that he was exiled to the island of Patmos (1:9) off the west coast of Asia Minor (modern Turkey), and that on the "Lord's Day" (Sunday) he was caught up "in the Spirit" (1:10) and saw the visions recorded in his book. An examination of the Greek language of the book of Revelation reveals that it has some strong similarities to the Gospel and Epistles of John, but also some striking stylistic differences. The author seems to think in Hebrew and write in Greek.

As a whole, this evidence points to John the Apostle, who spent his latter years in Ephesus or on the island of Patmos. The earliest church tradition was unanimous in attributing the Book of Revelation to John. Although later voices have found problems with the identification, the apostle John remains the strongest candidate for authorship. The book was probably written during the latter years of the reign of the Roman Emperor Domitian (A.D. 81–96).

HISTORICAL SETTING

John tells us, "The seven heads [of the beast] are seven mountains" (17:9), undoubtedly a reference to the famed seven hills of Rome. Chapter 13 tells us that the dragon (Satan) gave authority to the beast (Rome) to exact worship from its inhabitants (v. 4). The first Roman emperor to demand that his subjects address him as "Lord and God" on an empire-wide basis was Domitian. It was under Domitian that the apostle John was banished to Patmos. Christians, of course, were forbidden by the First Commandment (Ex. 20:3) to worship anyone other than God. In the Book of Revelation, John sounded the trumpet-alert to Domitian's challenge.

THEOLOGICAL CONTRIBUTION

The grand theme of the Book of Revelation is that of two warring powers, God and Satan, and of God's ultimate victory. It would be a mistake to consider the two powers as equal in might. God is stronger

A Concise Outline of
Revelation

If you look closely you can see an ancient oil lamp, resting on a ledge in this house in Qatzrin, now a major tourism center in the Golan Heights. (Todd Bolen, bibleplaces.com)

than Satan, and Satan continues his scheming plots only because God permits him to do so. Thus, at the final battle Satan and his followers are utterly destroyed—without a contest—by fire from heaven (20:7–10).

John portrays God's majesty and power through two key words. The first is the image of the throne. Elsewhere in the New Testament this word is found 15 times, but in Revelation it occurs 45 times! The throne stands for the rightful reign of God over the course of history. Angelic choruses bow before God's throne and chant, "Holy, holy, holy, Lord God Almighty" (4:8).

The second term is Almighty. Outside Revelation this term is found only once in the New Testament (2 Cor. 6:18), but here it occurs nine times (once as Omnipotent in 19:6). Almighty means "without contenders." No matter how fierce and wicked Satan may be, he cannot defeat God. In God's time and in His way, He will fulfill His promises and accomplish His sovereign purpose in history.

The central figure in the army of God the King is Jesus Christ. The Book of Revelation begins with the words, "The Revelation of Jesus Christ" (1:1). This is not a book of revelations, but of one revelation—Jesus Christ. John's first vision is of Christ standing in the midst of His churches with eyes like fire (all-seeing), feet like fine brass (all-powerful), hair like wool, white as snow (eternal and all-knowing), and with a sharp two-edged sword coming out of His mouth (the word of truth). Christ is "the First and the Last" (1:11; 22:13), whose final promise is "Surely I am coming quickly" (22:20).

Throughout the Book of Revelation Christ appears in various images, each illuminating a special function or characteristic. He appears as a lion (5:5), representing royal power. As a root (5:5; 22:16), He represents Davidic lineage. As the rider on a white horse (19:11), He symbolizes victory over evil. Most important is the symbol of the Lamb who was slain (5:6). By His sacrifice on the cross, Christ has redeemed humankind (1:5). Because of His humble obedience to the will of the Father, He alone is worthy to open the sealed book that discloses events to come (5:6–10).

This Lamb is victorious. He shares in the power of God's throne (7:17). At the end of time, He will come in judgment (19:11). Then He will reveal Himself as the Lord of the world who was foretold in the Old Testament (2:26; 12:5; 19:15) and the source of new life with God in the heavenly Jerusalem (21:22; 22:1).

In its own way, each metaphor tells an important truth about Christ. Christ is before all things, and all things were created in Him and for Him. This is the abiding message of Revelation: Jesus Christ is the fulfillment of the hopes of believers, no matter how grim circumstances may appear.

SPECIAL CONSIDERATIONS

Revelation was written originally for first-century Christians who faced severe trials under a totalitarian political system. Its imagery reflects the historical realities of that time. This is not to say, however, that it does not address succeeding generations, including our own. As is true of all biblical prophecy, God's Word comes to a particular situation; but it yields a harvest to later generations as they receive it. Thus, Revelation assures us that God is present, purposeful, and powerful today, no matter what forms the beast may take.

One of the unique characteristics of Revelation is its use of four, twelve, and seven. Thus, we find four living creatures, four horsemen, and four angels; twelve elders, twelve gates to the city of God, twelve foundations, and twelve varieties of fruit on the tree of life; and seven churches, seven spirits of God, seven thunders, seven seals, seven trumpets, seven bowls, and seven beatitudes. In apocalyptic literature these numbers represent completeness and perfection. Conversely, 3 1/2 is a number frequently associated with Satan (11:2; 13:5; 42 months or 3 1/2 years); this number symbolizes a fracturing and diminishing of God's unity.

With this in mind, the 144,000 elect in chapter 7 should not be taken literally. Immediately following this passage (7:9), John mentions that he saw "a great multitude [of the redeemed] which no one could number." Actually, the 144,000 refers to martyrs—12,000 from each of the twelve tribes of Israel. One hundred and forty-four thousand (12,000 times 12) stands for totality. This means that no martyr will fail to see God's reward.

Finally, the number of the beast, 666 (13:18), probably refers to Nero, or more specifically to the idea that Nero would return alive to lead the armies of Satan against God. In Hebrew and Greek, letters of the alphabet also served as numbers, and in this case the numerical value of "Nero Caesar" amounts to 666, the number of the beast.

A first-century lampstand, similar in design (if not in material) to what John wrote about in Revelation 1:12: "And having turned I saw seven golden lampstands" (NKJV). (Todd Bolen, bibleplaces.com)